Educational Opportunity in Rural Contexts: The Politics of Place

A Volume in:
Research in Educational Policy: Local, National, and Global Perspectives

Series Editor:
Kenneth K. Wong

Research in Educational Policy: Local, National, and Global Perspectives

Series Editor:

Kenneth K. Wong
Brown University

Charting Reform, Achieving Equity in a Diverse Nation (2013)
Gail L. Sunderman

Partnering for Progress: Boston University, the Chelsea Public Schools, and Twenty Years of Urban Education Reform (2009)
Cara Stillings Candal

Cross-National Information and Communication Technology Policies and Practices in Education (Revised Second Edition) (2009)
Tjeerd Plomp, Ronald E. Anderson, Nancy Law, and Andreas Quale

The Testing Gap: Scientific Trials of Test-Driven School Accountability Systems for Excellence and Equity (2007)
Jaekyung Lee

System-wide Efforts to Improve Student Achievement (2006)
Kenneth K. Wong and Stacey Rutledgey

Cross-national Information and Communication: Technology Policy and Practices in Education (2003)
Tjeerd Plomp, Ronald E. Anderson, Nancy Law, and Andreas Quale

Improving Results for Children and Families: Linking Collaborative Services with School Reform Efforts (2001)
Margaret C. Wang,and William Lowe Boyd

Educational Opportunity in Rural Contexts: The Politics of Place

Edited by
Sheneka M. Williams
Ain A. Grooms

INFORMATION AGE PUBLISHING, INC.
Charlotte, NC • www.infoagepub.com

Library of Congress Cataloging-in-Publication Data

Names: Williams, Sheneka Maria, editor. | Grooms, Ain A., editor.
Title: Educational opportunity in rural contexts : the politics of place / edited by Sheneka M. Williams, Ain A. Grooms.
Description: Charlotte, NC : Information Age Publishing, Inc., 2016. | Series: Research in educational policy : local, national, and global perspectives | Includes bibliographical references and index.
Identifiers: LCCN 2015028884| ISBN 9781681232485 (pbk. : alk. paper) | ISBN 9781681232492 (hardcover : alk. paper) | ISBN 9781681232508 (ebook : alk. paper)
Subjects: LCSH: Education, Rural–United States. | Rural schools–United States–Administration. | Academic achievement–United States.
Classification: LCC LC5146.5 .E48 2016 | DDC 370.9173/40973–dc23 LC record available at http://lccn.loc.gov/2015028884

Printed in the United States of America

CONTENTS

Preface: Educational Opportunity in Rural Contexts ix

The Politics of Place ix
Sheneka M. Williams and Ain A. Grooms

PART I

IMPLICATIONS OF STATE AND FEDERAL POLICIES ON RURAL SCHOOLS

1. **School Funding and Rural Districts** 3
Jerry D. Johnson and Brian P. Zoellner

2. **Location, Location, Location: School Choice in the Rural Context** 21
Ain A. Grooms

3. **The Unequal Impact of the Great Recession on the Instructional Capacity of Rural Schools** 39
John W. Sipple and Yuan Yao

4. **Literacy Education for the Lumps and Divots of Smart Cities and Rural Places** 59
Karen Eppley and Patrick Shannon

PART II

IMPLICATIONS OF LOCAL POLICY AND PRACTICE IN RURAL SCHOOLS

5. It Takes a Community: Preparing Teachers for Rural African American Early Childhood Students 77
Janeula M. Burt and Daniel Boyd

6. A New Narrative on Rural Education: How One High School Takes on 21st Century Challenges 107
Stephen Kotok, Erica L. Kryst and Annelise Hagedorn

7. The Political Economy of Rural Appalachian School Achievement 123
Craig B. Howley, Caitlin W. Howley, and Wesley A. Kuemmel

Biographies....................................155

PREFACE

EDUCATIONAL OPPORTUNITY IN RURAL CONTEXTS

The Politics of Place

Sheneka M. Williams and Ain A. Grooms

The impetus behind this volume stems from reflections on commemorations of the historic *Brown v. Board of Education* decision. *Brown* turned 60 in May of 2014, and many special issues of peer-reviewed journals were dedicated to that anniversary. Unlike most special issues and volumes, we sought to highlight a smaller part of *Brown*, though no less significant. More specifically, we thought to develop a volume that focused on rural education, given that the *Briggs* case included in the *Brown* decision originated in rural South Carolina. Most of the literature on education policy and education reform caters to urban and suburban contexts. Very few academic books and journal articles, focus on rural education in the United States. Thus, we wanted this volume to focus on the politics of educational opportunity in rural contexts.

There is a paucity of rigorous research that examines the impact of education policy on the conditions of rural schools. More specifically, research that examines the ways in which students in rural schools and districts have access to educational opportunities is scarce. Most education policy literature focuses on urban schools, and more recently, suburban schools. However, approximately one

Educational Opportunity in Rural Contexts: The Politics of Place, pages vii–xii.

third of all public schools are located in rural areas (Ayers, 2011). Educational opportunity in rural districts has been plagued by geographic isolation, loss of economic bases, and lack of capital (both financial and political) to voice the need for resources. To be clear, this volume does not present chapters that detail educational opportunity in rural districts and schools from a deficit perspective. Instead, chapters in this volume offer insight into both micro- and macro-level policies and practices that shape educational opportunities for students in rural schools and districts. As such, chapters in this volume investigate the "now" of educational opportunity for rural students and makes recommendations and suggestions for "later." Given that, we are reminded of James Coleman's (1975) thesis, "Education is a means to an end, and equal opportunity refers to later in life rather than the educational process itself" (p. 28).

This book will be organized into two distinct sections. The first section includes chapters that examine educational opportunity in rural districts from a micro-level perspective, taking a broad look at the implications of state and federal policy on educational opportunity in rural schools and districts.

The second section, which includes case studies of rural districts in the American South, Appalachia, and the Northeast, takes a macro-level approach to examining educational opportunity in rural districts. Combined, chapters throughout the book provide readers with both an overview and a specific view of educational opportunity in rural schools. Given the breadth and scope of chapters included in this volume, we believe this book adds tremendously to the education policy literature, as this vantage point has rarely been included in larger education policy discussions.

Part I: Implications of State and Federal Policies on Rural Schools

- School Funding and Rural Districts—Jerry D. Johnson and Brian P. Zoellner
- Location, Location, Location: School Choice in the Rural Context—Ain A. Grooms
- The Unequal Impact of the Great Recession on the Instructional Capacity of Rural Schools—John W. Sipple and Yuan Yao
- Literacy Education for the Lumps and Divots of Smart Cities and Rural Places—Karen Eppley and Patrick Shannon

In this section, the authors provide a broader landscape of the implications of federal and state policies on the rural locale. The section begins with an overview of school funding by authors Jerry D. Johnson and Brian P. Zoellner. The chapter, "School Funding and Rural Districts," provides an overview of how school funding is calculated and the ramifications that calculation has on rural districts. Their discussion of school funding as an important manifestation of the politics of educational opportunity in rural communities offers an opportunity for policymakers to leverage resident resources to create more effective policy. Following that discussion, the authors consider fiscally relevant demographic, geographic, and topographic characteristics of rural settings. They then draw on the previous two sections of the chapter to frame and develop a discussion of how policies could better support rural education and help achieve desirable outcomes for rural schools and the communities they serve.

Ain Grooms' chapter, "Location, Location, Location: School Choice in the Rural Context," details how choice is viewed and implemented (or not) in states with largely rural communities. Her chapter provides demographic data from NCES and the US Census Bureau. She begins by providing a definition of rural as defined by the US Census Bureau. She follows that by examining the types of school choice offerings that are available in states with high numbers of students who attend schools in rural districts. In sum, her chapter provides a picture of how rural districts "look" and the types of educational opportunities those districts offer its students.

The third chapter, "The Unequal Impact of the Great Recession on the Instructional Capacity of Rural Schools," authored by John W. Sipple and Yuan Yao, considers communities' capacities to staff schools in rural districts. The authors specifically conduct the study addressing concerns about whether the Great Recession reduced or exacerbated such differences in staffing with specific analysis of pre- and post-patterns of staffing across location and community wealth. In this study, the authors examine the resource distribution of teachers across states and school districts with special attention to the relative change in staffing levels over time in rural versus other geographic locales. Moreover, they examine this in light of the great recession of 2008 with special attention to how the resource constraints caused by the recession impacted educational opportunity (measured by staffing levels) in rural America.

The final chapter in this section, "Literacy Education for the Lumps and Divots of Smart Cities and Rural Places," authored by Karen Eppley and Patrick Shannon, examines Thomas Friedman's desire to provide top speed bandwidth to cities and towns that combine a university, an educated populace, a dynamic business community, and leave behind small towns and rural places. The authors use Fraser's (2005, 2009) work on justice to take the position that initiatives such as Friedman's plan for smart cities pit technological innovation and the manufacturing of products and services against the democratic projects of the United States. This undermines literacy education in rural places and it pushes a neoliberal agenda that goes against American ideals. Thus, the authors consider their objections to Friedman's thesis as fair, helpful, and rational.

Part II: Implications of Local Policy and Practice in Rural Schools

- It Takes a Community: Preparing Teachers for Rural African American Early Childhood Students—Janeula M. Burt and Daniel Boyd

- A New Narrative on Rural Education: How One High School Takes on 21st Century Challenges—Stephen Kotok, Erica L. Kryst, and Annelise Hagedorn
- The Political Economy of Academic Achievement in Appalachia—Craig B. Howley, Caitlin W. Howley, and Wesley A. Kuemmel

This section of the book takes a macro-level approach to examining educational opportunity in rural districts. More specifically, the chapters in this section include case studies that hone in on local level policies and practices that impact the ways in which students in rural districts experience school. The first chapter in this section, "It Takes a Community: Preparing Teachers for Rural African American Early Childhood Students," authored by Janeula M. Burt and Daniel Boyd, reminds us that while the intent and purpose of No Child Left Behind's highly qualified teacher requirements were well intentioned, the legislation imposed a more negative effect and significant impact on rural school districts. Unequal resources, inadequate numbers of teachers, geographical challenges, shifting student demographics, and limited school choice options are several of the issues that make it difficult for rural schools to keep pace with their suburban and urban counterparts. Their chapter examines the unique strategies that were implemented by a predominately African American rural school district in order to meet the NCLB highly qualified teacher, early childhood requirement. The authors also examine the post-NCLB impact and outcomes of having varying levels of "highly qualified" preschool teachers within predominately African American rural classrooms.

The second chapter in this section, "A New Narrative on Rural Education: How One High School Takes on 21st Century Challenges," examines how high schools in rural communities prepare students for postsecondary options in terms of course offerings and guidance. The authors, Stephen Kotok, Erica L. Kryst, and Annelise Hagedorn draw on Carr and Kefala's (2009) framework of "stayers," "achievers," "seekers," and "leavers" to analyze how the Brockway district and school officials negotiate the dual challenge of readying students for postsecondary options while also considering how they can make Brockway a desirable place for young professionals to settle. Brockway provides a unique policy landscape for a rural study given the existing presence of the Marcellus Shale gas industry and rural school choice via cyber charter schools. The study finds that Brockway has been successful in accessing resources, motivating students with a diverse set of interests, and retaining strong faculty. However, some issues of equity exist, mainly through a rigid tracking system in which 40% of students take noncollege preparatory courses. Additionally, while Brockway might serve as a model for developing and integrating school and community resources, it should be noted that the district benefits from key local benefactors including the current President pro tempore of the State Senate and a wealthy family with business interests throughout the Northeast.

The final chapter in the volume, "The Political Economy of Academic Achievement in Appalachia," authored by Craig B. Howley, Caitlin W. Howley, and Wesley A. Kuemmel, (a) connects the history of the Appalachian "resource curse" (Douglas & Walker, 2013) to the early phase of the region's industrialized schooling, (b) suggests how "high modernism" (Scott, 1998) underwrote Appalachian achievement deficiency, with particular reference to West Virginia, and (c) plots the issues for the policy future of Appalachian schooling in a neoliberal context, including some unpopular realism about alternatives. This chapter serves as a summation chapter for this volume because it infuses politics and economy to detail the academic achievement of students in Appalachia, one of the largest rural regions in the United States.

This book makes a major contribution to education policy, in general, and the discussion of educational opportunity, in particular. While we have commemorated many historical landmarks over the past year (*Brown v. Board*, the Civil Rights Act, and the Voting Rights Act), there is still much work to do in terms of educating the nation's future. To that end, this book will be used as a gauge to measure progress in educational opportunity provided for students in rural contexts.

The audience for this book includes academic and education policy audiences, at the international, national, and state levels. This book should be marketed to the following Special Interest Groups associated with the American Educational Research Association: Rural Education SIG, Politics of Education Association, the School Finance SIG, and the Sociology of Education SIG. As a result, we expect readers to use this book in their education policy and teacher education classes. We also envision that readers will use this book to frame larger discussions around educational opportunity. In the end, the main purpose of this book is to one day end discussions on educational opportunity across contexts. Ultimately, we envision a day when there is no difference in the educational opportunities afforded a child who attends school in a small town in rural Alabama and one who grows up in an affluent suburb in the Northeast.

ENDNOTE

1. This is a pseudonym for the actual name of the town.

REFERENCES

Ayers, J. (2011). *Make rural schools a priority: Considerations for reauthorizing the Elementary and Secondary Education Act*. Washington, DC: Center for American Progress.

Carr, P. J., & Kefalas, M. J. (2009). *Hollowing out the middle: The rural brain drain and what is means for America*. Boston, MA: Beacon.

Coleman, J. S. (1975). Equal educational opportunity: A definition. *Oxford Review of Education, 1*(1), 25–29.

Douglas, S. M., & Walker, A. (2013). Sample selection in Appalachian research. *The Review of Regional Studies, 42*(2), 143–159.
Fraser, N. (2005). Reframing justice in a globalizing world. *New Left Review, 36,* 69–88.
Fraser, N. (2009). *Scales of justice: Reimagining political space in a globalizing world.* New York, NY: Columbia University Press.
Scott, J. (1998). *Seeing like a state: How certain schemes to improve the human condition have failed.* New Haven, CT: Yale University Press.

PART I

IMPLICATIONS OF STATE AND FEDERAL POLICIES ON RURAL SCHOOLS

CHAPTER 1

SCHOOL FUNDING AND RURAL DISTRICTS

Jerry D. Johnson and Brian P. Zoellner

SCHOOL FUNDING AND THE POLITICS OF EDUCATIONAL OPPORTUNITY IN RURAL COMMUNITIES

Viewed (metaphorically) from 10,000 feet, all rural districts probably seem much the same to the casual observer. Indeed, from such a vantage point, in some ways rural school districts may even resemble urban school districts (Provasnik et al., 2007).For example, rural areas have higher poverty and lower budgetary revenue than their suburban counterparts, just like urban areas. Similar to those in urban schools, parents of rural school children tend to have lower levels of educational attainment than parents in suburban schools. In reality, though, there is considerable variability both among rural districts (Johnson, Showalter, Klein, & Lester, 2014) and between rural and nonrural districts (IES, 2007). When that variability is accounted for, what emerges (or should emerge, to the careful observer) is the recognition that each rural district operates with its own set of strengths and challenges (cf. Hobbs, 1998). Federal and even state policymakers tend to treat urban, suburban, and rural schools the same, using a one-size-fits-all approach in addressing diverse issues that play out in diverse settings (Johnson & Howley,

Educational Opportunity in Rural Contexts: The Politics of Place, pages 3–20.

2015); such an approach fails to address the specific needs of each educational setting and can end up doing more harm than good. Understanding varied rural contexts—from the perspective of both strengths and challenges—and their effects on rural schools is an important step in crafting effective and responsive fiscal policy for these districts.

In this chapter, we begin with a discussion of the unique strengths of rural districts. We begin with strengths because policymakers often fail to realize them when crafting policy—a missed opportunity to leverage resident resources and the assets of the school setting to create more effective policy. That discussion is followed by a consideration of salient demographic, geographic, and topographic elements informing the contexts of rural settings. These contexts, and comprising elements, are important to understand as they heavily impact the fiscal realities of rural districts in ways that distinguish them from suburban and urban districts. Finally, we will draw on the previous two sections to craft a discussion of how policies could better support rural education and help achieve desirable outcomes.

Of note, most studies comparing achievement in rural and nonrural schools find no significant overall difference when appropriate statistical controls are imposed (e.g., see Fan & Chen, 1999, for mathematics achievement). That means outcomes in rural schools vary, and the variations are closely related to student and community characteristics that are typically used to describe *achievement gaps*. In other words, the same challenges (e.g., poverty, transience) that characterize schools generally are present in rural places and result in similar patterns in the distribution of achievement. These challenges tend to manifest differently in rural settings, however, because rural areas often face higher concentrations of traditional barriers to educational achievement than do their nonrural counterparts, and geographic and organizational characteristics of rural schools present challenges to delivering the kinds of programs and services that are typically applied to address barriers and promote improvements in educational achievement. A primary purpose of this chapter is to unpack those manifestations and move the dialogue forward about how to better address such challenges. Before engaging that unpacking and discussing salient issues and topics related to school funding, we offer a brief overview of some key strengths in order to establish some context for the analyses that follow. Of note, this is far from a comprehensive listing.

Strengths of Rural Schools

Primary strengths associated with rural schools include their often smaller size and stronger community attachments. These characteristics are not universal among rural schools, of course—there are indeed some very large rural schools and some that do not maintain close community connections. These are nonetheless typical characteristics of schooling in rural areas, and smaller size and community ownership represent strengths that can have the potential for benefit to the school and the community when appropriately cultivated and supported.

To capture the benefits of smaller organizational scale for improved schooling outcomes, we offer the following list of 10 *reasons why small works*, as described by Jimerson (2006):

- Participation in co-curricular and extracurricular activities (a measure that is linked to academic success and general well-being) is greater;
- Students, educators, and others are safer;
- Students feel a greater sense of belonging;
- Smaller classes allow for more individualized instruction;
- Good teaching methods are easier to implement;
- Teachers feel better about their work;
- Mixed-ability classes are more commonly utilized, resulting in fewer students facing institutionalized low expectations;
- Multiage classes are more likely to be utilized, an arrangement that promotes personalized learning and positive social interactions;
- Smaller districts generally mean less bureaucracy and thus increased transparency and better access to policymakers and leaders;
- Schools are more likely to be organized with broader grade spans (more grades in a single school), mediating or even eliminating problems associated with student transitions to a new school.

Of note, some of the strategies that rural schools have used to address generally perceived limitations stemming from their smaller organization size have merit beyond simply finding a way to do what larger schools do. An example of this dynamic would be how rural schools overcome the inability to provide traditional workshop-based professional development due to cost and access to traditional educational experts. These schools may provide this professional development utilizing community resident resources by collaborating with schools to build capacity among the entire faculty (Howley & Howley, 2005). Such an approach has the added benefit of reinforcing the notion of the school and community as *intradependent* resources (Theobald, 1997), a process that validates the contributions of both entities and promotes mutual understanding and the opportunity for synergy (cf. Longo, 2007).

Close community ties in a rural setting represent an opportunity for both the school and the community. Explicitly connecting what is learned in school (the formal curriculum) to students' experiences within their own communities (their own social realities) and to the broader experiences of the community itself (its history, natural environment, culture, and economy) has been linked to positive academic and social outcomes among those students, especially among students who are not otherwise engaged or have been historically underserved by schooling (Fontaine, 2000; Lieberman & Hoody, 1998; NEETF, 2000; Schneider & Atkin, 2000; SEER, 2000). Moreover, the benefits of this kind of approach to schooling (which notably includes service to the community as an authentic outcome of the teaching and learning process) extend equally, if not more substantively, to the community (Gruenewald, 2003; Hutchison & Orr, 2004; Smith, 2002; Smith & Gruenewald, 2007; Smith & Sobel, 2010; Sobel, 2004).

Teachers in rural schools often come from nearby, and many have graduated from the very schools in which they teach. These jobs are valuable, especially in impoverished locales, because they provide well-paid local jobs that permit well-schooled rural people to avoid outmigration—to stay where they were raised, close to family, and in a rural place (Burnell, 2003; Carr & Kefalas, 2009; Corbett, 2007). These "homegrown" teachers often better understand the context of the school and the community in which they are working as well, and are better positioned to deliver culturally responsive (Gay, 2010) and place-conscious (Johnson, Shope, & Roush, 2009; Johnson, Thompson, & Naugle, 2009) instruction and related academic support.

While rural schools possess key strengths that, when understood and appropriately marshaled, can play a vital role in promoting desirable schooling outcomes, those same strengths can be converted into weaknesses by policies that are inattentive and/or unresponsive. It is important to point out that policymakers often do not intend harm to rural schools; it is rather their ignorance of the unique assets and challenges of rural schools and communities that results in unintended and often harmful policy outcomes. The typically smaller size of rural schools is a legitimate strength. Indeed, particularly in urban settings, *intentionally* smaller schools are viewed as a reform strategy intended to promote improved academic and social outcomes among students and closer relationships with communities (Ayers, Klonsky, & Lyon, 2000; Klonsky & Klonsky, 2011). But at almost every turn, traditional policymaking has converted the size of *naturally* small schools and districts into a weakness. These small rural schools cannot, within the context of existing policy structures and requirements, provide the right kinds of programs, staffing, or results (DeYoung, 1989; Howley, Pendarvis, & Woodrum, 2004; Kannapel & DeYoung, 1999). These policies have made small schools and districts inefficient and, by a perception lacking in empirical support, ineffective. In contrast to the urban reform movement of creating smaller schools, used as a strategy to promote desirable outcomes, in rural settings the primary policy movement has been to close schools and consolidate districts (Howley, Johnson, & Petrie, 2011). Rural resistance has been fierce however (Haller & Monk, 1988), and in some states has enjoyed limited success—some states still sustain many hundreds of small rural school districts.

Community engagement too figures as a prominent strength in the rural education literature, but the modern-day professionalization-of-schooling movement has pushed community engagement to the margins of the contemporary schooling experience. Community people, especially rural community people (deemed less educated, less ambitious, less promising as candidates for global competitiveness), were judged an unhealthy influence on the operation of schools (DeYoung, 1995), and contemporary policy debates have indeed considered eliminating school boards altogether, partly because of this history (Land, 2002). We see a parallel to this in the teacher qualification provisions of recent federal legislation—provisions that effectively devalue the kind of local knowledge that is a recognized strength of rural educators (Eppley, 2009; Johnson, Shope et al., 2009).

Despite the ways in which strengths get turned into weaknesses through policy, both rural communities and rural education advocates have sustained the sense of opportunity inherent in small size and community ownership, and have, with surprising regularity, sometimes realized associated opportunities (e.g., see Howley & Harmon, 2000; Lyson, 2002). The defeats are more numerous than the victories, but the existence of some success demonstrates the continuing existence of (largely unrealized) opportunities. In writing about the rural policy issues surrounding *No Child Left Behind* (NCLB), Reeves (2003) stated that the "law will challenge states, districts, and schools in ways that will require them to rethink the structure, organization, and delivery of education in public schools" (p. 1). For rural educators and educational leaders, rethinking structure, organization, and delivery has been largely a matter of reshaping rural schools to look and operate more like urban and suburban schools. Most of the challenges NCLB presents to rural schools are still present and, in many ways, have been increased with recent policies like Race to the Top (Johnson & Howley, 2015).

Related to these policy challenges unique to rural schools, we turn next to a consideration of several topics and issues salient to school funding in rural districts. To begin, we describe several sociodemographic characteristics of rural schooling that impact funding directly (i.e., in terms of the costs of providing services) and indirectly (i.e., as a result of policies that do not adequately account for salient rural characteristics). Next, we examine extant funding mechanisms (local, state, and federal) and how they intersect with those characteristics. Finally, we consider educational policies that directly impact school funding in rural areas. Of particular note, and in direct contrast to the earlier-described metaphorical 10,000 feet perspective, here we are highlighting three notions of diversity relative to rural schools: diversity of student needs and rural contexts, diversity of organizational issues and impacts on these rural schools, and diversity of funding requirements as related to rural contexts and organization.

Contextual Characteristics Influencing Educational Costs in Rural Schools

In this section, we describe and discuss key sociodemographic characteristics of rural schooling—characteristics related to student needs and local geography/topography. These factors directly and indirectly influence the costs of providing educational services and the ability of local communities to generate revenue to support public education. A major challenge to creating state and national education policy that is rurally responsive is the variance of sociodemographic characteristics among rural districts: "Distances, human resources, physical and technological resources, and a wide range of contextual situations appear far more variable for rural schools" (Imazeki & Reschovsky, 2003, as cited in Hudson &

Hudson, 2008, p. 68). Understanding this variability is essential to develop meaningful understandings of rural-specific challenges related to the level of available resources (revenues) and the costs of providing educational services (expenditures).

Schooling costs and revenue-generating potential in rural settings are influenced by a number of sociodemographic characteristics. Among the most relevant are socially ascribed characteristics of students that have consistently been linked to schooling outcomes (i.e., characteristics used to measure and describe *achievement gaps*): socioeconomic status, racial and ethnic background, English language learner (ELL) status, individualized educational plan (IEP) status, and mobility/transience. These characteristics describe certain student populations that have not historically fared well in public schools (hence, the presence of achievement gaps between these students and students who do not demonstrate these characteristics) and so require additional resources and supports (instructional materials, specially trained teachers, specialized professional development for in-service teachers, etc.). A review of national-level data for rural student populations gives a sense of how these characteristics manifest (see Table 1.1).

These figures represent higher levels of *at-risk* characteristics (e.g., lower parent education, household poverty) than are present in town or suburban schools, and as high or nearly as high as in urban schools (Provasnik et al., 2007). It is also very important to recognize that these student characteristics are not uniformly distributed in rural settings across the United States; on the contrary, states vary considerably in terms of their rural student population characteristics, and community characteristics vary considerably within individual states. The following ranges give some sense of the variation among states (Table 1.2). And variation within states can be even more dramatic, as populations of students with specialized needs (e.g., students who are learning English) tend to be clustered in distinct communities in rural areas (Johnson & Strange, 2009). These variations create a great diversity of student need among and within rural districts. In the case of teaching students of limited English language proficiency, Jimenez-Castellanos and Topper (2012) described the importance of understanding local context in

TABLE 1.1. National Rural Statistics (2010–2011)

Percentage of rural schools	32.9%
Percentage of rural students	20.4%
Percentage of rural students in poverty	46.6%
Percentage of rural minority students	26.7%
Percentage of rural ELL students	3.1%
Percentage of rural IEP students	12.8%
Percentage of rural student mobility/transience	11.6%

Source: Johnson et al. (2014)

TABLE 1.2. National Rural Statistics—State Ranges (2010–2011)

Percentage of rural schools	6.5% (MA)–75.3% (MT)
Percentage of rural students	3.9% (NV)–57.5% (VT)
Percentage of rural students in poverty	11.8% (CT)–81.8% (NM)
Percentage of rural minority students	4.6% (RI)–82.5% (NM)
Percentage of rural ELL students	<1% (VT)–23.4% (NM)
Percentage of rural IEP students	<1% (VT)–17.5% (WY)
Percentage of rural student mobility/transience	4.1% (RI)–21.0% (NV)

Source: Johnson et al. (2014)

understanding the financial needs of rural districts: "Contextualizing the diversity of ELL students in cost study research protocols is another way to further include ELLs in each of these methodological approaches" (p. 205). An explicit accounting for different costs across districts is an important method to better understand and address these costs (Imazeki & Reschovsky, 2003). The implications of rural diversity for rural school funding are clear: Challenges that necessitate equitable and adequate resource levels are present and substantial, and variation in the distribution of those challenges within rural America and within the rural areas of individual states demand fiscal policies that are rurally responsive and attentive to the varying needs of rural schools and school districts.

The smaller organizational scale of rural schooling is also associated with challenges related to the availability of specialized staff and support services (Levin, Manship, Chambers, Johnson, & Blankenship, 2011). Put simply, the smaller size of rural schools makes it more difficult to provide specialized course offerings and services (e.g., instruction for ELLs) through traditional delivery methods (i.e., by employing a full-time qualified ELL teacher who might only serve a few students). Additionally, student support service functions that are typically handled by district-level staff, like screening for special education programs by a licensed school psychologist, also present challenges to many rural districts that do not serve a large enough student population to justify the need for a dedicated staff person and/or a large enough population to generate funding for such a position within the context of the typical per-pupil funding model. And remote settings make it more difficult and more costly to obtain such specialized services from private agencies. Additionally, the policies that regulate such provisions are framed with both metropolitan purposes and metropolitan circumstances in mind, as these areas have a greater number of students with special needs, but also have greater revenue to fund the programs to serve these students.

Geographic and topographic characteristics of rural school districts that impact schooling costs are present and substantial, and also vary greatly among and within states. Population sparsity and geographic isolation, which can occur because of wide spacing of schools and/or of students' homes within an attendance zone, creates additional costs for pupil transportation and increases the cost of goods and services that must be delivered to the school (Howley, Howley, & Shamblen, 2001; Levin et al., 2011). Challenging topography can also affect expenditures, as administrators addressing transportation needs may encounter land that includes mountains, oceans, deserts, and prairies. Variation in state attention to infrastructure needs (e.g., roads, public transportation) also affects district transportation costs. This may have an especially large influence in rural districts where weather and geology exert substantial impacts on the maintenance of roads (e.g., flooding, freeze/thaw patterns, heavy snowfall).

Both the nature and variability of sociodemographic and geographic/topologic factors of rural settings uniquely affect the costs of operating rural districts. This difference in cost presents challenges to these schools when meeting the policy requirements to screen and provide programs (e.g., special education services) to qualified students. In the next section, we will describe some of the contexts of these policies and how they affect cost in rural districts.

Policy Contexts Influencing Educational Costs in Rural Schools

Our purpose in this section is to describe nonfiscal educational policies that impact the costs of providing educational services in rural schools. In general, the policies discussed here create additional costs for rural schools because they fail to account for rural characteristics such as those described in the previous section (i.e., because they construe the objectives and the needs of rural school as being exactly the same as those of nonrural schools), and/or because they fail to account for the diversity in rural school settings as described in the previous section (i.e., because they construe the objectives and the needs of all rural schools as being exactly the same). We focus attention on three broad policy categories: accountability, curriculum, and teacher quality.

Policies related to accountability impact rural school finance in a variety of ways. Most directly, accountability policies create additional demands for schools and school districts with regard to data management and data analysis. Many (or most) larger urban and suburban districts have dedicated specialized staff to fulfill these roles. In smaller rural districts, though, these added responsibilities must be borne by existing staff and added to the existing responsibilities of generalists (Fox & Van Sant, 2011).

Less directly, actions taken against schools and districts as a result of accountability policies also influence cost in ways that create differential impacts on rural schools. Here's how and why. State and federal accountability policies require schools to meet assessment goals (e.g., the Adequate Yearly Progress [AYP] requirements under NCLB each year). Because of their small size, rural districts are disproportionally affected by statistical anomalies (Coladerci, 2003). Minor fluctuations in the measured achievement outcomes for subgroups (e.g., minority students, economically disadvantaged students) can be the difference between schools meeting AYP or being designated as *needing improvement*. That designation has substantive financial consequences, as it requires districts to provide students with supplemental services and school choice.

For rural schools that are required under NCLB to provide supplemental services (e.g., tutoring, after-school programs) to students who are not proficient in reading and mathematics, staffing can be a serious challenge. With already high demands placed on faculty members, rural schools may not have the resources to provide these programs themselves. Outsourcing services and programs is an option exercised by suburban and urban schools, but private providers may not choose to work in rural areas, as there may not be a large enough population to make operations profitable (Reeves, 2003). Online options may exist, but this approach can be just as problematic in rural settings, as Internet access and technological support can be highly variable in rural areas. Additionally, technology often requires specialized personnel with the capacity to operate and maintain hardware and software (personnel that may be as difficult to attract as those providing supplemental services).

Additionally, as a major policy lever of NCLB, students enrolled in schools designated as *needing improvement* are free to transfer to a school (that was determined to be successful based on NCLB accountability measures) that they and their family believe better meets their needs. Setting aside the broader issue of pulling funding from already underfunded schools (state federal dollars follow the student, as funding allocations are based on the number of students served by a school or district), rural students may not have ready access to another school option, and the student's home district (i.e., the *needs improvement* district) must provide for those transportation costs. Because of geographic isolation and the small number of schools in rural districts, many of which may have only one school at the high school or middle school level, intradistrict school choice may not be a viable option for students seeking educational alternatives, especially at the secondary level.

State policy initiatives related to course offerings create fiscal challenges for rural high schools, where curriculum breadth tends to be narrower because of lower enrollments and smaller faculties. Specifically, state policies that specify the number and type of courses to be offered (without consideration of the capacity of existing schools to meet those mandates) result in what is essentially an unfunded mandate to hire additional faculty and/or create additional learning opportunities (Johnson, 2006). Such policies can often accelerate the movement toward school consolidation, as districts look for ways to provide the additional courses without receiving any additional funding to support them. This process of using policy to force rural high schools to broaden curriculum, regardless of the hardships that accompany it, would seem like a reasonable course of action if it resulted in enhanced learning opportunities and improved student outcomes; that is, it might be understood as a necessary cost in reforming and modernizing rural schools. There is, however, no empirical evidence to support the belief that this type of policy action will benefit students. On the contrary, the empirical evidence suggests that (a) increasing the number of courses available in a high school typically results not in more academic offerings but in the addition of less rigorous options for academic content (i.e., more ability-level tracking) and nonacademic electives, and (b) the extent of participation in the curriculum as a whole is higher in smaller high schools (Oxley, 1994; Uerling & Dlugosh, 1999). In short, increasing the number of available courses generally results in more places for students to hide and/or fall through the cracks.

NCLB (and most state) policy requires that teachers have specialized licensure in each area they teach. These requirements are especially challenging in the sciences, as licenses typically are specific to the scientific discipline (i.e., earth science, biology, physics, chemistry). Rural schools must be able to hire separate teachers for each discipline for which a course will be offered or attract and retain a teacher who is certified in multiple areas of science. The first option is often problematic, as rural schools, which, again, are typically smaller, may not have the enrollment to warrant multiple sections of any one particular course, thus making it difficult to justify keeping a full-time specialist on staff. The second option is a better structural fit for meeting rural school needs, but is also problematic. Because of the requirement of teachers needing to prepare for multiple courses (e.g., a science teacher needing to prepare to teach biology, physics, earth science, and chemistry each day), isolation from content-specific colleagues (individual teachers might be a department or their school might be a great distance from the nearest school), and lower salary, rural school districts may not be the most attractive sites for such cross-certified (and, because of that, highly sought after) teachers.

As an additional constraint, access to the resources and services available from higher education institutions (e.g., faculty expertise, graduate programs, research support, in-service training) might be limited in rural schools and communities because of geographic isolation and/or transportation logistics (Johnson, Thompson et al., 2009). New teacher candidates from urban and suburban settings might lack the necessary professional development opportunities because of the location of their programs. Additionally, since programs typically seek out local districts as partners for such things as field placements as well as data collection and analysis, the needs of these urban and suburban districts may dictate the areas of focus for programs (e.g., an urban teacher-education program might focus on curriculum and experiences to prepare preservice teachers to work in the local urban district). Candidates may not even be aware of the selection biases, as described by a participant in an Australian rural education program:

> Before going on the "Over the Hill" trip I had every intention of staying on the coast and in my local area to teach. The thought of going out west for a rural [practicum] was intimidating and the last thing that I wanted to happen, I had a very negative outlook on rural teaching. In a rural setting you come to [realize] how important education is and how valued it can be. The level of involvement of the teachers in the community of a rural setting is enormous and overwhelmingly rewarding. After

> having spent some time in a country setting it has now changed my views in regards to teaching in a rural setting and I would be more happy to head out west after graduation. (Hudson & Hudson, 2008, pp. 72–73)

Another student described the recruitment hurdle of ignorance about rural settings: "I was not really even considering a rural teaching placement prior to the trip [a guided rural school experience], however after seeing the environment and community where we were taken, I now want to teach there" (Hudson & Hudson, 2008, p. 72).

Building on the discussion here and in the previous section of contextual characteristics and policy structures that influence costs, in the next section we describe and discuss the ways in which the existing mechanisms for distributing local, state, and federal education funds are responsive (and not responsive) to rural schools.

Funding Mechanisms and Rural Schools

Fiscal challenges for rural schools are fundamentally the result of policymaking and its intersection with rural school and community characteristics at every turn. In the United States, this policymaking is constitutionally authoritative, and the development of state systems of education has centered on a record of battles over school funding (Johnson, 2014; Johnson, Malhoit, & Shope, 2012; Malhoit, 2005). Overall, state and federal funding schemes tend to treat rural, suburban, and urban schools the same way. Moreover, even those schemes that do purport to address rural needs generally do not account for salient differences among rural districts. That there are differences in the costs of education and the funding needed to meet those costs between, say, Los Angeles, California, and Whitesburg, Kentucky, is a fairly straightforward argument to make (though much of the current fiscal policy context is not attentive to such differences); the argument that a rural district in Arizona has different needs than one in West Virginia is a little more difficult to process, at least for policymakers who have little or no firsthand experience working in and with rural schools and communities.

A brief overview of local, state, and federal funding policy is probably in order here: the purported role of each policy level, how they intersect with one another, and how they operate in today's fiscal policy context. Local revenue to support public schools relies largely on *ad valorum* taxes—real estate and personal property taxes.The value of real estate and personal property, and thus the corresponding available tax base, varies dramatically among communities. Wealthier communities have higher real estate property values and higher income individuals possess more expensive non–real estate property, so school districts that serve wealthier communities have access to a more substantial tax base. Of importance to this chapter, these disparities in the tax base fall not just along the lines of wealthy versus impoverished communities, but also along rural versus nonrural lines. Specifically, developed real estate (even if inner city) has a higher value and provides a more substantial tax base than undeveloped real estate, and personal property is more concentrated where population is concentrated. Thus, the extent to which the level of funding available to schools is derived from local funding is a good measure of the extent to which funding levels align with a community's wealth and, to a somewhat lesser extent, its urbanity. The larger the role played by local funds, the more inequitable the funding levels are.

That's where state funding mechanisms come in. State funds are generally intended to level the playing field by providing more money to districts with a smaller tax base and less money to districts with a larger tax base. Most (40 of 50 states in 2006–2007) follow a *foundation formula* approach, establishing a minimum level of funding for all districts in the state and then providing in state funds what is needed to bridge the gap between the local contribution and the minimum level (Verstegen & Jordan, 2009). States vary in terms of both the established minimum level and the aggressiveness with which they redistribute dollars within the state. So, paralleling the discussion about the role of local funds and inequity, the larger the proportional contribution of state dollars (or the larger the state *slice* in a pie representing the total level of funding available to schools), the more equitable we might expect the distribution of funding to be in that state.

Federal funds to school districts play a decidedly different role than state or local funds. Historically, federal funds were tied to specific and exceptional needs, and were intended to *supplement, not supplant* other funding sources. Unlike state dollars, federal funds were not intended to level the playing field between districts; rather, they were intended to provide additional resources, and programs and services beyond the typical teaching and learning experience. For example, programs for students requiring special education services and/or students designated as at-risk. Rural schools did reasonably well under this system, since rural students by and large are characterized by higher levels of such needs. More recently, the federal government has shifted priorities from this needs-based approach to a competitive-grants approach; instead of providing grants based on need, the United States provides awards based on proposals. The shift has not been beneficial to rural school districts, in part because of the proposal specifications (some grants required proposed projects to serve a student enrollment size far larger than most rural school districts) and in part because of the proposal process (preparing successful proposals required research design and program evaluation expertise not accessible to most rural school districts). In sum, this shift has resulted in additional federal dollars going to urban and suburban districts with larger enrollments and dedicated grant writers with access to relevant experts (Strange et al., 2011).

Problems emerge when policymakers treat school districts as monoliths in their development and implementation of these funding distribution mechanisms. As an example, most state and federal funding allocations are set on a per-pupil basis. While fixed costs (e.g., the cost of a school principal) might be the same in absolute terms for schools of varying sizes, they are more expensive per pupil in smaller schools, an aspect of what economists term *economies of scale*. Thus, rural districts are affected to a greater extent because the costs per pupil are higher while the funding per pupil is the same. The majority of state funding mechanisms (30 of 50 states) include some formula elements or categorical provisions that attempt to account for increased costs in small, sparsely populated, and/or remote districts (Education Commission of the States, 2011); however, these elements and provisions vary considerably from state to state, and are generally considered to be insufficient to account for the additional costs associated with smaller districts (Levin et al., 2011). As Imazeki and Reschovsky (2003) stated, "Among the most important factors contributing to high costs in rural districts is their small size—a reflection of the low populations of the communities they serve" (p. 138). They continued, "Rural districts are more likely to have small enrollments and large proportions of economically disadvantaged students: factors our results show clearly increase costs" (p. 152).

In addition to challenges posed by the smaller size of rural districts, declining enrollment creates its own financial hardships in terms of lost revenue and unstable revenue flows, both with regard to availability and allocation. When students leave a district, per-pupil revenues leave with them. Again, some states do include provisions that attempt to cushion the blow (e.g., through the use of a multiyear average enrollment for allocation purposes and/or short-term hold harmless provisions), but the specifics vary considerably from state to state (Levin et al., 2011).

Another fiscal challenge comes from the inability of existing formulas to account for additional costs associated with transporting students in sparsely populated areas (Howley et al., 2001). Often faced with less than ideal travel conditions because of topographic and weather challenges, rural districts must bear an additional financial burden. To illustrate, transportation in sparsely populated areas is inherently more costly because of efficiency issues associated with fewer students and more miles, and because of additional maintenance costs stemming from travel over poorly maintained roads.

The rural student population is considerably more diverse than is generally recognized, and this diversity is rapidly increasing (Strange, Johnson, Showalter, & Klein, 2012). With that increasing diversity comes an increase in the range and amount of student needs that must be met—needs that pose unique challenges for rural schools. When rural students require specialized expertise to aid their learning (because of issues like learning disabilities or limited English language proficiency), policies require rural districts to provide the personnel, regardless of how many students need these services. With funding for specialized services tied to the number of students served, rural schools are presented with what is essentially an unfunded mandate. For example, a district with seven English Language Learners is tasked with providing ELL services to those students, though it might need an enrollment of 20 ELL students to qualify for a funded teacher—if it could even find one.

In the previous sections, we have described general characteristics of rural districts including their unique strengths, demographics, and geography/topography. We then discussed the rural policy contexts generally and policies centered on funding mechanisms more specifically. The diverse characteristics of rural districts bring challenges when these schools work within a policy environment that often treats them as urban settings. This approach fails to meet the goal of creating opportunity, through public schooling, for underserved students. In the next section, we address the politics of educational opportunity in rural contexts and share our recommendations for improving policies to better meet the needs and challenges faced by rural districts through examples of promising federal and state policies and local practices.

DISCUSSION

The survival and success of rural schools and the communities they serve depend largely on their ability to marshal their strengths to overcome their challenges, a process that is constrained more often than facilitated by existing policy structures that emphasizes top-down, one-size-fits-all approaches (Johnson & Howley, 2015). Attentive policies that operate with appropriate commitments open opportunities by activating strengths to engage whatever challenges present themselves. These may include use of local experts and community members to increase student engagement. Ignorant policies frustrate opportunities by converting strengths into weaknesses and then seeking to eliminate the strengths. And funding is not merely a concern about numbers, but about direction, vision, and priorities. Indeed, school funding represents the direct intervention of policy at all levels—federal, state, and local—into the organization and operation of schools.

Some compensatory funding has been created in acknowledgement of these issues. On the federal level, this has included policy from NCLB, the Rural Educational Achievement Program (REAP) in Title IV, and Race to the Top. Some states (e.g., Wisconsin and Texas) have also created funding formulas to address the additional expenses that rural districts face (Imazeki & Reschovsky, 2003).

We recommend that policies be authentically responsive to rural schools and communities by building on their strengths to address their challenges and meet their diverse needs. Specific recommendation include:

- Designing more equitable funding formulas that adequately address issues of outmigration, low property values, and differences in fixed costs (e.g., transportation) among districts;
- Creating more flexibility in the requirements for certified specialists (e.g., a rural science generalist certification);
- Diminishing the effects of geographic isolation by utilizing distance learning for students and professional development for teachers (with accompanying funding for infrastructure and technological support);

- Leveraging the typically smaller class sizes to address the shortage of special education specialists by focusing on greater individualized attention and greater teacher freedom from administrative duties to be more innovative in course design (e.g., using data for effective mixed-skill grouping);
- Allowing districts to meet supplemental service policy requirements through the utilization of community members;
- Increasing funding and supporting innovative approaches for recruitment and retention of rural teachers;
- Creating greater emphasis on rural education, through on-campus courses and field experiences, in teacher education programs.

Overall, there must be greater flexibility in federal and state mandates to better match the realities that rural schools face. Additionally, school funding must also match the variable costs facing rural districts and support districts in finding creative ways to manufacture *economies of scale* through, for instance, sharing specialized staff or administrators. Using a one-size-fits-all approach to federal and state policy fails to address the diverse issues in these settings, and policies that drive funding levels represent perhaps the most dramatic example of the damage that such an approach can do. With a greater understanding of the variability in rural settings, policymakers can ensure that rural schools have the funding needed to effectively meet the unique needs of those schools and increase/expand educational opportunities.

ENDNOTE

1. Some states (e.g., Ohio) also rely on income taxes administered at the school district. The same observations made here about *ad valorum* taxes hold true for school district–level income taxes

REFERENCES

Ayers, W., Klonsky, M., & Lyon, G. H. (2000). *A simple justice: The challenge of small schools.* New York, NY: Teachers College Press.

Burnell, B. (2003). The real-world aspirations of work-bound rural students. *Journal of Research in Rural Education, 18*(2), 104–113.

Carr, P., & Kefalas, M. (2009). *Hollowing out the middle: The rural brain drain and what it means for America.* Boston, MA: Beacon.

Coladerci, T. (2003). *Gallup goes to school: The importance of confidence intervals for evaluating "adequate yearly progress" in small schools.* Washington, DC: Rural School and Community Trust.

DeYoung, A. (1989). *Economics and American education: A historical and critical overview of the impact of the economic theories on schooling in the United States.* New York, NY: Longman.

DeYoung, A. (1995). *Parent participation, school accountability, and rural education: The impact of KERA on Kentucky school facilities policy.* Washington, DC: Policy Program, Annenberg Rural Challenge.

Education Commission of the States. (2011). *Funding formulas at a glance: 50-state information on school finance formulas.* Denver, CO: Author.

Eppley, K. (2009). Rural schools and the highly qualified teacher provision of No Child Left Behind: A critical policy analysis. *Journal of Research in Rural Education, 24*(4), 1–11. Retrieved from http://jrre.vmhost.psu.edu/wp-content/uploads/2014/02/24-4.pdf

Fan, X., & Chen, M. J. (1999). Academic achievement of rural school students: A multi-year comparison with their peers in suburban and urban schools. *Journal of Research in Rural Education, 15*(1), 31–46.

Fontaine, C. (2000, June). School and community partnerships: A model for environmental education. A report to the community-based environmental education program, Antioch New England Graduate School. Retrieved from http://www.peecworks.org/peec/peec_reports/I01795F26.0/99-00_CO-SEED_Eval.pdf

Fox, P, & Van Sant, D. (2011). *A rural needs study: Improving CDE services to rural school districts.* Boulder: Colorado Department of Education.

Gay, G. (2010). *Culturally responsive teaching: Theory, research, and practice.* New York, NY: Teachers College Press.

Gruenewald, D. (2003). The best of both worlds: A critical pedagogy of place. *Educational Researcher, 32*(4), 3–13.

Haller, E. J., & Monk, D. (1988). New reforms, old reforms, and the consolidation of small rural schools. *Educational Administration Quarterly, 24*(4), 470–483.

Hobbs, D. (1998). Foreword. In R. M. Gibbs, P. L. Swaim, & R. Texeira (Eds.), *Rural education and training in the new economy* (pp. v–viii). Ames: Iowa State University Press.

Howley, A., & Howley, C. (2005). High-quality teaching: Providing for rural teachers' professional development. *The Rural Educator, 26*(2), 1–5.

Howley, A. A., Pendarvis, E., & Woodrum, A. (2004). *The rural school principalship: Promises and challenges.* Charleston, WV: AEL.

Howley, C. B., & Harmon, H. (Eds.). (2000). *Small high schools that flourish: Rural context, case studies and resources.* Charleston, WV: AEL.

Howley, C. B., Howley, A. A., & Shamblen, S. (2001). Riding the school bus: A comparison of the rural and suburban experience in five states. *Journal of Research in Rural Education, 17*(1), 1–22.

Howley, C., Johnson, J., & Petrie, J. (2011, February 1). Consolidation of schools and districts: What the research says and what it means. *National Education Policy Center.* Retrieved from http://nepc.colorado.edu/publication/consolidation-schools-districts

Hudson, P., & Hudson, S. (2008). Changing preservice teachers' attitudes for teaching in rural schools. *Australian Journal of Teacher Education, 33*(4), 67–77.

Hutchison, D., & Orr, D. (2004). *A natural history of place in education.* New York, NY: Teachers College Press.

Imazeki, J., & Reschovsky, A. (2003). Financing adequate education in rural settings. *Journal of Education Finance*, 137–156.

Jimenez-Castellanos, O., & Topper, A. (2012). The cost of providing an adequate education to English language learners: A review of the literature. *Review of Educational Research, 82*(2), 179–232.

Jimerson, L. (2006). *The hobbit effect: Why small works in public schools.* Washington, DC: Rural School and Community Trust.

Johnson, J. (2006). *More doesn't mean better: Larger high schools and more courses do not boost student achievement in Iowa high schools. Washington, DC: Rural School and Community Trust.*

Johnson, J. (2014). School funding in Mississippi: A critical history and policy analysis. In C. Howley, A. Howley, & J. Johnson (Eds.). *Dynamics of social class, race, and place in rural education* (pp. 165–192). Charlotte, NC: Information Age.

Johnson, J., & Howley, C. (2015). Contemporary federal education policy and rural schools: A critical policy analysis. *Peabody Journal of Education, 90*(2), 224–241.

Johnson, J., Malhoit, G., & Shope, S. (2012). Rural-specific strategies and concerns in the budget process. *School Business Affairs, 78*(3), 24–26.

Johnson, J., Shope, S., & Roush, J. (2009). Toward a responsive model for educational leadership in rural Appalachia: Merging theory and practice. *Education Leadership Review, 10*(2), 93–103.

Johnson, J., Showalter, D., Klein, R., & Lester, C. (2014). *Why rural matters 2013–14.* Washington, DC: Rural School and Community Trust.

Johnson, J., & Strange, M. (2009). *Why rural matters 2009: State and regional challenges and opportunities.* Washington, DC: Rural School and Community Trust.

Johnson, J., Thompson, A., & Naugle, K. (2009). Place-conscious capacity-building: A systemic model for the revitalization and renewal of rural schools and communities through university-based regional stewardship. *Rural Society, 19*(3), 178–188.

Kannapel, P., & DeYoung, A. (1999). The rural school problem in 1999: A review and critique of the literature. *Journal of Research in rural Educaiton, 15*(2), 67–79.

Klonsky, M., & Klonsky, S. (2011). *Small schools: Public school reform meets the ownership society.* New York, NY: Routledge.

Land, D. (2002). Local school boards under review: Their role and effectiveness in relation to students' academic achievement. *Review of Educational Research, 72*(2), 229–278.

Levin, J., Manship, K., Chambers, J., Johnson, J., & Blankenship, C. (2011). *Do schools in rural and nonrural districts allocate resources differently? An analysis of spending and staffing patterns in the west region states.* Washington, DC: National Center for Education Evaluation and Regional Assistance, U.S. Department of Education.

Lieberman, G., & Hoody, L. (1998). *Closing the achievement gap: Using the environment as an integrating context for learning.* San Diego, CA: State Environment and Education Roundtable.

Longo, N. (2007). *Why community matters: Connecting education with civic life.* Albany: SUNY Press.

Lyson, T. (2002). What does a school mean to a community? Assessing the social and economic benefits of schools to rural villages in New York. *Journal of Research in Rural Education, 17*(3), 131–137.

Malhoit, G. (2005). *Providing rural students with a high quality education: The rural perspective on the concept of educational adequacy.* Washington, DC: Rural School and Community Trust.

National Environmental Education and Training Foundation (NEETF). (2000). Environment-based education: Creating high performance schools and student. Washington, DC: NEETF.

Oxley, D. (1994). Organizing schools into smaller units: Alternatives to homogenous grouping. *Phi Delta Kappan, 75*(7), 521–526.

Provasnik, S., KewalRamani, A., Coleman, M. M., Gilbertson, L., Herring, W., & Xie, Q. (2007). *Status of education in rural America* (NCES 2007-040). National Center for Education Statistics. Retrieved from http://files.eric.ed.gov/fulltext/ED497509.pdf

Reeves, C. (2003). *Implementing the No Child Left Behind Act: Implications for rural schools and districts.* Naperville, IL: North Central Regional Educational Laboratory. Retrieved from http://c3ta.org/kb_files/NCLB_RuralPolicyBrief.pdf

Schneider, B., & Atkin, J. M. (2000). *Raising standards in environmental education: Evaluation report executive summary.* Sausalito, CA: Yosemite National Institutes.

Smith, G. A. (2002). Place-based education: Learning to be where we are. *Phi Delta Kappan, 83*(8), 584–595.

Smith, G. A., & Gruenewald, D. (2007). *Place-based education in the global age: Local diversity*. Mahwah, NJ: Erlbaum.

Smith, G. A., & Sobel, D. (2010). *Place- and community-based education in schools*. New York, NY: Routledge.

Sobel, D. (2004). *Place-based education: Connecting classrooms and communities.* Great Barrington, VT: Orion Society.

State Education and Environment Roundtable (SEER). (2000). *California Student Assessment Project: The effects of environment-based education on student achievement.* San Diego, CA: SEER.

Strange, M., Harrison, L., Johnson, J., Lambert, R., Mahaffey, R., & McCullough, P. (2011). *Taking advantage: The rural competitive preference in the Investing in Innovation program*. Washington, DC: Rural School Community Trust.

Strange, M., Johnson, J., Showalter, D., & Klein, R. (2012, January 10). Why rural matters 2011–12: The condition of rural education in the 50 states. *Rural School and Community Trust.* Retrieved from http://www.ruraledu.org/articles.php?id=2820

Theobald, P. (1997). *Teaching the commons: Place, pride, and the renewal of community.* Boulder, CO: Westview.

Uerling, D., & Dlugosh, L. (1999). *Selected indicators of a quality high school: Program offerings and student participation.* Paper presented at the annual conference on Creating the Quality School, Memphis, TN.

Verstegen, D., & Jordan, T. (2009). A fifty-state survey of school finance policies and programs: An overview. *Journal of Education Finance,* 213–230.

CHAPTER 2

LOCATION, LOCATION, LOCATION

School Choice in the Rural Context

Ain A. Grooms

INTRODUCTION

Since the first charter school opened in 1991 in Minnesota, and charters rose in popularity in the 20 years that followed, school choice has become a familiar topic of conversation among families, educators, and policymakers alike—despite the fact that homeschooling has existed since the founding of the country, religious-based private schools began operating in the 1600s, and magnet schools were created in response to desegregation in the 1970s. School choice is often thought of as an "urban issue," as most of the media attention and policy discussions tend to focus on urban school districts, with little to no regard for rural families and rural schools. This chapter serves to bring attention to the availability and popularity of school choice options in rural settings.

According to the National Center for Education Statistics (NCES, 2014e), from 2010 to 2011, of the estimated 54.8 million children enrolled in both public and private schools across the country, approximately 25% (or 13.1 million children)

Educational Opportunity in Rural Contexts: The Politics of Place, pages 21–38.

were enrolled in rural public and private schools. The overwhelming majority of the 13.1 million rural students attend public schools, while just over 700,000 attend private schools. Despite low private school enrollment, it remains evident that school choice is a viable option for families living well outside of urban areas.

As with urban and suburban families, rural students can choose from a variety of alternatives to traditional public schools, including charter, magnet, virtual/online, and private schools, as well as homeschooling. These choice options will be explored in greater detail later in the chapter. The purpose of this chapter is neither to discuss student achievement, education funding, curriculum, student assignment, or teacher and administrator preparation, recruitment, and training, nor is it to serve as advocacy or critique of the various school choice options available to rural families; that is outside the scope of this particular research. Rather, the intent here is to outline the choice options in which rural families participate in order to, first, bring continued visibility to rural education and second, to expand the school choice conversation with a conscious effort to avoid "placism," or bias based on where a person lives (Jimerson, 2005).

DEMOGRAPHICS OF RURAL COMMUNITIES AND SCHOOLS

In order to understand choice in the rural context, it is crucial to first understand how *rural* is defined. The U.S. Census Bureau (2014) defines rural as being neither an urbanized area (50,000 people or more) nor an urbanized cluster (between 2,500 and 50,000 people). Every state has at least 50% of its geographical area classified as rural (the District of Columbia is the only area that is 100% urban) (U.S. Census Bureau, 2014), yet there is no monolithic version of what rural looks like—rural communities in West Virginia differ from those in Alaska, Louisiana, Massachusetts, New Mexico, or Utah. Further classification by the NCES (2014f) explains the variations among rural areas: rural fringe (less than or equal to 5 miles away from an urban area, or less than or equal to 2.5 miles away from an urban cluster), rural distant (between 5 and 25 miles away from an urban area, or between 2.5 and 10 miles away from an urban cluster), and rural remote (more than 25 miles away from an urban area or more than 10 miles away from an urban cluster). These distinctions assist in providing a deeper contextual understanding of rural areas and the school choice options being utilized by rural students.

Despite each state being majority rural space, the percentage of the state's population that lives in these rural areas varies tremendously. Data collected from the 2010 U.S. Census (2014) finds that Maine has the highest percentage of its total population living in rural areas, at 61.3%, followed by Vermont (61.1%), West Virginia (51.3%), Mississippi (50.65%), and Montana (44.1%). This may come as a surprise to those who do not think of Maine and Vermont as rural in the traditional sense. School enrollment data from the 2011–2012 school year finds that the five states with the highest number of rural students enrolled in public schools are Texas, North Carolina, California, Georgia, and Florida, totaling approximately 3.9 million students, or 31% of the nation's total rural public school

TABLE 2.1. Top Five States, Rural Public School Enrollment

State	Number of Rural Students	State	Percentage of Rural Students
Texas	1,285,592	Maine	58.6
N. Carolina	722,818	Vermont	56.9
California	698,698	Mississippi	52.3
Georgia	646,453	West Virginia	50.5
Florida	541,931	N. Carolina	48.2

Source: National Center for Education Statistics, 2014c

population. However, the five states with the highest number of rural students as a percentage of total public school enrollment are Maine, Vermont, Mississippi, West Virginia, and North Carolina (NCES, 2014e). Only one state, North Carolina, has one of the highest numbers of rural public school students and one of the highest percentages of rural students. Table 2.1 outlines rural public school enrollment data in greater detail.

Rural schools are predominately White (70%), with 13% of students identifying as Hispanic/Latino, 10% Black, 2% Asian, and the remaining 5% identifying as either Hawaiian/Pacific Islander, American Indian, or Biracial/Multiracial (NCES, 2014e). Of the three rural classifications, the fringe areas (closest to cities) are the most diverse, at 65% White, while rural distant areas are the least diverse, at 80% White. Rural remote areas (the farthest from cities) are 75% White (NCES, 2014e). A significant portion, 44%, of rural students attending public schools qualify for free and/or reduced lunch nationally, as compared to 48% of all public school students nationally. New Mexico has the highest percentage of rural students that qualify for free and/or reduced-price lunch (71%) followed by Mississippi (66%), Louisiana (63%), Oklahoma (61%), and Arkansas (60%) (NCES, 2014b).

Despite the stereotype that rural schools and communities are generally deficient, data from the 2008–2009 school year finds that the high school graduation rates of rural students (80%) were higher than the national average (77%) and exceed the average of high school students in urban areas (68%). Of the three rural classifications, the graduation rates were minimally distinct, with graduation rates being the highest in rural distant areas (80.1%) followed by rural fringe (79.9%) and rural remote (79.5%) (NCES, 2014e).

SCHOOL CHOICE IN THE RURAL CONTEXT

The five school choice options outlined in this chapter (not including traditional, assigned, public schools) are charter, private, magnet, and virtual/online schools as well as homeschooling. Continuing the trend found in urban centers across the country, there is less information and data available about noncharter choice options. The following sections provide numerical data about rural student enrollment across each of the five options.

Rural Charter Schools

Charter schools are typically the most commonly considered school choice option, regardless of locale. Approximately 2.1 million students attended 5,700 charter schools across the country during the 2011–2012 school year (NCES, 2014a.) During that same year, there were 983 rural charter schools across the United States, constituting approximately 4% of 27,816 total rural public schools and 17% of total charter schools. Rural charters educate over 327,000 students, or 15% of all charter school students, in 35 states.[1] These numbers (17% of all charter schools and 15% of all charter school students) are similar to those reflecting rural enrollment as approximately 25% of all public school students.

The following eight states have not presently authorized charter school law and are not included in these particular analyses: Alabama, Kentucky, Montana, Nebraska, North Dakota, South Dakota, Vermont, and West Virginia. This is especially important because each of these states has at least 30% of its student population classified as rural and rank in the following order among all 50 states in terms of percentage of rural students: Vermont (2nd), West Virginia (4th), Alabama (6th), South Dakota (7th), North Dakota (8th), Kentucky (11th), Montana (15th), and Nebraska (36th). It may be that charter school law in these states would affect a significant portion of their overall student enrollment and their rural school enrollment.

The five states with the highest total number of rural charter schools are as follows: California (158), Arizona (116), Florida (90), Texas (74), and Oregon (50). The number of rural charter schools in just these five states total 488, or 50% of all rural charter schools nationally. These states are not necessarily the states with the highest number of rural charter school students—a trend similar to the differences in the states with the highest number of rural school students and the states with the highest percentages of rural school students. The five states with the highest rural charter enrollments are California, Florida, Arizona, Colorado, and Georgia. These five states account for 56% of all rural charter school students (NCES, 2014c).

Further, of the 983 rural charter schools, 61% (636 schools) are in rural fringe districts (located the closest to urban areas), with another 224 in rural distant areas. Some 13% (123 schools) of all rural charter schools are located in rural remote areas, the farthest distance from urban centers (NCES, 2014d). Upwards of 84% of all rural charter school students attend a rural fringe charter school, and 4% attend rural remote charter schools. Nine states have 100% of their rural charter school students attending rural fringe charter schools. Oregon only has 25% of its rural charter school population attending rural fringe charters. Conversely, Wisconsin has the highest percentage of students attending rural remote charter schools (28%), and 16 states have no students attending rural remote charter schools. These data provide evidence that students and families living in even the most remote areas are taking advantage of the choice options being provided in their school districts. Table 2.2 lists the states with the highest numbers of charter schools by locale as well as the states with the highest enrollment as a percentage of total rural charter enrollment.

Of the 327,000 students attending rural charter schools, the majority (60%) are White, with 19% of rural charter school students identifying as Hispanic/Latino, 11% identifying as Black, and the remaining 10% identifying as American Indian, Asian, Hawaiian/Pacific Islander, and biracial/multiracial (NCES, 2014d). These data show that rural charter school enrollment is slightly more diverse than rural public school enrollment (NCES, 2014e): 70% White, 13% Hispanic, 10% Black, and the remaining 6% identifying as American Indian, Asian, Hawaiian/Pacific Islander, and biracial/multiracial. However, the demographics of rural charter school students differ substantially from national data, which shows more overall diversity—36% of public charter school students nationally were White, 29%

TABLE 2.2. Highest Number of Rural Charter Schools and Highest Percentages of Rural Charter School Students by Locale

Rural Fringe		Rural Distant		Rural Remote	
Highest Number of Charter Schools	**Highest Percentage of Charter School Students**	**Highest Number of Charter Schools**	**Highest Percentage of Charter School Students**	**Highest Number of Charter Schools**	**Highest Percentage of Charter School Students**
California (117)	Delaware/ Illinois/ Maryland/ New Hampshire/ Nevada/New York/Oklahoma/ Rhode Island/ Tennessee (100%)	Arizona (34)	Oregon (52.6%)	Wisconsin (22)	Wisconsin (28.0%)
Florida (77)	Utah (97.9%)	California (27)	Louisiana (35.5%)	Arizona (16)	Oregon (22.2%)
Texas (66)	Ohio (97.5%)	Wisconsin (26)	Alaska/ Wisconsin (31.7%)	California/ Oregon (14)	Wyoming (18.4%)
Arizona (62)	Texas (94.9%)	Oregon (20)	New Mexico/ Arizona (27.8%)	Minnesota (13)	Idaho (15.8%)
Michigan (36)	(91.0%)	Minnesota/N. Carolina (13)	Kansas (27.7%)	Colorado (7)	Minnesota (13.9%)

Source: National Center for Education Statistics, 2014d

were Black, 28% were Hispanic/Latino, 4% were Asian/Pacific Islander, and 1% were American Indian/Alaskan Native (NCES, 2014a).

However, when focused only on the 129,000 non-White rural charter school students, we find the racial demographics are much more pronounced: 48% of the non-White rural charter school students are Hispanic/Latino, 27% are Black, 9% are Asian, 8% are biracial/multiracial, 4% are American Indian, and 3% are Hawaiian/Pacific Islander. Rhode Island has the least diverse rural charter school enrollment at 90.7% White, while Tennessee has the most diverse rural charter school enrollment at 99.8% non-White (NCES, 2014d). The states with the highest percentages of non-White rural charter school students vary, as evidenced in Table 2.3.

Approximately 34% of rural charter school students qualify for free and/or reduced-price lunch (NCES, 2014d) as compared to 48% of public schools students nationally, and 44% of rural public school students (NCES, 2014b). A total of 81% of the rural charter school students who qualify for free and/or reduced-price lunch attend rural fringe charter schools, and only 6% of students who attend rural remote charter schools qualify. New York has the highest percentage of rural charter school students who qualify for free and/or reduced-price lunch (78.9%), followed by Louisiana, (65.1%), Arkansas (54.5%), Georgia (51.9%), and Hawaii (51.6%) (NCES, 2014d). Three of these states also have the highest percentages of non-White students—Hawaii (third), New York (fourth), and Louisiana (fifth)—indicating that the rural charter school population is growing more racially and socioeconomically diverse.

TABLE 2.3. Highest Percentages of Rural Charter School Student by Racial Demographic

American Indian Rural Charter School Students	Asian Rural Charter School Students	Black Rural Charter School Students	Hispanic/ Latino Rural Charter School Students	Hawaiian/ Pacific Islander Rural Charter School Students	Biracial/ Multiracial Rural Charter School Students
Wyoming (31.8%)	Illinois (13.2%)	Tennessee (93.3%)	Texas (41.7%)	Hawaii (43.1%)	Hawaii (6.6%)
Oklahoma (16.7%)	Hawaii (10.7%)	Louisiana (48.4%)	New Mexico (40.4%)	Nevada (2.0%)	California (5.7%)
Alaska (12.1%)	Texas (7.2%)	Maryland (40.9%)	Florida (36.6%)	Utah (1.2%)	Maryland (5.5%)
New Mexico (8.5%)	Michigan (6.15%)	New York (39.6%)	Colorado (26.0%)	Alaska (0.6%)	Nevada (5.11%)
Arizona (5.4%)	California (5.9%)	S. Carolina (35.8%)	California (25.7%)	California (0.5%)	Massachusetts (4.97%)

Source: National Center for Education Statistics, 2014d

Distance Education/Virtual Schools

A growing trend across the country is the increase in the number of students participating in distance (online) learning. Distance education is defined as credit-granting courses delivered via technology, with the instructor and students in different locations. Instruction is either provided in real time or through email and discussion boards (Queen, Lewis, & Coopersmith, 2011; Watson, Murin, Vashaw, Gemin, & Rapp, 2012). During the 2009–2010 school year, 55% of the nation's public school districts had students enrolled in distance education courses, educating 1.8 million students, up from 36% of districts during the 2002–2003 school year, when 317,000 students took advantage of online courses. Data from the 2010–2011 school year finds that 59% of public rural districts had 329,000 students enrolled in distance education courses, as compared to 654,000 students from 37% of urban districts (Queen et al., 2011). The number of rural students enrolled in distance education courses constitutes 3% of total rural public school enrollment and was greater than each of the student enrollments in rural charter and magnet schools.

Regardless of geographic location (urban, suburban, town, or rural), the vast majority of districts—no less than 95%—had students enrolled in distance education at the high school level; however, rural districts had the lowest percentage (95%) while cities and towns had the highest percentage (98%). Rural districts also had the lowest percentage of districts with students enrolled in distance education at the elementary (4%) and middle school (16%) levels (Queen et al., 2011). On average, 75% of all districts (and 76% of rural districts) with students enrolled in distance education reported courses created by organizations other than the school district itself. These organizations included independent vendors (used by 37% of rural districts), online charter schools (3% of rural districts), postsecondary institutions (61% of rural districts), the state's virtual school (34% of rural districts), and another school district within the state (29% of rural school districts) (Queen et al., 2011).

Independent vendors offer a significant portion of online courses for students across the country, and two such companies are K12 Inc. and Connections Academy. Through these organizations, students are able to enroll in an online school (either a tuition-free public school or a private school), or students can purchase individual courses (appropriate for homeschooled children). K12 Inc. (2014) claims to be the largest provider of online courses, having offered over one million to date.

As participation in distance education increases, it also allows for growth in the number of full-time online (or "virtual") schools, in which all instruction is delivered primarily via technology. Nationally, there were approximately 275,000 students enrolled in full-time virtual schools during the 2011–2012 school year in 31 states and Washington, DC (Watson et al., 2012). Of the 311 full-time virtual schools in operation during the 2011–2012 school year, 58 were operated by K12 Inc. and enrolled 77,000 students (Miron, Horvitz, & Gulosino, 2013).

The growth in online charter schools is synonymous with the growth in fully online schools. These virtual schools operate much in the manner of traditional charter schools, except that they offer instruction through technology as opposed to in brick-and-mortar buildings. Online charter schools constitute 41% of fully online schools and the majority (67%) of student enrollment (Miron et al., 2013). Arizona, California, Colorado, Florida, and Ohio house the majority of fully online schools, with each state having at least 25 schools. Ohio and Pennyslvania have the most students enrolled in fully online schools, with each state enrolling over 30,000 students.

Rural Magnet Schools

Magnet schools, sometimes referred to as the "forgotten choice" (Frankenberg & Siegel-Hawley, 2008) were originally created in the 1970s as a means of circumventing forced busing. The NCES (2014a) reports that there were approximately 3,000 magnet schools nationwide during the 2011–2012 school year, educating 2.2 million children. There is almost half the number of magnet schools nationally as compared to charter schools, yet they educate slightly more children. While most, if not all, states have magnet schools, there are 323 rural magnet schools—accounting for 12% of all magnet schools—in 26 states[2] (NCES, 2014d). Most (197) of these rural magnet schools are located in rural fringe communities, followed by 96 in rural distant areas, and 30 in rural remote areas. These rural magnet schools educate approximately 190,000 students, or 9% of all magnet school students (NCES, 2014d).

Michigan has by far the greatest number of rural magnet schools, and at 150 schools, the state alone represents 46% of all rural magnet schools. Michigan has 69 rural fringe magnet schools (out of 197 total), 59 rural distant magnets (out of 96), and 22 rural remote magnets (out of 30). Michigan also has the highest magnet school enrollment as a percentage of total rural magnet enrollment (30%), or 58,090 students. Florida has the second-highest number of rural magnets (35 schools), educating 22% of rural magnet school students, followed by South Carolina (34 schools), educating 13% of rural magnet students. None of the remaining states have more than 15 rural magnet schools or educate more than 7% of the rural magnet students (NCES, 2014d). Table 2.4 outlines the number of rural magnet schools and the percentages of rural magnet school students by locale.

The racial demographics of rural students who attend magnet schools are similar to those of the students who attend rural charter schools. The majority of rural magnet school students are White (63%), with 18% identifying as Black, 13% identifying as Hispanic/Latino, and the remaining 7% constituting Asian, American Indian, Hawaiian/Pacific Islander, and biracial/multiracial students (NCES, 2014d). Upon closer examination of the 119,000 non-White rural magnet students, we find that Black students represent almost half (49%), with Hispanic/La-

TABLE 2.4. Highest Number of Rural Magnet Schools and Highest Percentages of Rural Magnet School Students by Locale

Rural Fringe		Rural Distant		Rural Remote	
Highest Number of Magnet Schools	**Highest Percentage of Magnet School Students**	**Highest Number of Magnet Schools**	**Highest Percentage of Magnet School Students**	**Highest Number of Magnet Schools**	**Highest Percentage of Magnet School Students**
Michigan (69)	Alabama/ Connecticut/ Georgia/ Idaho/Illinois/ Maryland/ Nevada/ Tennessee/ Texas/Utah/ Virginia (100%)	Michigan (59)	Delaware/Maine (100%)	Michigan (22)	Arizona (100%)
Florida (28)	Florida/ Colorado (91.7%)	S. Carolina (9)	Pennsylvania (85.4%)	Kansas (3)	Kansas (70.0%)
S. Carolina (25)	N. Carolina (86.5%	Florida (7)	New York (66.0%)	Louisiana/ California/ Colorado/ Georgia/Arizona (1)	Colorado/ Michigan (8.3%)
Virginia (13)	Minnesota (83.6%)	Louisiana (4)	Arkansas (34.2%)		Louisiana (6.1%)
Tennessee/Texas (7)	S. Carolina (82.1%)	Minnesota/New York (3)	Michigan (33.9%)		California (0.6%)

Source: National Center for Education Statistics, 2014b

tino students composing another 34% of non-White rural magnet school students. Of the 26 states with rural magnet schools, 15 have student populations composed of at least 45% non-White students. Pennsylvania has the least diverse rural magnet school enrollment at 93.4% White, while Georgia has the greatest diversity among rural magnet school students at 99.1% non-White (NCES, 2014d). Table 2.5 provides information about rural magnet school enrollment across individual racial groups.

There is a significant number, 46%, of rural magnet school students that are eligible for free and/or reduced-price lunch, as compared to 34% of rural charter school students (NCES, 2014d). Some 75% of rural magnet school students who qualify for free and/or reduced-price lunch attend rural fringe magnet schools, while just 5% of students who attend rural remote magnet schools qualify. Georgia has the highest percentage of rural magnet school students who qualify for

TABLE 2.5. Highest Percentages of Rural Magnet School Students by Racial Demographic

American Indian Rural Magnet School Students	Asian Rural Magnet School Students	Black Rural Magnet School Students	Hispanic/ Latino Rural Magnet School Students	Hawaiian/ Pacific Islander Rural Magnet School Students	Biracial/ Multiracial Rural Magnet School Students
Arizona (18.0%)	Nevada (18.5%)	Georgia (98.7%)	California (50.3%)	Nevada (2.0%)	California (7.1%)
N. Carolina (2.8%)	Maine (11.1%)	Louisiana (62.4%)	Texas (43.5%)	Utah (0.9%)	Virginia (6.9%)
Kansas (2.5%)	Illinois (8.2%)	Connecticut (48.5%)	Nevada (36.7%)	Arizona (0.6%)	Nevada (5.9%)
Michigan (1.6%)	Virginia (7.7%)	N. Carolina (47.2%)	Arizona (32.8%)	Maryland (0.5%)	Colorado (4.8%)
California (1.0%)	Maryland (6.9%)	Maryland (39.2%)	Illinois (22.8%)	California (0.4%)	Maryland (4.7%)

Source: National Center for Education Statistics, 2014d

free and/or reduced-price lunch (89.6%), followed by Louisiana, (74.3%), Kansas (68.4%), North Carolina (56.8%), and Texas (52.9%). Three of these states also have the highest percentages of non-White rural magnet school students—Georgia (first), Texas (second), and North Carolina (fourth)—indicating that the rural magnet school population is racially and socioeconomically diverse, similar to student enrollments in rural charter schools (NCES, 2014d). Of the 26 states with rural magnet schools, 15 have student populations of 40% or more who qualify for free and/or reduced-price lunch.

Rural Private Schools

The National Center for Education Statistics reports that, in the 2011–2012 school year, there were a total of 30,861 private elementary and secondary schools across the country, educating 4.5 millions students (Broughman & Swaim, 2013). Some 46% of the private schools were non-Catholic religious (14,214), while 32% (9,775 schools) were nonsectarian, and the remaining 22% (7,100) were Catholic schools. Geographic data finds that the majority of the approximately 31,000 private schools were located in either suburban areas (10,911) or urban areas (10,005). There were 7,045 rural private schools, and the remaining 2,900 private schools were located in towns (Broughman & Swaim, 2013).

Data from the 2010 Private School Universe Survey (NCES, 2014c) reports that during the 2009–2010 school year, approximately 600,000 students attended 5,623 rural private schools. As with the other brick-and-mortar school choice options, most of the rural private schools (58%) were located in rural fringe areas, with another 33% in rural distant areas, and the remaining 7% in rural remote areas. Rural private school students are dispersed across the country more evenly than rural charter or magnet school students. Pennsylvania has the most rural private school students as a percentage of the total rural private school population at 7%, followed by Georgia, Texas, and Florida (5% each), and California and Virginia (4% each). Pennsylvania has the highest number of rural private schools (716), followed by Indiana (277), Wisconsin (254), California (234), and Ohio (215) (NCES, 2014c). Table 2.6 outlines the states with the highest number of rural private schools and highest percentages of rural school students by locale.

Just under 600,000 students attended roughly 5,600 rural private schools in 2010, accounting for 13% of total private school enrollment and 5% of all rural school enrollment. When disaggregated by private school type, data shows that the majority of rural private schools are religious schools (66%), followed by nonsectarian schools (24%), and Catholic schools (10%). Unlike the student

TABLE 2.6. Highest Number of Rural Private Schools and Highest Percentages of Rural Private School Students by Locale

Rural Fringe		**Rural Distant**		**Rural Remote**	
Highest Number of Private Schools	**Highest Percentage of Private School Students**	**Highest Number of Private Schools**	**Highest Percentage of Private School Students**	**Highest Number of Private Schools**	**Highest Percentage of Private School Students**
Pennsylvania (400)	Pennsylvania (7%)	Pennsylvania (268)	Pennsylvania (9%)	Wisconsin (55)	Maine/ Mississippi (9%)
California (188)	Texas/Florida/ Georgia (6%)	Indiana (147)	Virginia/Indiana (6%)	Minnesota (40)	Minnesota/ Wisconsin/ Alabama/ Nebraska (7%)
Florida (167)	California (5%)	Ohio (116)	Wisconsin/ Michigan (5%)	Missouri (37)	Missouri (5%)
Texas (151)	N. Carolina/ Maryland/Ohio/ New Jersey (4%)	Wisconsin (110)	Georgia/Ohio/ Mississippi/ Alabama/ Missouri (4%)	Nebraska (34)	Michigan (4%)
Georgia (132)	S. Carolina/ Virginia/ Mississippi/ Tennessee/ Illinois/Indiana/ Alabama (3%)	New York (102)	S. Carolina/N. Carolina/New York/Minnesota/ Iowa/New Hampshire (3%)	Michigan (28)	Vermont (3%)

Source: National Center for Education Statistics, 2014c

enrollment evident in rural charter and magnet schools, enrollment in rural private schools is far less diverse. In 2011, rural private schools were 74% White (NCES, 2014c), and by 2012, almost 84% of rural private school students were White (Broughman & Swaim, 2013). The demographics of the remaining rural private school students were 5% Black, 3% Asian, 5% Hispanic/Latino, and the remaining 4% were American Indian, Hawaiian/Pacific Islander and/or biracial/multiracial (Broughman & Swaim, 2013). Student-level data obtained from the 2009–2010 Private School Universe Survey was not as extensive as that collected from the Public School Universe Survey; state-level analyses on the racial demographics of rural private school students (similar to Tables 2.3 and 2.5) will not be included in this particular analysis.

Rural Homeschooling

Data from the 2011–2012 school year found that approximately 1.7 million children were homeschooled, or 3% of all school-aged children (Noel, Stark, Redford, & Zukerberg, 2013). Homeschool data and research is not as expansive or as readily available as that collected on the other school choice options, and it is possible that this particular data may overlap with the numbers of students who participate in distance education.

Of the almost two million children who are homeschooled, there is almost a fairly even split between urban (28%, or 489,000 students), suburban (34%, or 601,000 students), and rural (31%, or 584,000 students) families (Noel et al., 2013). The remaining 7% of homeschooled students live in towns. Based on absolute numbers, homeschooling is the second-most popular school choice option among rural families after private schools. Demographically, the racial makeup of rural homeschooled students reflects rural public school enrollment—68% of rural homeschooled students are White (as compared to 70% of rural public school students), 15% are Hispanic /Latino (compared to 13% of rural public school students), 8% are Black (10% of rural public school students are Black), and the remaining 9% identify as American Indian, Asian, Hawaiian/Pacific Islander, and biracial/multiracial (6% of rural public school students).

THE NEED FOR CONTINUED RESEARCH ON RURAL SCHOOL CHOICE

Arnold, Newman, Gaddy, and Dean (2005) suggest that there has been a lack of high-quality research conducted on issues pertaining to rural education, and point to the fewer than 500 articles published on rural education between 1991 and 2003. Further still, only 30 of the 498 articles were focused on educational policy issues specific to rural communities (the more popular topics were students with special needs, instruction, school safety, and student acheivement) with 7 of those 30 addressing school choice.

Stuit and Doan (2012) contend that although the educational needs of those living in cities often overshadow the needs of those in rural communities, data suggests that rural students and families face more severe problems, including small district size, rapid population declines or increases, teacher and administrator recruitment and hiring, inadequate funding, and achievement concerns (Jimerson, 2005; Stuit & Doan, 2012). Jimerson (2005) argues that recent educational policies, including 2001's No Child Left Behind Act, are biased against rural communities and "devalues some of the most positive attributes of small rural schools, and undermines many other current efforts to improve rural education" (p. 211).

The data presented in this chapter paints a positive picture about school choice options for and participation by rural families, yet school choice is still a hot-button issue in many states, and especially for some rural families, and demands continued attention. For example, the Alabama Accountability Act, passed in 2013, provided school choice options for students in failing schools by allowing them to transfer to nonfailing schools and also provided a $3,500 tax credit to all families, regardless of income, if they wish to send their child to a private school (Alabama House Republicans, 2014). The Southern Poverty Law Center (SPLC) filed a lawsuit opposing the Act, calling it "a perverse interpretation of school choice" (Gadd, 2014, para. 12) as "non-failing schools were not required to admit a child from a failing school" (Gadd, 2014, para. 11). The SPLC lawsuit, filed on behalf of eight students living below the poverty line in rural counties, argued that the Alabama Accountability Act "creates two classes of students assigned to failing schools—those who can escape them because of their parents' income or where they live, and those, like our Plaintiffs here, who cannot" (C.M. v. Bentley, 2013, para. 3). Alabama has the sixth-highest percentage of rural students (48%) (NCES, 2014e) and 55% of its rural student enrollment qualifies for free and reduced-price lunch (NCES, 2014b). Although the SPLC lawsuit was dismissed in April 2014, the Act was eventually overturned in May 2014, with the judge ruling that it violated the state's Constitution (Cason, 2014). Legislation such as this could have affected a significant portion of the state's schoolchildren, and provides another lens through which to discuss not only school choice but issues of access and equity as well.

Similar to the pushback in Alabama as a response to the state's Accountability Act, enrollment in private schools, especially through the use of vouchers, still enjoys a lively debate in other parts of the country as well, especially across political lines. Although Democrats, including President Obama, have openly supported school choice, and in particular, charter schools, Republicans have been pushing for the use of vouchers to support school choice and student enrollment in private schools. Many of those who oppose the use of vouchers disagree with the use of public funding to support private education, especially problematic when used in schools with religious-based practices and curriculum. Interestingly, many rural Republicans oppose vouchers as well (Bump, 2014), arguing that rural schools presently receive little funding and a voucher program would siphon off what little monies they do receive. Additionally, some rural Republicans don't support voucher programs because there are few rural private schools from which to choose (Bump, 2014). Here again, place plays a role in support or rejection of a particular choice option—in this case, voucher programs.

Finally, it is necessary to continue to focus on rural school choice because the population in and demographics of rural communities are changing rapidly. Between 2000 and 2010, the population in rural counties increased by 2.2 million people (4.5% growth), with growth across all classifications of rural areas—rural fringe areas grew by 5.5% and rural remote areas grew by 2.7%. Across those 10 years, minorities accounted for 83% of the population growth in rural areas, with Hispanics/Latinos constituting 54% of the rural population gain (Johnson, 2012). Rural areas are still less diverse than cities, but it is evident that the diversity is increasing dramatically. There are almost 600 counties nationally that have more non-White students than White students, and over half (356 counties) are located in rural districts. An additional 300 counties are near "majority-minority," in that they are between 40% and 50% minority youth. Of those, 178 are rural and are concentrated in the Mississippi Delta, the Rio Grande area, the Southeast, and the Northern Great Plains (Johnson, 2012).

Scholars have argued that choice exacerbates racial and socioeconomic segregation in schools (Butrymowicz, 2013; Erickson, 2011; Frankenberg, Seigel-Hawley, & Wang, 2010; Renzulli & Evans, 2005; Saporito, 2003). While much of this research points to the growing number of non-White schools of choice (including charter and magnet schools), Butrymowicz (2013) points to growing numbers of predominately White charter schools located in suburban areas. Chingos (2013) revisited the research on school choice and segregation and analyzed 10 years of data taken from the Common Core. His findings suggest that charter schools are not necessarily causing school segregation to increase; however, "school choice policies come in a variety of flavors which may have different effects on the demographic makeup of schools" (para. 12).

Consistent research has shown that racially isolated minority schools have access to fewer resources, larger class sizes, and inadequate facilities (Orfield, Frankenberg & Garces, 2008). Stuit and Doan (2012) note that schools in rural fringe areas have better access to the human, cultural, and fiscal resources located in central cities, while schools in rural remote areas tend to be more autonomous. Although the majority of research on school choice and segregation has traditionally been conducted on public schools in many of the country's largest metropolitan areas, these studies raise important questions about school choice in rural areas, where schools and communities are often faced with additional challenges, including geographic isolation, less funding, and rapidly increasing racial diversity.

CONCLUSION

Arnold et al. (2005) contend that the dearth of research focused on rural school choice may be based on the assumption that geography negates choice. Of the 13 million rural students across the country (which constitute roughly 25% of the nation's schoolchildren), approximately 2.03 million children (15%) are participating in some sort of school choice option—with 600,000 attending rural private schools, 584,000 homeschooling, 329,000 participating in distance education, 327,000 attending rural charter schools, and 190,000 attending rural magnet schools. Based on these data, it is evident that parents in rural locations, and even those in the most rural remote locations, are exercising choice and sending their children to nonassigned schools. This chapter provides evidence that rural families are not concentrated in one particular area of the country nor do they all look the same. Further, rural families participating in school choice cross racial, socioeconomic, and geographic boundaries.

Public schools of choice, specifically charter and magnet schools, often provide targeted curricula, and schools of choice in rural areas are no different. Where the differences do lie, however, are often in the academics offered by rural schools. While many rural schools of choice focus on leadership development and college readiness (just like those in urban and suburban areas), some target the needs of rural communities by focusing on agriculture and farming. There exists far less information about rural charter and magnet schools and the curriculum being taught in these schools, as compared to their urban and suburban counterparts, but the lesson here is not only what these rural schools teach but that they exist and provide viable options for families.

Regardless of school setting or choice option studied, there has been no definitive research to date which finds that participation in school choice has a clear positive impact on student achievement (Bifulco & Ladd, 2006; Center for Research on Educational Outcomes, 2009; Wolf, 2012). As such, Jimerson (2006) argues that the impact of school choice and school choice policies on rural students, schools, and districts should be closely evaluated over time. This is especially important given the range in political climates at the local, state, and national levels in support or opposition of various school choice laws and policies in general, and charters and vouchers, in particular.

The intent of this chapter was not to promote or critique school choice, school choice in the rural settings, the reasons why parents choose, or student achievement as a result of participation in school choice options. While the academic and political attention paid to rural education and rural schools is growing, there remains a lack of research specifically targeting rural school choice. The evidence provided throughout this chapter serves as a foundation for the continued in-depth discussion of rural school choice and brings a new perspective to the relationship between place and choice. As rural schools and communities diversify, research addressing school choice should follow suit.

NOTES

1. The seven states that do not have rural charter schools, but have passed charter school laws are Alaska, Connecticut, Iowa, Maine, Missouri, Virginia, and Washington.

2. Alabama, Arkansas, Arizona, California, Colorado, Connecticut, Delaware, Florida, Georgia, Idaho, Illinois, Kansas, Louisiana, Maryland, Maine, Michigan, Minnesota, North Carolina, Nevada, New York, Pennsylvania South Carolina, Tennessee, Texas, Utah, and Virginia.

REFERENCES

Alabama House Republicans. (2014). *Accountability Act of 2013.* Retrieved from http://alhousegop.com/accountability/

Arnold, M. L., Newman, J. H., Gaddy, B. B., & Dean, C. B. (2005). A look at the condition of rural education research: Setting a direction for future research. *Journal of Research in Rural Education, 20*(6), 1–25.

Bifulco, R. P., & Ladd. H. F. (2006). The impacts of charter schools on student achievement: Evidence from North Carolina. *Education Finance and Policy, 1*(1), 50–90.

Broughman, S. P., & Swaim, N. L. (2013). *Characteristics of private schools in the United States: Results from the 2011–12 Private School Universe Survey*. Washington, DC: National Center for Education Statistics.

Bump, P. (2014, January 22). Why don't Republicans want school vouchers in places Republicans actually live? *The Wire.* Retrieved from http://www.thewire.com/politics/2014/01/why-dont-republicans-want-school-vouchers-places-republicans-actually-live/357277/

Butrymowicz, S. (2013, July 15). A new round of segregation plays out in charter schools. *The Hechinger Report.* Retrieved from http://hechingerreport.org/content/as-charter-schools-come-of-age-measuring-their-success-is-tricky_12647/

Cason, M. (2014). *Montgomery County judge rules Alabama Accountability Act unconstitutional.* Retrieved from http://blog.al.com/wire/2014/05/montgomery_county_judge_rules.html

C.M. et al. vs. Robert J. Bentley, M.D. et al. (2013). Retrieved from http://www.splcenter.org/sites/default/files/downloads/case/stamped_complaint.pdf

Center for Research on Education Outcomes. (2009). *Multiple choice: Charter school performance in 16 states*. Stanford, CA: Stanford University.

Chingos, M. M. (2013, May 15). Does expanding school choice increase segregation? *Brookings.* Retrieved from http://www.brookings.edu/blogs/brown-center-chalkboard/posts/2013/05/15-school-choice-segregation-chingos

Erickson, A. T. (2011). The rhetoric of choice: Segregation, desegregation, and charter schools. *Dissent, 58*(4), 41–46.

Frankenberg, E., & Siegel-Hawley, G. (2008). *The forgotten choice? Rethinking magnet schools in a changing landscape.* Los Angeles, CA: Civil Rights Project/Proyecto Derechos Civiles at UCLA.

Frankenberg, E., Siegel-Hawley, G., & Wang, J. (2010). *Choice without equity: Charter school segregation and the need for civil rights standards*. Los Angeles, CA: Civil Rights Project/Proyecto Derechos Civiles at UCLA.

Gadd, M. G. (2014, January 29). Alabama Accountability Act leaves disadvantaged children trapped in failing schools. *Southern Poverty Law Center.* Retrieved from http://www.splcenter.org/get-informed/news/Alabama-Accountability-Act-leaves-disadvantaged-children-trapped-in-failing-schools

Jimerson, L. (2005). Placism in NCLB—How rural children are left behind. *Equity & Excellence in Education, 38*, 211–219.

Jimerson, L. (2006). *Breaking the fall: Cushioning the impact of rural declining enrollment.* Arlington, VA: Rural School and Community Trust.

Johnson, K. (2012). Rural demographic change in the new century: Slower growth, increased diversity. Durham: Carsey Institute, University of New Hampshire.

K12 Inc. (2014). *Online public schools.* Retrieved from http://www.k12.com/schools-programs/online-public-schools#.U439mi-7m70

Miron, G., Horvitz, B., & Gulosino, C. (2013). *Virtual schools in the U.S.: Politics, performance, policy, and research evidence.* Boulder, CO: National Education Policy Center.

National Center for Education Statistics (NCES). (2014a). *Number and enrollment of public elementary and secondary schools, by school level, type, and charter and magnet status: Selected years 1990–91 through 2011–12.* Retrieved from http://nces.ed.gov/programs/digest/d13/tables/dt13_216.20.asp

National Center for Education Statistics (NCES). (2014b). *Number and percent of students in city, suburban, town, and rural regular public elementary and secondary schools with membership who are eligible for free or reduced-price lunch, by state or jurisdiction: School year 2010–11.* Retrieved from http://nces.ed.gov/pubs2012/pesschools10/tables/table_07.asp

National Center for Education Statistics (NCES). (2014c). *Private school universe survey, 2009–10.* Retrieved from http://nces.ed.gov/surveys/pss/

National Center for Education Statistics (NCES). (2014d). *Public elementary/secondary school universe survey, 2011-2012.* Retrieved from http://nces.ed.gov/ccd/pubschuniv.asp

National Center for Education Statistics (NCES). (2014e). *Rural education in America: Data on schools and school districts.* Retrieved from http://nces.ed.gov/surveys/RuralEd/index.asp

National Center for Education Statistics (NCES). (2014f). *School locale definitions.* Retrieved from http://nces.ed.gov/surveys/ruraled/definitions.asp

Noel, A., Stark, P., Redford, J., & Zukerberg, A. (2013). *Parent and family involvement in education, from the National Household Education Surveys Program of 2012.* Washington, DC: National Center for Education Statistics.

Orfield, G., Frankenberg, E., & Garces, L. M. (2008). Statement of American Social Scientists of research on school desegregation to the U.S. Supreme Court in *Parents v. Seattle School District* and *Meredith v. Jefferson County*. *Urban Review, 40*, 96–136.

Queen, B., Lewis, L., & Coopersmith, J. (2011). *Distance education courses for public elementary and secondary school students: 2009–10.* Washington, DC: National Center for Education Statistics.

Renzulli, L. A., & Evans, L. (2005). School choice, charter schools, and White flight. *Social Problems, 52*, 398–418.

Saporito, S. (2003). Private choices, public consequences: Magnet school choice and segregation by race and poverty. *Social Problems, 50*, 181–203.

Stuit, D., & Doan, S. (2012). *Beyond city limits: Expanding public charter schools in rural America.* Washington, DC: National Alliance for Public Charter Schools.

U.S. Census Bureau. (2014). *2010 census urban and rural classification and urban area criteria*. Retrieved from http://www.census.gov/geo/reference/ua/urban-rural-2010.html

Watson, J., Murin, A., Vashaw, L., Gemin, B., & Rapp, C. (2012). *Keeping pace with K–12 online and blended learning 2012: An annual review of policy and practice.* Durango, CO: Evergreen Education Group.

Wolf, P. J. (2012). *The comprehensive longitudinal evaluation of the Milwaukee Parental Choice Program: Summary of final reports.* Fayetteville: University of Arkansas Press.

CHAPTER 3

THE UNEQUAL IMPACT OF THE GREAT RECESSION ON THE INSTRUCTIONAL CAPACITY OF RURAL SCHOOLS

John W. Sipple and Yuan Yao

INTRODUCTION

The investment made by federal, state, and local governments in U.S. public schools is, by any measure, substantial. Collectively, more than $560 billion are spent to educate our nation's children in Kindergarten[1] through twelfth grade—roughly $11,300 for every pre-K–12 student in the country. Of course, these resources are not allocated evenly, with state averages ranging from just over $6,000 in Utah to more than $19,000 in New York. But while state averages are salient and illustrative, the within-state differences can be a telling tale of the (in) equitable distribution of educational opportunity within the same state. This can be particularly apparent when documenting within-state differences in investment among urban, suburban, and rural areas. This chapter focuses attention on these inter- and intrastate resources—resources closely related to the core functioning of schools—with special attention given to rural communities and inequalities.

Educational Opportunity in Rural Contexts: The Politics of Place, pages 39–58.

Much research on teacher staffing highlights the challenges of recruitment and retention of adequate numbers of qualified teachers. Specifically, there is a great challenge in incentivizing quality teachers into hard-to-staff school placements, which include school demographics, salary schedules, location and nonmonetary benefits (Kolbe & Rice, 2012; Kolbe & Strunk, 2012; Miller, 2012; Opfer, 2011; Reininger, 2012). This study, however, does not examine the strategies to lure individuals to specific instructional positions, but rather examines the overall instructional capacity of school districts to serve their communities in the form of staffing levels and ratios. Specifically this study addresses concerns about whether the Great Recession (December 2007–June 2009; NBER, 2015) reduced or exacerbated such differences in teacher staffing with specific analysis of pre- and post-recession patterns of staffing across location and community wealth. It has been documented that the recovery from the recession has been uneven (Wilson, 2014) and understudied, especially given the continued push for higher academic standards, an increasingly demographically diverse student body, enhanced teacher accountability policies, and the Common Core curriculum initiative across the nation.

Within- and between-state staffing differences are important to study in light of the requisite attention paid to differential educational opportunity since the *Brown* decision of more than 60 years ago, the Coleman (1966) and Jencks (1969) studies of the late 1960s, and the series of adequacy and equity-based court cases adjudicated across 40 states since the 1970s (e.g., see Baker & Green, 2011; Jackson & Johnson, 2013). Complicating the longer-term historical differences is the impact of the recession of 2008 and how it likely impacted some states and regions more than others. Recently, the Economic Policy Institute (Gould, 2014) published a brief on the gap in the number of teachers, nationally, between what staffing levels might have been without the recession and compares it with the actual number of teachers employed in the years since the recession (see Figure 3.1). The EPI estimates that the nation employs about 377,000 fewer teachers today than it would have without the recession. This includes the actual reduction in the number of teachers employed in public schools but also the increase in the number of teachers who likely would have been hired given the 1.6% increase in the total enrollment of students over this time period from 2008 to 2013. This brief is useful in highlighting, nationally, the loss of instructional positions but provides no insight into state differences and certainly no insight on within-state changes in instructional capacity.

Background

It is well known that schools are a human endeavor with fully 65% of all school district budgets paying for teachers and at least 85% of all expenditures paying for teachers, administrators, and other, nonacademic support staff. U.S. public schools currently educate 49.5 million children by employing 3.1 million

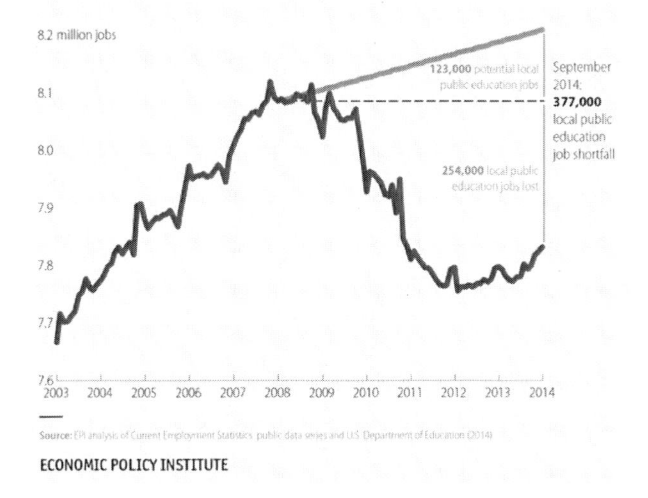

FIGURE 3.1. Local public education jobs (2013–2014). Source: Gould (2014).

teachers, which results in a ratio of 16 students for every teacher across the nation (NCES, 2014). This investment in reducing the student-to-teacher ratio is up from 1990 when the ratio was just over 17 students per teacher, and 1970 when there were 22.3 students per teacher. National- and state-level trends over time reveal steady declines in these ratios signaling a steady increase in investment in the instructional capacity of schools across the nation. While this is true in national terms, the relative levels and trend patterns vary substantially by state and year (Sipple, 2007) and with only limited evidence that staffing is related to "evidenced-based" practices (Cohen-Vogel, 2011). The total bill for this increase in staffing is large, though the public consistently reports that lack of financial support remains a key challenge for local public schools (PDK, 2014). Given that the majority of all dollars spent on public education is for teachers and that most agree that teachers are central to a quality educational experience, it seems wise to examine the trends of rural vs. nonrural staffing patterns, especially in light of the post-recession budget cuts caused by shrinking property values and freezes or cuts in state and federal aid.

Given the tension between calls for more centralized influence over public schools and the decentralized governance and funding of public schools in the United States (see Marsh & Wohlstetter, 2013), we choose to focus our analyses on a small number of states to allow for more careful comparison of intrastate analyses to explore the (in)equitable distribution of funding pre- and post-2008 recession. In selecting these states, we chose a mix of large states (e.g., New York, California, Texas, and Pennsylvania) with substantial numbers of urban and suburban school districts, and historically important states with regard to educational opportunity and equity (e.g., Arkansas, Kansas, and Iowa). Arkansas was the home of the *Little Rock Nine* and served at the forefront of the battle to integrate schools. Kansas, of course, was the genesis of the *Brown v. Topeka School Board* court case. And Iowa has received much attention regarding the widespread arguments and concerns about the "hollowing out" of rural America (Carr & Kefalas, 2009), as evidenced by population decline and net losses of in- vs. out-migration movements. It should be further noted that prior analysis of staffing trends across the U.S. highlighted substantial within- and cross-state differences among these states (Sipple, 2007). We intentionally do not include predominantly rural states (e.g., Vermont, the Dakotas, Wyoming, Mississippi), as our analytic focus is on the (in)equitable distribution of staffing levels within states across various locales. For this reason, we focus on states with large urban and rural populations.

Policy

Throughout history, policies that impact staffing patterns predominately include (a) those that legislate the ability of local school districts and/or communities to raise revenues (e.g., fiscally independent or dependent districts); (b) state formulas and mechanisms to distribute state tax dollars through school aid programs (e.g., foundation or equalization formulas, per-pupil grants); and (c) the small but important federal aid for compensatory and special education teachers since the 1960s (i.e., Title 1 and P.L. 94-142). But beyond targeted funding mechanisms, staffing-relevant policies can also include classroom quality measures, such as class size minimums or caps (see California and Florida) and teacher qualifications or licensure requirements (e.g., state-defined licensure requirements and the federal *Highly Qualified Teacher* initiative).

While it is clear that there are key staffing decisions at the local, state, and federal levels, federal policy has only a modest impact on core staffing levels, with the vast majority of federal aid (together making up only 5%–10% of a local school budget) geared toward staffing special education and compensatory programs in higher need school buildings (e.g., P.L. 94-142 and Elementary and Secondary Education Act's Title 1). State policy, however, is where about half of all K–12 dollars are allocated through myriad of funding formulas and allocations (Jackson & Johnson, 2013). These state finance reform initiatives are often court driven and related to spending differentials and achievement differences.

Recession Policy

The most visible policy change related to school staffing levels during and after the 2008 recession was the action taken by Congress to stem the tide of massive budget cuts and near-certain staffing reductions. This was widely known as ARRA, or the *American Recovery and Reinvestment Act of 2009*. ARRA funds were aimed to soften the blow of the recession by generating federal stimulus spending to stem the threat of public and private sector layoffs. If the recession was quick, the ARRA funds might provide the bridge needed to sustain service provision through to the other side of the recession. However, if the recession dragged on, the stimulus funds would simply delay the inevitable layoffs and could be viewed as an expensive and only temporary band-aid.

Between 2009 and 2012, Congress awarded a total of $283 billion to a variety of departments and programs (see Recovery.gov). The Departments of Commerce, Agriculture, and Defense each received about $6 billion in ARRA funds, while Health and Human Services, Energy, and Transportation received $27, $35, and $47 billion, respectively. Dwarfing these numbers, however, was the nearly $100 billion ($97,280,522,191) received by the U.S. Department of Education to then spend on stimulus programs. It is from these ARRA funds that both competitive (e.g., the *Race to the Top*) and noncompetitive grants to states were awarded (see Kolbe & Rice, 2012).

Moreover, in 2010, President Obama signed the *Education Jobs Fund* into law (Public Law No. 111-226, August 10, 2010). This appropriated an additional $10 billion dollars to "rehire, retain, or hire" instructional employees (specifically not allowing these funds to supplant state funds, retire local debt, or create "rainy-day funds") in school districts across the nation. While these funds were allocated based on a state's population (and guided by the distribution of Part A, Title 1 funds), the distribution of the dollars within a state allowed some flexibility for how each state would distribute the aid to local districts. Secretary of Educaiotn Arne Duncan stated, "There is a huge sense of urgency to get these funds out the door. . . . These education dollars will help these states keep thousands of teachers in the classroom working with our students this school year" (U.S. Department of Education, 2010).

It is in this light that we analyze a small number of states to trace the trajectory of enrollment and staffing changes. More specifically, we examine whether there was any pattern to the changes in staffing levels related to locale (urban, suburban, rural), wealth, or size. Our null hypothesis is that there will not be a differential impact of the recession, there will not be differences between states, and that there will not be differences within states by geography. In testing these hypotheses, we look for variables that would explain or uncover differences (if any) within and between states. Regarding the aforementioned federal attempts to stave off local layoffs, Table 3.1 displays the various awards including the ARRA funds, Education Jobs Fund, and the Race-To-the-Top awards. The *ARRA* funds

TABLE 3.1. Federal Recession-Motivated Program Allocations by State

	ARRA (millions)	Education Jobs Fund (millions)	Race To the Top (millions)	Total (millions)	Estimated # of Teachers ($75K) from Education Jobs Fund
AR	$2,134	$93		$2,227	$1,235
CA	$29,460	$1,218		$30,678	$16,240
IA	$2,043	$98		$2,141	$1,309
KS	$2,097	$94		$2,191	$1,252
NY	$13,650	$617	$697 (2011)	$14,963	$8,220
PA	$8,724	$391	$413 (2013)	$9,528	$5,213
TX	$15,603	$842		$16,445	$11,222

Sources: https://www2.ed.gov/programs/racetothetop/awards.html; http://www.recovery.gov/arra/Pages/; http://www.recovery.gov/ejf/Pages/home.aspx

RTT funds distributed over three years.

range from just over $2 billion to each of the three smaller states (Arkansas, Iowa, Kansas) up to nearly $30 billion allocated to California. The *Education Jobs Fund* included similarly proportioned allocations with just over $90 million to each of the three smaller states, $391 million to Pennsylvania, $617 million to New York, $842 million to Texas, and $1.2 billion to California.

Data and Methods

The data for this study comes from the publicly available *Common Core of Data* (CCD) collected by National Center for Education Statistics (NCES). The CCD is an annual collection of fiscal and nonfiscal data about all public schools, public school districts, and state education agencies in the United States. After initial analyses of national- and state-level data, the study zeroes in on district-level data within states to capture the variation (if any) in the distribution of staffing levels across locations (e.g., rural vs. urban).

We extracted 12 years of state- and district-level data from the CCD, beginning with the 2000/2001 school year and ending with 2011/2012 school year. This set of data captures reforms beginning with the roll out of the *No Child Left Behind Act of 2001* and before the Great Recession of 2008, but then allows us several years of data to measure the impact of the recession and the infusion of the ARRA funds through 2012. Key variables include basic demographic information, staffing levels, and student enrollment. We include in our analyses states that have significant historical roles and demonstrate interesting trends in our initial state-level data analysis (Arkansas, Iowa, Kansas, and Pennsylvania). These states also have a substantial number of rural districts in addition to their more populated urban centers. We include California, New York, and Texas as three of the largest states in any national policy discussion, but which also have great variety of school district locales and were featured centrally in the recession and policy discussions following the recession.

Before regression analyses were performed, we engaged in substantial data checking and cleansing to ensure meaningful results for the study. Due to data availability,[2] New York City was dropped from the New York State data in these analyses. Charter schools, officially not part of any school district, were aggregated to the county level to draw useful information on their impact in their local regions. We used this dichotomous charter variable simply as a control for the differential funding and size of charter schools across five of the selected states (Iowa and Kansas have no charter schools).

For the main analysis, we analyze staffing trends in light of key contextual variables. These variables include an indicator of locale (i.e., rural, urban, suburban, town) by using the National Center for Education Statistics Urban-Centric Local Codes (NCES, 2007). These include 12 codes broken into four distinct categories:

Urban

11 = Large City with population of 250,000
12 = Medium City with population of 100,000 to 250,000
13 = Small City in "urbanized area" with population of less than 100,000

Suburban

21 = Suburb of a large city
22 = Suburb of a medium city
23 = Suburb of a small city

Town

31 = Urban Fringe Town less than 10 miles from urban center
32 = Distant Town located more than 10 but less than 35 miles from urban center
33 = Remote Town located more than 35 miles from urban center

Rural

41 = Rural Fringe, a census-defined rural area less than 5 miles from an urbanized area or 2.5 miles from an urban cluster
42 = Rural Distant, more than 5 miles but less than 25 miles from an urbanized area or more than 2.5 miles but less than 10 miles from an urban cluster
43 = Rural Remote, more than 25 miles from urbanized area or more than 10 miles from an urban cluster.

Our prior analyses have suggested that the remote towns (code 33) look and act much more like the rural districts (codes 41, 42, and 43) than do the urban fringe (code 31) and distant towns (code 32). For this reason, we include districts with a local code of 33 with the rural locale. There is some reason to believe that the rural fringe districts (code 41) look and act more like towns or even suburbs, but in this analysis, we keep the three rural codes together along with the remote towns.

In addition to locale, we use a single measure of local wealth, free and reduced price lunch (%FRPL). This measure of aggregated individual student wealth is a rough proxy for community wealth but is a related variable that is available for all districts across all years. We also use an indicator of school agency type (e.g., public school district, charter school). This is important to distinguish between traditional school districts and charter schools as another opportunity for staffing inequalities. We use the total pre-k–12 enrollment (including ungraded students) as our indicator of district size. This is a critical indicator when assessing relative staffing patterns as changes in staffing may result from changes in enrollments or from more or less generous distribution of state or federal aid. Finally, to allow for the estimation of trends over time and for nested time-series regression modeling, we include the year from which the data was gathered. This is typically referred to by the academic year (e.g., 2010/11 academic year).

Given the nested nature of the data (i.e., multiple years of data for each individual district), we conducted random-effects longitudinal linear regression, accounting for clustering the panel data by district over time. We ran the same model for each of our seven states, with the only difference being the exclusion of the charter school dummy variable for Iowa and Kansas. The dependent variable, full-time teachers (Teacher FTEs), is standardized (mean = 0, st. dev. = 1) to make interpretation and comparability across states easier and more appropriate.

Findings

National

As discussed above, it does not seem fruitful to simply conduct an aggregate national analysis of school staffing differences between locales (rural, suburban, and urban) and wealth. While examination at the national level between urban and rural, wealthy and poor districts may yield some differences, the significant policy and budgeting decisions that impact local staffing levels are deeply institutionalized at the state and local level.

Nevertheless, the general trend of public school teacher FTEs is steadily increasing with slight fluctuation around the 2008 recession. Figure 3.2 displays the number of teacher FTEs in all public schools and the ratio of students to teachers (FTE) over the same time period. Over time (2000/2001 through 2011/2012), the figure displays the steady increase in the sum total of teachers across the nation. The one exception to the steady increase is seen at the time of the start of the recession (2008/2009 through 2009/2010) when the number of teachers flattens out (see left vertical axis). Using the right vertical axis, we see the steady decline in

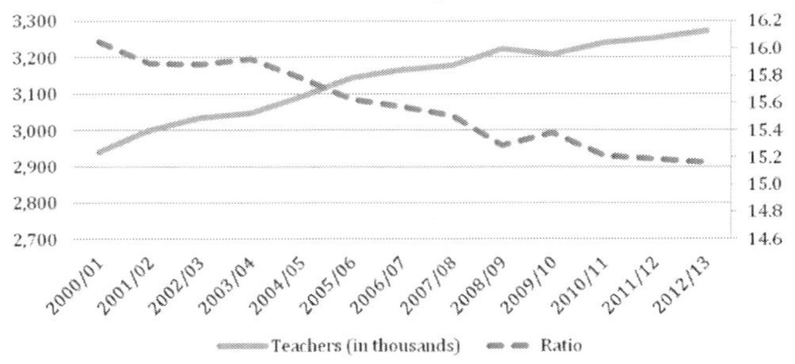

FIGURE 3.2. Total teacher FTEs and student-to-teacher ratios (2000–2012).

the overall ratio of students to teachers with the one exception marked by the start of the recession. What is not shown is the change in the number of students (see Table 3.2) that has steadily increased from 47.2 million in 2000 to 49.6 million in 2012. From Figure 3.2, it is clear that whatever the collective investment local school districts are making in teachers is outpacing the increase in the number of students.

TABLE 3.2. Numbers of Public School Teachers, Students, and the Ratio of Students to Teachers from 2000 to 2012

Year	Teachers (in thousands)	Enrollment (in thousands)	Ratio
2000	2,941	47,204	16.0
2001	3,000	47,672	15.9
2002	3,034	48,183	15.9
2003	3,049	48,540	15.9
2004	3,091	48,795	15.8
2005	3,143	49,113	15.6
2006	3,166	49,316	15.6
2007	3,178	49,293	15.5
2008	3,222	49,266	15.3
2009	3,210	49,373	15.4
2010	3,240	49,306	15.2
2011	3,253	49,422	15.2
2012	3,274	49,642	15.2

Source: Table 691. Public and private elementary and secondary teachers, enrollment, and pupil/teacher ratios: Selected years, fall 1955 through fall 2020.

Selected States

So while we can see the broad national trend in Figure 3.2, we now turn to a select number of states to more closely examine public school staffing trends. Table 3.3. details the numbers of teachers, students, and ratios for our analytic sample across the seven states. Again, these states were selected to allow for more careful and detailed analysis of changes in local investment in teachers (as measured by teacher FTEs). What becomes apparent is the skewing of the district size toward smaller districts and the great variation in school district size from small rurals to large cities. For instance, while the average rural district has around 90 teacher FTEs, one half (median) of all the rural districts have teaching staffs of just over 50 FTEs across the illustrated time period of 2005–2011. Similar patterns exist for the other locale types indicating how a smaller number of much larger districts (within each local category) skew the means upward. Moreover, the median rural district across our sample has just over 50 teacher FTEs and 650 students (ratio

TABLE 3.3. District-Level Teachers, Enrollment and Ratios From 2005–2006 to 2011–2012

	2005/6	2006/7	2007/8	2008/9	2009/10	2010/11	2011/12
Rural							
Mean Teachers	87	90	91	92	92	90	90
Median Teachers	53	55	53	54	55	53	53
Mean Enrollment	1,243	1,259	1,263	1,265	1,270	1,281	1,283
Median Enrollment	682	678	666	658	656	665	660
Student/Teacher Ratio	13	13	13	13	13	14	13
City							
Mean Teachers	1,245	1,250	1,252	1,282	1,262	1,225	1,214
Median Teachers	532	541	545	525	528	516	516
Mean Enrollment	21,389	21,247	21,224	21,258	21,498	21,636	21,781
Median Enrollment	9,041	8,924	8,856	9,071	9,238	9,400	9,619
Student/Teacher Ratio	17	17	18	17	17	19	19
Suburb							
Mean Teachers	382	387	399	398	391	379	376
Median Teachers	246	250	257	253	249	241	239
Mean Enrollment	6,530	6,587	6,604	6,640	6,636	6,678	6,675
Median Enrollment	3,818	3,862	3,841	3,786	3,788	3,791	3,780
Student/Teacher Ratio	16	16	16	16	16	17	17
Town							
Mean Teachers	161	163	166	165	163	158	155
Median Teachers	131	135	136	137	134	129	125
Mean Enrollment	2,472	2,476	2,466	2,455	2,448	2,444	2,432
Median Enrollment	1,949	1,928	1,930	1,923	1,913	1,908	1,886
Student/Teacher Ratio	15	15	15	15	15	15	15

Source: NCES Common Core, authors' calculations. Years prior to 2005 are not shown.

of between 13 and 14). This is in contrast to the cities where the median number of teacher FTEs is over 500 with a median enrollment of over 20,000 students.

With regard to rural school districts and their capacity to staff their schools, Figure 3.3 displays the average student-to-teacher ratio in rural districts from 2000/2001 through 2011/2012 across the seven states. What stands out is the relatively high ratio for California districts. Even before the recession, the ratio held steady at around 18 students per teacher, but in the post-recession years, the ratio increased to 20 students per teacher until finally, in the 2011/2012 year, it began to drop. This includes the sizable allocation of federal funds (e.g., ARRA, Education Jobs Fund) to California, which makes one wonder how much worse the increase in the student to teacher ratio would have been absent federal help. Conversely, New York, Kansas, and Iowa all exhibit ratios around 12 or 13 students per teacher and were slowly but steadily decreasing in the years prior to the recession. Pennsylvania's ratio started at just over 15 students per teacher but steadily dropped to around 13 before a slight uptick around 2010. Arkansas appears to have had the most volatile ratio over these 12 years. The ratios increase until 2004/2005, and then decrease before spiking around 2007/2008. Like California and Iowa, Arkansas increased its ratio in 2008 and 2009, but then saw drops in ratios at the time the federal ARRA and Education Jobs funds were initiated in 2010.

A closer examination of Arkansas' volatility reveals the fluctuation in ratios is found in the rural and town communities and not in the suburbs or cities (see Figure 3.4). Note that the capacity gains (e.g., adjusting teacher levels to reduce

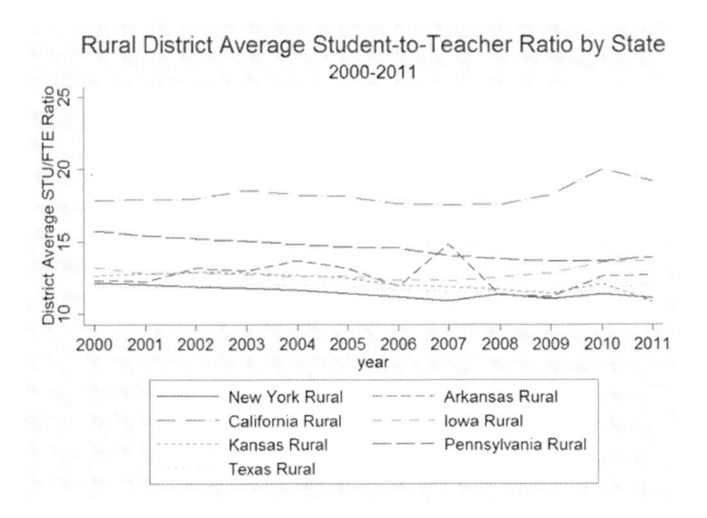

FIGURE 3.3. Instructional capacity in rural districts by state and year (2000–2001/2001–2002). *Source*: Authors calculations using NCES Common Core of Data (CCD).

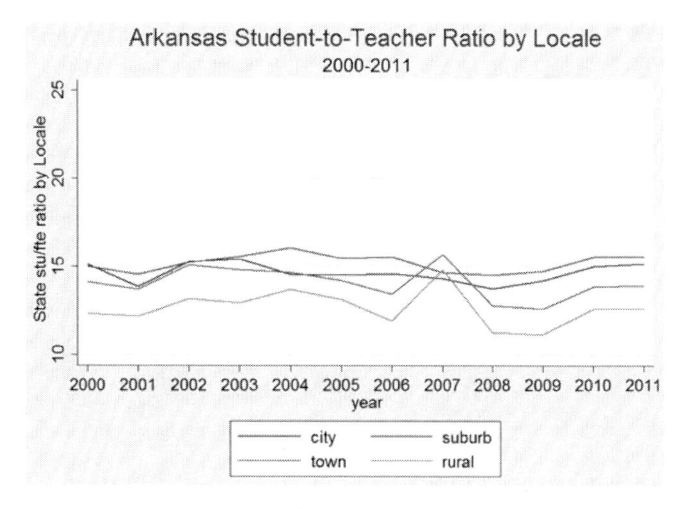

FIGURE 3.4. Arkansas student to teacher ratios by district locale and year. Source: Authors calculations using NCES Common Core of Data (CCD).

the ratio of students to teachers) made by the 2008/2009 school year disappeared by 2010/2011 with only a leveling off by the 2011/2012 school year.

California, with the highest ratios (e.g., least substantial investment in instructional capacity), illustrates how the variation across locales was exacerbated by the 2008 recession (see Figure 3.5). The staffing reductions began with the 2009/2010 year and hit their peak in 2010/2011 before retreating in the 2011/2012 year, presumably aided by the federal investment. Rural districts consistently have the greatest relative investment in staffing and are represented by the lowest student-to-teacher ratios.

Finally, in Iowa, it is worth noting that the concerns about the "hallowing out" of rural America is at least hinted at by the trends illustrated in Figure 3.6. Beginning in the 2007/2008 year, the ratio steadily increases before, during, and after the recession. While there is some apparent investment in the nonrural districts during this time, it appears as if the rural districts are experiencing a steady erosion of their staffing ratios.

Multivariate Regression Analyses

We use random-effects longitudinal regression analyses to estimate the effects of rural location net the effects of wealth, year, and charter school status. We model the change in teacher FTE (standardized z-scores) in districts in each of the seven states by regressing the teacher FTEs on the full set of independent variables. We model each state independently because of the salience of state and local district authority (and resources) to invest in teaching staffs to teach their

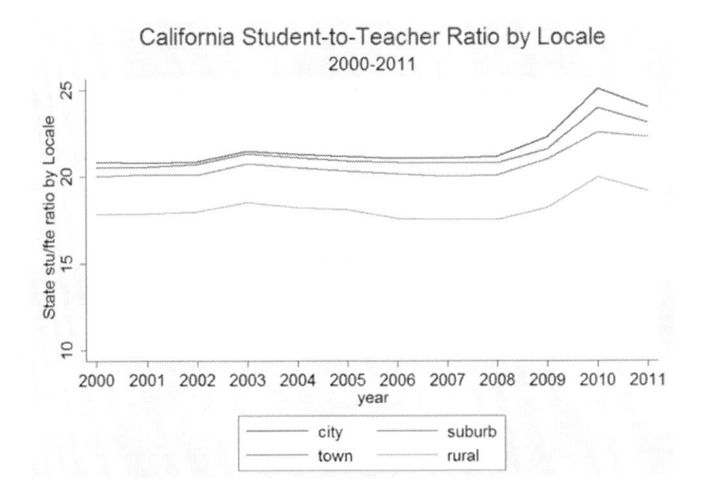

FIGURE 3.5. California student to teacher ratios by district locale and year. Source: Authors calculations using NCES Common Core of Data (CCD).

students. The models are easily comparable across states in Table 3.4 as we use standardized units for key variables.

Independent variables in these models include district-level characteristics. These include the total district enrollment (standardized) to control for variation in student enrollment changes over time, and hence, necessary additions or subtractions to the number of teachers needed in the district. As a way to adjust for the particular staffing needs and resource constraint of poverty, we include the number of students who qualify for free and reduced price lunch (FRPL) in each district (standardized). We include the year (centered at 2007) to allow for the estimate of the average annual change in the Teacher FTE from 2000 to 2012. Given the salience of the years during and post-recession, we include indicator variables for each of the years 2008/2009, 2009/2010, 2010/2011, and 2011/2012 to estimate the differential effect of these key years on the model. We also include the urban-centric district locale of each school district to estimate the effect of being located in a city, town, or a rural locale in comparison with the suburban districts.

We begin by observing the estimates of the effect of school size on teacher FTEs. Across the seven state models and above and beyond the effects of the other independent variables, we see consistent, significant, and positive enrollment coefficients indicating that as district enrollments increase, the teacher FTEs increase. But despite the broad and expected positive relationship, there are important differences to note across the states. Specifically, California has the lowest rate of increase in teacher FTEs as the number of students increase across all California districts. For each one standard deviation increase in enrollment across all California school districts, the districts only increase their staffing FTE by 0.909

TABLE 3.4. Longitudinal Regression Modeling of Teacher FTEs by State

zFTE	AR	CA	IA	KS	NY	PA	TX
zEnrollment	1.094**	0.909**	1.279**	1.226**	1.318**	1.046**	1.186 **
zFRPL	0.218**	0.011**	0.020*	0.021*	0.171**	0.032**	0.002**
Charter	–0.002	0.026			–0.049 **	– 0.082	– .087 **
YearC	0.000	–0.001**	0.001**	0.001**	0.003**	0.005**	0.001**
y2008	0.018**	0.006*	–0.002*	0.002	– 0.007**	0.005**	0.001**
y2009	0.018**	–0.029**	– 0.003	–0.017 **	– 0.005**	0.008	0.019**
y2010	–0.010**	– 0.082 **	– .019**	–0.025**	– 0.018**	–0.001	0.003
y2011	– 0.015**	–0.048**	–0.019**	0.000	–0.020**	–0.020**	–0.050**
City	0.006	0.001	0.008	0.023	–0.006	0.107**	0.073**
Town	0.015*	0.026**	0.018**	–0.014	–0.004	–0.015*	–0.013
Rural	0.014*	0.017**	0.016**	– 0.027*	– 0.011**	– 0.017**	–0.320**
RuralX2009	–0.001	0.031**	– 0.001	0.018 **	– 0.006**	– 0.018**	–0.020**
RuralX2010	0.013**	0.080**	0.010**	0.022**	0.000	–0.015*	–0.006*
RuralX2011	0.016**	0.048**	0.009**	0.006	0.001	– 0.006	0.040**
_cons	0.018	– 0.083	0.031**	0.063	0.106	0.039	0.064

z Standardized with a mean of 0 and standared deviation of 1.
* $p \leq 0.05$; ** $p \leq 0.01$
Year is centered at 2007.

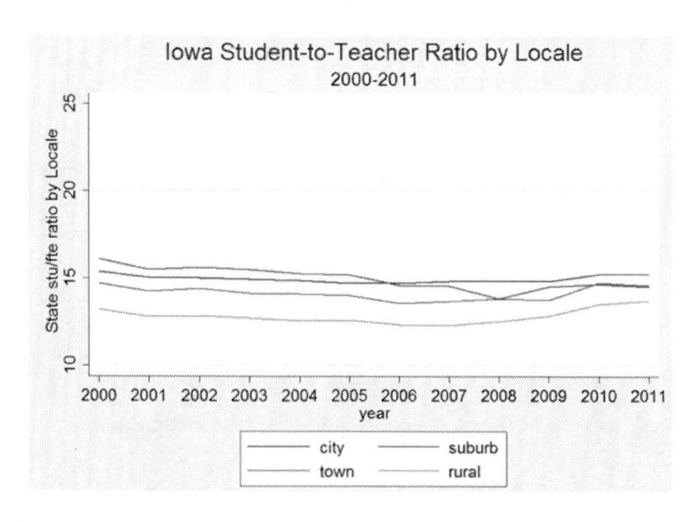

FIGURE 3.6. Iowa student to teacher ratios by district locale and year. *Source*: Authors calculations using NCES Common Core of Data (CCD).

standard deviation units. Put another way, as district enrollment increases (in any year), the pace of teacher staffing in larger schools falls behind the staffing levels for smaller districts.

Arkansas and Pennsylvania each exhibit slight increases in staffing as enrollment increases across districts, a pattern favoring the larger districts. In Texas, Iowa, Kansas, and New York, as enrollments increase in standard units, the teacher FTEs also increase, but at a higher rate, again favoring the larger districts. For each standard deviation increase in Texas school districts, the teacher FTEs increase by 1.186 standard deviations. On the high end, for each standard deviation increase in district enrollment (in any year) in New York, the districts increase their teacher FTE by 1.3 standard deviation units, a substantial commitment to enhancing capacity in larger districts when compared with smaller districts.

Further delving into the models reveals some interesting and important state-level differences. As the rate of FRPL-eligible students in a district increases, the models estimate, on average, districts have slightly more teacher FTEs. Specifically, for each standard unit of increase in FPRL rates across all districts in the state, there are significant increases in staffing levels in six of the seven states. With the exception of Texas, in which there is no relationship between FRPL rates and staffing levels, the other six states varied from a low of .01 standard deviation increase in teacher FTEs in California to a high of 0.218 standard unit increase in Arkansas. This suggests Arkansas districts staff at higher levels for the instruction of low-income children than do other states, particularly in Texas where there is no change in staffing levels as the number of low-income students increase.

While not a focus of this study, we did control for the staffing levels in charter schools in five of the seven states (there are no charter schools in Iowa and Kansas). In Arkansas and California, there is no statistically significant difference between the staffing rates of charter versus noncharter schools, once controlling for the full set of independent variables. However, in New York, Pennsylvania, and Texas, we find similar negative effects of charter school status in terms of teacher staffing levels. The effects are not large, but a comparably sized charter school with similar demographics has about 0.05 to 0.08 standard deviations fewer teacher FTEs than their traditional public school counterparts.

To capture the change in staffing levels over time, we estimate average year-to-year changes in staffing above and beyond the variation explained by enrollment, FRPL, charter status, and locale. We find that in Arkansas, there is no annual change in staffing levels over time, and in California, there is a statistically significant, though small (0.001 standard deviation), *drop* in teacher FTEs year after year. Conversely, Iowa, Kansas, and Texas exhibit an equally small but positive year-to-year change. New York and Pennsylvania have larger positive increases at the level of 0.003 and 0.005, respectively. We tested to see if this relationship was nonlinear across the 12 years, but found no statistically significant effect, thus indicating a fairly steady though slight increase in the relative staffing levels in these states (as illustrated nationally in Figure 3.2).

We added interaction terms to estimate the effect of the 2008 recession on staffing levels. These interaction terms reveal a very interesting set of staffing increases and decreases between 2008/2009 and 2011/2012, suggesting that the recession had differential effects within each state. This variation can be attributed to the variation of the local economies, particularly changes in property values and state policies, as well as the infusion of the federal ARRA support. For instance, in Arkansas, there were increases in teacher FTEs in 2008 and 2009, though decreasing teacher FTEs in 2010 and 2011 relative to the change in teacher FTEs in the pre-recession years. Hence, we conclude that the effect of the recession in Arkansas was not impactful on teacher FTE staffing levels until the 2010/2011 academic year. In contrast, California experienced the effects of the recession on its districts' staffing levels one year before Arkansas. In 2008, districts in California were, on average, able to increase their staffing levels relative to pre-recession years (2000–2007). However, in 2009, 2010, and 2011, the teacher FTEs were reduced by .029, .082, and .048 standard deviations, respectively, signaling the reduction in instructional capacity.

In Iowa, the reductions began in 2008 (as did New York) with -0.0002 standard deviation changes in teacher FTE level. In 2009, there was no difference in the staffing levels when compared with the pre-recession levels. But in 2010 and 2011, the reductions became significant again with nearly .02 standard deviation reduction in teacher FTE levels. In Kansas, there was no change in staffing levels in 2008 as compared to pre-recession years; but in 2009 and 2010, Kansas school districts, on average, saw reductions. In New York, we see a steady and consistent impact of the recession as illustrated by a reduction in staffing levels when compared to pre-recession levels.[3]

Pennsylvania and Texas illustrate different experiences with regard to the recession. Pennsylvania school districts appear to have no change in staffing levels when comparing pre-recession years to each of 2008, 2009, and 2010. Finally, in 2011, Pennsylvania districts appear to have reductions in teacher FTEs (–0.02). Texas districts actually increased staffing levels in 2008 and 2009 when compared to the prior years, showed no difference in 2010, and finally a reduction in 2011; truly a state where the effects of the recession on school staffing were delayed.

We now turn to the major focus of this study, the location of school districts within each of the selected states. With regard to rural school districts, we find, net the effects of the independent variables already described, a mixed set of experiences across these states of interest. On average, rural districts in Arkansas, California, and Iowa have significantly greater staffing levels than do suburban districts in their respective states. Rural districts in Iowa, Kansas, New York, Pennsylvania, and Texas have, on average, significantly lower teacher FTEs than do suburban districts in the same states. Towns have very similar patterns to rural districts though districts in towns in Kansas, New York, and Texas have staffing levels no different than suburban districts. With regard to city school districts, there are no statistically significant differences between city and suburban districts in any of the states except for Pennsylvania and Texas, in which city districts have teacher FTEs 0.10 and 0.07 standard deviations, respectively, higher than the suburban districts.

Finally, we added additional interaction terms to estimate the effect of staffing changes in rural districts in post-recession years (2009/2010, 2010/2011, 2011/2012). Again, there are clear state-to-state differences that illustrate the importance of following up with analyses of state-level policies and local school district differences in wealth and priorities. In 2009, we find two states, California and Kansas, with a positive effect (increased staffing levels) of rural location relative to suburban districts, two states with no effect (Arkansas and Iowa), and three with negative effects (New York, Pennsylvania, and Texas) indicating reduced staffing levels in rural districts when compared with suburban districts. By 2010, this shifts to four states with positive rural effects (Arkansas, California, Iowa, and Kansas), one state with no difference (New York), and two with negative effects (Pennsylvania and Texas). By 2011, we see that Arkansas, California, and Iowa continue to have positive rural effects on staffing. But now, Texas, for the first time, has a positive effect and Kansas, New York, and Pennsylvania now show no significant rural effect in the post-recession years when compared with the other locales (city, suburb, town) in the pre-recession years and in 2008.

DISCUSSION AND CONCLUSION

So what does this all mean in terms of rural communities, the 2008 recession, and equality of educational opportunity? Most importantly, we found substantial differences within and between states in the absolute staffing levels, relative staffing levels in rural versus nonrural districts, and the impact of the 2008 recession. This study highlights the importance of individual state analyses and the need to avoid broad national claims and trends.

There is not a single story, a single impact, or a single interaction between rural location, year, and staffing levels. But within specific states (i.e., in Iowa, Kansas, New York, Pennsylvania, and Texas) we find examples of relative underinvestment in the staffing levels of rural schools, regardless of year, while relative overinvestment in Arkansas and California relative to suburban schools. These effects, however, changed as the recession dragged on and then subsided.

We find variation in the year in which states "felt" the impact of the recession through staffing reductions. Texas and Pennsylvania experienced the longest effect of the recession and did not see any reduction in staffing levels until the 2011/2012 academic year. Alternatively, California, Kansas, and New York felt the effects early and persistently.

Specifically, with regard to the effect of the recession on rural school districts within the seven states, we find two different stories. First, as the post-recession years passed by Arkansas, California, Iowa, and Kansas, all made statistically significant gains in staffing levels of rural districts over the rates of increase prior to the recession. Second, New York, Pennsylvania, and Texas all experienced negative rates of increase in the 2009/2010 academic year, and Pennsylvania and Texas continued this negative pattern through the next year. Texas seems to have rebounded in 2011/2012.

The staffing levels of schools signal one of the most important investments in the education of a community's children. The degree to which staffing levels vary by community wealth, location, and size has been a matter of great debate in equity and adequacy court cases since the 1970s. We aim to add three conclusions from our analysis to this debate. First, there is no single story or set of relationships that holds across the nation. We find strong evidence that staffing levels vary across states and vary within states across various demographic and fiscal measures. Second, we find strong evidence that the impact of the recession varied by state with some reducing staffing levels (above and beyond changes due to enrollment) immediately and other states (i.e., Pennsylvania) not reducing staffing levels until 2012. Enhanced federal aid (e.g., ARRA, Education Jobs Fund, RTT) was proportionately constant (for each state) and so cannot explain the varied response in the years after the recession. Further investigation beyond this study into each of these states is necessary to explain why such differences exist. Finally, rural school districts have advantageous staffing levels in some states when compared with suburban districts and are disadvantaged in others. These (dis) advantages also vary by year as the recession continued and then ended.

ENDNOTES

1. Including pre-Kindergarten in states with K–12 school-based pre-K programming.
2. Including direct phone calls with data officials at the NYS Education Department who informed us that there were at least 2 years that they did not receive staffing data from New York City schools. In total, NYC represents over 1.1 million schoolchildren, but officially is only 1 of New York's 697 school districts.
3. A confounding issue in NY is the introduction of a property tax cap in 2011. This was coupled with cuts in state aid leaving NY's school districts without an ability to levy local taxes to offset cuts in state aid.

REFERENCES

Baker, B. D., & Green, P. C. (2009). Equal educational opportunity and the distribution of state aid to schools: Can or should school racial composition be a factor? *Journal of Education Finance, 34,* 289–323.

Berry, B. (2008). Staffing high-needs schools: Insights from the nation's best teachers. *The Phi Delta Kappan, 89*(10), 766–771.

Bushaw, W. J., & Calderon, V. J. (2014). The 46th annual PDK/Gallup poll of the public's attitudes toward the public schools. *Phi Delta Kappan, 96*(2), 49–59.

Carr, P. J., & Kefalis, M. J. (2009). *Hollowing out the middle: The rural brain drain and what it means for America*. Boston, MA: Beacon Press.

Cohen-Vogel, L. (2011). "Staffing to the test": Are today's school personnel practices evidence based? *Educational Evaluation and Policy Analysis, 33*(4), 483–505.

Coleman, J. S., Campbell, E. Q., Hobson, C. J., McPartland, J., Mood, A. M., Weinfield, E. D., & York, R. L. (1966). *Equality of educational opportunity*. Washington, DC: U.S. Government Printing Office.

Gould, E. (2014, October 8). The teacher gap: Strong gains but large jobs gap remains. *Economic Policy Institute*. Retrieved March 30, 2015, from http://www.epi.org/publication/teacher-gap-strong-gains-large-jobs-gap/

Jackson, C. K., Johnson, R. C., & Persico, C. (2015). *The effects of school spending on educational and economic outcomes: Evidence from school finance reforms*. Cambridge: National Bureau of Economic Research, Inc. doi:http://dx.doi.org/10.3386/w20847

Jencks, C. (1972). *Inequality: A reassessment of the effect of family and schooling in America.* New York, NY: Basic Books

Jencks, C., Bartlett, S., Corcoran, M., Crouse, J., Eaglesfield, D., Jackson, G., . . . Williams, J. (1979). *Who gets ahead? The determinants of economic success in America.* New York, NY: Basic Books.

Kolbe, T., & Rice, J. K. (2012). And they're off: Tracking federal race to the top investments from the starting gate. *Educational Policy, 26*(1), 185–209.

Kolbe, T., & Strunk, K. O. (2012). Economic incentives as a strategy for responding to teacher staffing problems: A typology of policies and practices. *Educational Administration Quarterly, 48*(5), 779–813.

Marsh, J. A., & Wohlstetter, P. (2013). Recent trends in intergovernmental relations: The resurgence of local actors. *Education Policy, 42,* 276–283.

Miller, L. C. (2012). Situating the rural teacher labor market in the broader context: A descriptive analysis of the market dynamics in New York State. *Journal of Research in Rural Education, 27*(13), 1.

National Bureau of Economic Research (NBER). (2015). *US business cycle expansions and contractions.* Retrieved March 30, 2015, from http://www.nber.org/cycles.html

National Center for Education Statistics (NCES). (2007). *Common Core of Data (CCD). Identification of rural locales.* Retrieved from http://nces.ed.gov/ccd/rural_locales.asp

National Center for Education Statistics (NCES). (2014). *Digest of education statistics: Advance release of selected 2013 digest tables*. Retrieved from http://nces.ed.gov/programs/digest/2013menu_tables.asp

Opfer, D. (2011). Defining and identifying hard-to-staff schools: The role of school demographics and conditions. *Educational Administration Quarterly, 47*(4), 582–619.

Reininger, M. (2012). Hometown disadvantage? It depends on where you're from: Teachers' location preferences and the implications for staffing schools. *Educational Evaluation and Policy Analysis, 34*(2), 127–145.

Shierholz, H. (2013, October 23). The teacher gap: More students and fewer teachers. *Economic Policy Institute*. Retrieved from http://www.epi.org/publication/teacher-gap-students-teachers/

Sipple, J. (2007). Bolstering capacity for heightened state and federal standards? In J. K. Rice & C. Roellke (Eds.), *High stakes accountability: Implications for resources and capacity* (pp. 117). Charlotte, NC: Information Age.

U.S. Department of Education. (2010, August 31). New York, Georgia, and American Samoa will receive funds to support education jobs [Press release]. Retrieved from http://www.ed.gov/news/press-releases/new-york-georgia-and-american-samoa-will-receive-funds-support-education-jobs

Wilson, V. (2014, October 27). Virginia boasts smallest gaps in unemployment rates by race in third quarter, but no state leads in race to recovery for all groups. *Economic Policy Institute.* Retrieved from http://www.epi.org/publication/virginia-boasts-smallest-gaps-in-unemployment-rates-by-race/

CHAPTER 4

LITERACY EDUCATION FOR THE LUMPS AND DIVOTS OF SMART CITIES AND RURAL PLACES

Karen Eppley and Patrick Shannon

We are reading educators in the middle of Pennsylvania, the state with the third highest rural population. In this chapter, we outline our fears that neoliberal urbancentric policies position rural citizens (and many other groups) as servants of concentrated innovation ecosystems where an elite, highly educated populace will invent the future. We begin with Friedman's candid call to redirect the distribution of resources from rural areas to urban ecosystems in order to save the middle class, and we follow the broadband wires and waves to rural schools where reading education is to be reduced to direct instruction of basic skills. We understand these actions as unjust because they reinforce institutional obstacles, limiting rural citizens' participatory parity with others in American and global democratic projects.

The Call

In an op-ed piece for the *New York Times*, Thomas Friedman (2012) asked politicians to concentrate their attention on "the world in which we're living and how we adapt to it." Information and communication technology (ICT) has flat-

Educational Opportunity in Rural Contexts: The Politics of Place, pages 59–73.

tened Frideman's world, providing faster and cheaper tools with which anyone anywhere can innovate, collaborate, and create. The fittest of these adaptations, he reported, integrates more and more empowered "anyones" into ecosystems, which act as petri dishes for imagining, designing, and manufacturing products that "make people's lives more healthy, educated, entertained, productive, and comfortable." The politicians, therefore, should explain, and then act on, their plans for the development of these smart ecosystems across America in order to win the 21st century.

Friedman (2012) provided a glimpse of his 21st century. He quoted Blair Levin, former chair of the Federal Communications Commission, criticizing the current American agenda to democratize the use of the Internet in under- and unserved rural areas ("the last 5 percent of the country"), arguing that, instead, we should provide "'ultra-high-speed bandwidth' to the top 5 percent, in university towns, who will invent the future." According to Friedman, "the best of these ecosystems will be cities and towns that combine a university, an educated populace, a dynamic business community, and the fastest broadband connections on earth," enabling the mining of "Big Data" in order to discover and claim new commodities and services to be manufactured and reproduced anywhere. Other nations are ahead of us, Friedman warned, and this adaptation is America's "only way [to] maintain a middle class." At the end of his essay, Friedman posed a technical and then a tactical question for politicians: "How (do) we deploy more ultra-high-speed networks and applications in university towns" and "How do we educate more workers to do these jobs?"

Its Meaning

Before we address how federal and state policies anticipated and responded to these questions, we slow down to trace and react to Friedman's remarks from his representation of the world to his frame for our adaptation and through to the ideology that supports both and drives much of current domestic and international policies. According to Friedman, the world in which we are living is one of scarcity and competition, requiring speed, cunning, and sacrifice in order for nations to gain advantage. American politicians, and the public, have not and are not paying enough attention to this world, and therefore we are losing ground to other nations in this race for prosperity. Friedman chooses a simple change in the direction of broadband from open spaces to concentrated nodes as the metaphor for this recommended adaptation. Worried that he might not be accepted as an authority on this specific topic, he quoted the chairman of the FCC that the broadband flip would be from one 5% of the population to another and bring an upgrade in technical service for the good of the country. Friedman frames his adaptation as the sole salvation of the middle class, suggesting that politics must sacrifice democratizing the Internet to the economic necessities of the real world.

A neoliberal ideology stands behind Levin's remarks and Friedman's promotion of them, proposing that human well-being can best be advanced by the maximization of entrepreneurial freedoms through institutional frameworks. The central role of government is to create the conditions for such frameworks and then to let them work according to the invisible hand of markets. Friedman cloaks this government role, acting as if ecosystems, the information technology revolution, and globalization were natural phenomena instead of the artifacts of previous governments and supranational institutions' decisions and actions. Accordingly, the transfer of resources from rural to urban, and the likely consequences of this adaptation, make common sense, and any objection is positioned as injurious to all, unnatural, and senseless.

Our Reaction

Despite these warnings, we object to Friedman's call and its meaning because we consider neoliberal representations of and frames for policy and action to be undemocratic, establishing unjust barriers to participatory parity among all people (Fraser, 2009). We take this social justice stance in order to think more deeply, not only about Friedman's views on access to broadband, but also about the application of such "flat world" initiatives to education policy and school curriculum. We use Fraser's (2005, 2009) work on justice to take the position that initiatives such as Friedman's plan for smart cities pit technological innovation and the manufacturing of products and services against the democratic projects of the United States. We understand our objections as fair, helpful, and rational.

In *Scales of Justice*, Fraser (2009) outlines her vision of the globalized world in which we're living and how we might adapt, employing multiple meanings of scale for an audience broader than Friedman's. First, she uses scale to explain the moral balance in weighing the relative merits of conflicting claims. What does it mean for whom when we choose one course of action rather than others? And second, Fraser offers scale as a geographic metric, recognizing that transnational flows contest the modern national and traditional regional frames in which such weighing could take place. How do those "who" subjects assume meaningful places in the weighing of consequences in a globalized world? Fraser's frames for her adaptations center on participation parity in making decisions that will affect our lives. She understands parity as expressed through economic, cultural, and political (what, who, and how) dimensions, resting on a "radical democratic interpretation of the principle of equal moral worth, [in which] justice requires social arrangements that permit all to participate as peers in social life" (p. 16).

From this vantage point, Friedman's (2012) call for adaptation misframes the scales of justice because it excludes some (many) from full participation. Fraser's frame enables us to analyze the metaphor of broadband access in order to weigh the consequences of Friedman's shift in the distribution of resources, the recognition of difference among social groups, and the boundaries of representation within globalization, obstructing participatory parity among peers. We can use Fraser's dimensions to explain the injustice in Friedman's call, and its likely consequences, as a prelude to discussing the educational consequences of such thinking.

Distributive justice addresses the fairness associated with the economic outcomes of policy decisions and actions. What resources are allocated, in what amounts, and does that distribution seem fair? Friedman and Levin's plan names the resource, evaluates it, and distributes it across three groups—"the top 5 percent, in university towns," "the last 5 percent . . . in rural areas," and the 90% ("a middle class"). Broadband facilitates the use of "more and more cheap IT tools of innovation, collaboration, and creativity," enabling individuals and society to prosper. Its value can be expressed along a speed continuum from ultra-high speed to average toward not being available. Friedman and Levin call for a re-allocation of resources in order to enhance the position of the urban 5% to compete globally, implying that their profits will trickle down to the middle class. The "last 5 percent" are denied this resource, and without broadband are hindered systematically during interactions with the top and the middle as peers.

Status justice concerns the recognition of cultural differences and fair treatment among groups within societies. Who (which groups) are acknowledged as having legitimate yet distinct identities, deserving universal respect and membership as peers? Friedman recognized that globalization, and the IT revolution has empowered many, but he draws distinctions among the human capital potential among groups. People welcomed into innovation ecosystems possess abundant human intellectual capital, which when combined with the dynamic people of business will become catalysts for jobs and societal prosperity. According to Levin and Friedman (2012), the last 5% in rural areas are not yet empowered by the IT revolution and have insufficient potential to warrant the expense of bringing broadband to their doors. No other social group could suffer such misrecognition so openly. More than a decade ago, noting the struggle of rural people relative to other groups, Howley and Howley wrote,

> the rural is emblematic of the most entrenched status quo and therefore represents—in contrast to the potentially transformative positioning conferred by other contexts (e.g., race, gender, ethnicity)—a hopelessly regressive condition. Even critical educators equate the rural with machine politics, inbreeding, and racism (2000, p. 75).

Representation justice considers the political stage on which fairness of distribution of resources and recognition of difference can be weighed. How can all peers participate as equals within the relevant environments of the issues to be addressed? Levin and Friedman (2012) choose the terms "last . . . in rural areas" and "top . . . in university towns" in order to make distinctions between geographies of the 5%s on a national scale. Accordingly, politicians are to connect the Top(s) internationally across the flat world in order use the IT revolution to engage in economic and cultural decisions that will affect the other 95%(s). To enable that representation for those Tops, politicians are to cut the Last(s) off from these connections. Our parenthetical plurals signify the global neoliberal plans for all modern nation states—the fastest broadband connects all the Tops, regardless of national boundaries, in order to set the economic, cultural, and political decision-making rules to direct the global future. Without broadband, the Lasts are denied equal access to participation in setting these rules or making decisions either nationally or globally.

Across these three dimensions, Levin and Friedman (2012) would have politicians regrade the flat world, scraping economic, cultural, and political resources from the rural and pushing them across the middle toward a few innovative ecosystems. The result would leave a topology of lumps and divots from which the aptly named Tops could look down the slopes in order to see the middle 90% coming to serve them and to descry the euphemistically labeled Lasts living disconnected lives from their peers. Such a landscape is unjust by design and unfortunately, by current enactment as well. Federal technological infrastructure policies and their connections to educational policies erect systemic, institutional obstacles for participatory party in the United States and globally. We turn to Friedman's questions for politicians at the end of his piece in order to name the injustices more specifically, to call for a different emphasis in reading education, and to suggest how coalitions might work to dismantle these obstacles.

How Do We Deploy More Ultra-High-Speed Networks?

The Telecommunications Act of 1996 introduced the Internet to the broadcasting and spectrum allotment. Its title expressed the four intentions for the Act: An Act to Promote Competition and Reduce Regulation in Order to Secure Lower Prices and Higher Quality Services for American Telecommunication Consumers and Encourage the Rapid Deployment of New Telecommunications Technologies. Section 706 of the Act required periodic updates on the rapid deployment of broadband. The Eighth Progress Report (2012) chronicles that the communications industry has invested billions in deployment of next-generation wired and wireless service and expansion of networks technically capable of 100 megabit-plus speeds to over 80% of the population (http://www.fcc.gov/reports/eighth-broadband-progress-report). Yet 19 million Americans (6% of the population) lack access, including nearly one quarter (14.5 million) of rural citizens.

In 2013, the National Telecommunications and Information Administration (NTIA) released a deeper analysis of the distribution of broadband resources (Beede & Neville, 2013). The researchers assigned communities to one of five categories in order to show variation of resources within rural and urban areas. Despite overall average high speed (50+ mbps), wireline availability levels of 63% in urban communities and 23% in rural areas, the report notes a continuum of service: 14% very rural, 32% exurban, 35% small town, 62% urban, and 67% suburban. For wireless distribution of 4G service (at least 6 mbps), 10% in very rural areas, 18% in small towns, and 36% in exurbs have access. Beede and Neville (2013) explain the exurbs' superior access to wireless over small towns through their inclusion within Metropolitan Statistical Areas, which connect multiple urban and suburban areas together. They argue that proximity to a central city is more closely association with higher broadband speeds than population density.

The Federal Communications Commission (FCC) unveiled Connecting America: The National Broadband Plan in 2010. Two of its goals were to ensure that every American had affordable access to "robust broadband service" and every community should have access of "at least 1 gigabit per second broadband service to anchor institutions." At the fourth anniversary of the Plan's release, Former Executive Director of the National Broadband Plan Blair Levin (2014) stated, "I'm a bit surprised, but delighted, that on driving fiber deeper and getting everyone online, we are doing better. Interestingly though, it's not due to federal government efforts but is largely due to private, non-profit and local government efforts." He mentioned three projects in particular: Google Fiber, Comcast Internet Essentials, and Gig.U. Google Fiber is a project to bring ultra-high speed (1,000 times regular) broadband to "low adoption" areas, beginning in Kansas City, Kansas, but with plans for 34 other cities that applied for service. Comcast Internet Essentials offers new low-income customers $10 per month 5-megabits-per-second connections, enrolling 300,000 urban families in three years. Gig.U, which Levin heads, "seeks to accelerate the deployment of ultra high-speed networks to leading U. S. universities and their surrounding communities" (www.gig-u.org).

However sincere, these public and private efforts to distribute high-speed broadband have rendered unequal results. In concert with neoliberal policies, government policies have opened markets for private companies to carry the service to citizens through supply (Google Fiber) or demand (Comcast Essentials) market forces. Gig.U channels private and public funding to innovation ecosystems as adaptation to the world in which we are living. Apparently some exurbs receive better wireless access than distant small towns because of their proximity to these hubs. Markets are good at distributing resources efficiently to the producers of commodities for which there is the most demand. Producers seek profits and competitive advantage to secure those profits, and consumers seek use and status through their purchase. Self-regulating exchange is a dispassionate individual cash transaction without regard for history, tradition, externalities, or need. Markets cannot and do not keep people in mind; even Adam Smith (1776) acknowledged that markets must be tempered with moral regulations of fairness and justice.

If as Congress argued in 2009, the broadband advances "consumer welfare, civic participation, public safety, community development, health care delivery, education, private sector investment, entrepreneurial activity and economic growth," (Federal Communications Commission, 2010) then one scale of justice weighs the fairness of direct access to this service for all Americans. The model for moral regulation of broadband distribution should not be based on misrecognition of the human potential of a particular group or profit. We agree with the Rural Broadband Policy Group that the diverse sets of people in rural areas deserve access to this tool that is acknowledged as fundamental to participatory parity in social life regionally, nationally, and globally (www.ruralstrategies.org/rural-broadband-policy-group). In order to achieve the goal of just redistribution, rural groups must work with other misrecognized and misrepresented groups to democratize the process of framing "who counts" in the continuous invention of the future. We see this as the role of education in general and the teaching of reading and writing in particular.

How Do We Educate More Workers to Do These Jobs?

Friedman (2012) and Levin's broadband adaptation plan creates a three-tiered framework for the education of workers in its wake. Although they do not name this differentiated curriculum and instruction explicitly, they identify three classes of "jobs." Some 5% of American citizens must be highly educated in order to innovate and decide the future; 90% should be educated to serve those ecosystems and enjoy the middle class; and the last rural 5% will be educated to live separate lives. Only rural children and youth are directed toward any tier. By comparing the rhetoric and service of two broadband policies—The Online Rural Community of Practice Group and ConnectEducators Initiative—we show how Friedman and Levin's neoliberal logic seeps into the educational practices in America's schools.

ConnectEd (www.whitehouse.gov/issues/eduction/k-12/connected) seeks to deliver Internet access to support digital learning in order to prepare students with the skills to obtain good jobs and compete with workers around the world. Although rural classrooms are not ignored in ConnectEd, they are not promised the same level of service. Rural schools will receive "better broadband," while suburban and urban schools will be supplied with "next-generation broadband." Neither "better" nor "next generation" is defined explicitly, but the terms are not treated as synonyms, and the "better" comparison is only offered in relation to existing rural broadband systems. While "better" implies improvement, it does not point to the future or innovation with the same connotations as "next generation." This differentiation is also underscored in the official content that the broadband is expected to bring officially to these schools. The ConnectEducators Initiative (www.ed.gov/connectededucators) is a subprogram of ConnectEd that is designed to provide professional development in the use of next-generation technologies. The Online Rural Community of Practice Group is a partnership between the White House Rural Council and the U.S. Department of Education that, according to Secretary of Education Arne Duncan, is expected to use "technology to overcome some of the unique challenges involved in rural schools" (Retrieved from https://www.youtube.com/watch?v=-KluZv3Y2hc, published 6/13/2012)

The official language surrounding these professional development programs presents the differentiated visions of broadband in classrooms serving different groups. Consider the opening statements and images of the official videos introducing these programs. ConnectEducators: "We live in a world fueled by technology and innovations." This statement is followed immediately with images of students describing their career aspirations. Technology figures prominently in their goals and also as an agent in their educational environments that are to be "connected, personalized, and collaborative." Accordingly, connected educators need more knowledge concerning the use of technology to "unlock exciting possibilities for learning" (www.ed.gov/blog/tag/connected/).

On the other hand, Secretary of Education Arne Duncan opens the video tour of the Online Rural Community of Practice Group website with the statement that users can find "various education resources, webinars, and featured content on school turnarounds and a variety of other topics as well" (www.ed.gov/blog/2012/06/connecting-educators-building-communities-across-rural-america). Duncan explains that this site is a tool to "collectively figure out how to give every child a world class education," and then he demonstrates how to open the link to the School Turnaround Learning Community (www.schoolturnaroundsupport.org). In the Race to the Top Initiative, school turnaround is the model for school improvement associated with the lowest 5% of American schools. Despite the 2011 National Assessment of Educational Progress (NAEP) evidence that rural students in fourth and eightth grades from fringe, distant, and remote schools outscored their peers in cities and towns (and trailed their suburban peers by only three percentage points) in both reading and math, Secretary Duncan conflates rural schools with "chronically low achieving" schools in need of drastic reform.

School Turnaround

School turnaround has a particular meaning for Secretary Duncan, who brought this model for school improvement to the Department of Education with him from Chicago, where he previously served as CEO of city schools. The turnaround model varies across schools, but typically includes replacement of the principal, competencies for review and decisions to select a teaching staff for the school (only 50% of existing staff can be rehired), job-embedded professional development to build capacity, continuous use of data to inform instruction, increased learning time for students and staff, and an instructional plan that will meet annual yearly progress goals for test scores within 3 years. Those turnaround schools that do not make their test score targets will be subject to progressively more direct state intervention (transformation, restart, or closure). Between 2001 and 2008, CEO Duncan closed 60 neighborhood schools in Chicago and "turned around" 12 others (www2.ed.gov/news/speeches/2009/06/06222009). Despite federal rhetoric of success surrounding turnaround schools, the Consortium on Chicago School Research at the University of Chicago found no lasting educational benefit for students relocated from those closed schools or attending the 12 turnaround schools (de la Torre & Gwynne, 2009). Despite the additional financial support for turnaround schools, Design for Change (Moore, 2012) judged that Chicago's schools relying on the reform strategy that preceded Duncan's tenure as CEO (School Based Democracy) outperformed Chicago's no excuses turnaround schools in reading achievement and teacher retention. Among the many findings, Moore (2012) concluded, "The study indicated that the high poverty schools achieving the high reading scores were governed by active Local School Councils who chose their principals, and experienced unionized teachers."

A basic distinction between high-scoring and low-scoring schools is that high-scoring schools carry out engaging instructional activities that help students master demanding standards, while low-scoring schools focus on various forms of test preparation. In the practice of School Based Democracy, the school community functions as a unified team and understands and acts on the close relationship between the issues facing the school and the community (Moore, 2012, p. 21).

Quoting from Trujillo and Renee (2012), the Rural and Community Trust doubts the likelihood that the RTTT turnaround school model can help rural schools. They cite the destabilizing consequences of required staffing changes, the too-narrow focus on test scores, and the neglect of parent and community knowledge as problems for rural districts. In an evaluation of rural turnaround schools, the National Center for Education Evaluations (2014) corroborated these concerns empirically and added low student motivation and staff morale as additional problems. On the official Online Rural Community of Practice blog, a schoolteacher questioned the motives behind the federal connections of rural schools and the turnaround model.

I applaud the Administration's push for greater Internet access for rural students and their schools, and for recognizing the power of teacher's networking. Some questions though: Is the idea to supplant or to unite already-existing networks for rural teachers? I'm thinking here of such longstanding groups as the Bread Loaf (Rural) Teachers Network, and several others. Why a "School Turnaround" network? Is this only for teachers who are in schools considered low performing? I think it is a great idea, but it gives the impression that the idea is starting from scratch when in fact it could build on existing work and take it to a higher level. (www.ed.gov/blog/2012/06/connecting-educators-building-communities-across-rural-america/)

With broadband comes popular social networking opportunities—Facebook, Twitter, Linkedin—enabling rural teachers to connect with whomever they choose. This blog mentions "Bread Loaf," "a formal teachers network existing for at least 20 years," and "others" (perhaps, American Social History Project, The Empire State Partnership, and 100Kin10), affording teachers networks of English, history, the arts, and STEM curricula and pedagogy. Although formal networks vary in their goals and practices, McDonald and Klein (2003) reported several functions that such networks perform in sustaining teachers' professional development: developing teacher content knowledge, enhancing pedagogical ideals and ideas, sharing content-focused expertise, and improving teachers' sense of efficacy. Beyond a commitment to the teachers in place in rural (and other) schools, these formal networks direct teacher and student engagement toward mastery of demanding standards as Moore mentioned in the successful School Based Democracies in Chicago. Test scores rise, but they are not the focus of the schools' work. The blogging teacher worries, and we concur, that the Online Rural Community of Practice Group's direct association with the turnaround model is intended to supplant rather than complement the work of these existing teacher networks. We see evidence of this intention in our work in rural schools.

For reading education since No Child Left Behind (2002), an acute focus on test scores in school reform leads most often to commercial curriculum and highly scripted instruction (Calfee, 2013). The NCLB's Reading First Initiative required that schools adopt a core reading program in order to facilitate teachers' devotion of more time and emphasis to explicit instruction, high-quality practice, and carefully sequenced texts in elementary grades. Powell, Higgins, Aran, and Freed (2009) confirmed that teachers in rural schools followed these directives. However, despite teachers' compliance with these guidelines, the Department of Education found that the Reading First Initiative did not raise students' reading comprehension test scores (Gamse et al., 2011). As a result of this study, Congress withdrew 60% of Reading First funding in 2007, and then completely in 2009. Yet the promotion of Direct Instruction of basic skills in reading for rural schools continues (see Stockard, 2011), with some suggesting Direct Instruction as the only means to raise rural students' reading achievement to globally competitive levels (Englemann, 2011).

A 2011 exchange in the *Journal of Research in Rural Education* expresses our concerns for this direction in reading education in rural schools. What counts as reading and what roles might reading play in current and future lives of students (Eppley & Corbett, 2011)? Advocates of Direct Instruction of basic reading skills argue that curricular decisions and instructional behaviors must be tightly controlled during reading instruction because schools cannot assume adequate preparation from either students or teachers (Stockard, 2011). Teachers cannot count on students' possession of requisite oral and written language skills that precede any reading lesson unless they have direct measurable evidence, and administrators cannot take for granted that all teachers can teach each new and necessary lesson with efficiency and effectiveness. Accordingly, reading must be divided into its elemental parts, encoded into a precise scope and sequence of lessons for those parts, and scripted tightly for both teacher and student to ensure standardization of delivery and mastery of each part in every classroom. Its proof, we were told, is in the arc of basic skills test scores and its popularity as a product on Amazon.com (Englemann, 2011).

Along with Bryk, Sebring, Allensworth, Luppescu, and Easton (2010), Moore, (2012), and Calfee (2013), we don't find the emphasis on basic skills and early testing compelling. In fact, we think advocates of Direct Instruction misunderstand people, reading, and learning. We bristle at the assumption of incompetence—Heath (1984), Hull and Schultz (2001), and Moll (1994) demonstrate that children and youth learn and practice literacy outside of school, often proficiently. Their literacies do not align neatly with any standardized sequence of basic skills; rather, as Luke and Freebody (1999) assert, right from the beginning and throughout life, readers need four cognitive and social resources in order to meet current societal demands for literacy—they must break code, make meaning, use text socially, and critique textual intentions. Instead of standardized, commercial scripts, teachers and student must recognize that literacy learning is situated in time and place and mediated by social and cultural interactions and tools (Street, 1984), that it occurs through a range and blend of explicit and implicit teaching (Wertsch, 1991), and that to learn literacy well, students need meaningful purposes for engaging in literate practices (Gee, 2003). Beyond alphabetic print, students must compose, interpret, and transform information and knowledge across various symbol systems forms (Hull & Moje, 2010). Direct Instruction in basic skills, then, is a barrier to students' immediate participatory parity in daily life, and it cloaks the agentive role of literacy in their later efforts to achieve parity in society.

CONCLUSION

Friedman (2012) and Levin's neoliberal three-tiered educational system appears to be based on assessments of the human capital potential of three groups. Each group will contribute accordingly to the economic well-being of the nation, although the top 5% will be wired into ecosystems globally. If politicians, policymakers, and educators will enact the plan, then America should keep its competitive advantage. Resources, then, should be allocated accordingly, and we have endeavored to demonstrate that federal broadband policies are directly implicated in the plan and its execution. Even when the line or waves make it to rural schools through ConnectED, the type of service will pale in comparison (better vs. next generation) to that received in schools serving the top or middle. Once there, the broadband brings differentiated professional development through ConnectEducator or Online Rural Community of Practice Group, suggesting that maybe it is not only rural students' human capital that is undervalued. ConnectEducator asks teachers to "unlock exciting possibilities," and the latter tells rural teachers to turn their schools around. In schools serving the top and middle, teachers will "engage students" and "personalize the learning experience," while rural teachers must take care of basics in order to secure whatever human capital could be aroused.

If as neoliberals contend that education and continuous development of human capital is indeed the individual adaptation to the world in which we are living, then rural citizens, young and mature, have the right to a just distribution of resources and the recognition that inhabitants of the last 5% of rural areas and students who attend these schools have similar capacities for education attainment as any other group. For reading educators, this means they have a right to participate in the development of curriculum and pedagogy as the School Based Democracies in Chicago demonstrate.

But this penchant for "getting the basics under control" often only exacerbates the problems of student disengagement and absenteeism. Students are more likely to be engaged in schools using an interesting curriculum, where they can take an active role in instructional activities and exercise some choice in their work as well as be regularly exposed to new problems and ideas through a well-paced set of courses. In contrast, didactic instruction, which typically places students in a passive role, can create a deadening experience, especially when combined with a "drill and kill" repetition of the same basic skills, over and over (Bryk et al., 2010, pp. 103–104).

How can an argument for broadband in rural places sit alongside the degradation of rural places within economic globalization? We do not seek an increased rural contribution within a neoliberal framework. Instead, we argue that current iterations of broadband and curricular policies are institutionalized obstacles to participatory parity for rural (and other) groups in the framing of the present and future. We label this unjust and argue that the devaluing of the rural has occurred, not naturally, but artificially. Past and current actions led to and maintained distributive injustice, status injustice, and representation justice. Our primary concern then is to disrupt the neoliberal market ideology behind those decisions over the last 40 years. And our primary focus is reading education.

We acknowledge that broadband is an economic tool, but it must also be understood as a cultural and political force. As a metaphor, current broadband policies represent the sacrifice of rural populations for the good of the middle class and elite innovators in smart cities. Changes in those policies, on the other hand, should recognize that rural citizens could be as highly educated and innovative as any other group and that rural students are not academically behind their peers in other geographic locations. Moreover, we agree with the United Nations that policies should represent high-speed broadband as a human right needed to connect us universally to the decisions that affect our immediate world. In their current forms, policies for access to broadband are institutionalized barriers for participatory parity for the existing generation, and Direct Instruction of basic skills in reading is an institutionalized barrier for the next generation. We agree with Fraser, "overcoming injustice means dismantling institutionalized obstacles that prevent people from participating on par with others as full partners in social interactions" (2009, 16).

For us, an important first step is to reframe reading education from its current neoliberal structure (Shannon, 2007, 2013), in which learning to read is understood as the accumulation of capital that individuals can exchange later in order to earn a living. As capital, reading is fetishized and becomes an object of competition measured early and often through abstract tested means. Because accumulation is its goal, reading education takes on the characteristics of the "world in which we are living" in which individuals (and social groups of which they are members) work to gain advantages. Our current array of reading achievement gaps attests to the consequences of past unjust decisions, policies, and actions within this frame. Perhaps ironically, we look back more than a century in order to see justice as the future for reading education.

Instead, the child is led by other means to feel the motives for acquiring skill in the use of these symbols, motives which persist when competition, often the only motive in the early years of many schools, ceases. If a child realizes the motive for acquiring skill, he is helped in large measure to secure the skill. Books and the ability to read are therefore regarded strictly as tools. The child must learn to use these, just as he would any other tool (Dewey, 1897, p. 72).

Dewey connected learning, the child, and the place in which the learning is relevant. In this way, reading becomes a tool with which students learn to make sense of themselves, others, and their environments. Accordingly, reading instruction (in which broadband represents and delivers text) could be framed around the development of sociological imagination. "To learn to live the sociological life is to learn to accept things as they come down, then to imagine why they are what they are" (Lemert, 2008, p. x). We tried to demonstrate this type of reading in this chapter—identifying how things come down for rural citizens and investigating why they came down that way. Lemert (2008) followed his definition with a statement of agency. "We live now in a time when life requires us to refrain from jumping too quickly to conclusions shaped by what we once believed to be true and good." We interpret this statement as an affirmation of what Fraser called "a radical democratic interpretation of the principle of equal moral worth" (2009, p. 16), leading to expectations of universal participatory parity. This—the right and ability to ask and pursue questions of interest in a sociological life—then, becomes Dewey's motive for learning to read and write.

Although just reading education cannot be fully specified because it requires democratic participation in a particular time and place, we find support for important elements in the work we've cited in the previous section. Bryk et al. (2010), Moore (2012), and the existing formal teacher networks tell us to assume that dynamic levels of competence among students, teachers, and community members already exist and can contribute to the invention of curriculum, pedagogy, and institutional structures that will mediate school-based democracies. That curriculum should be personal, but with imaginative ties to the social connections among us. Through implicit and explicit instruction on codes, meaning, use, and power in multimodal texts, teachers should encourage students to recognize how the development of self-knowledge invites interest in others and openness to the world. And teachers and community members must write these elements into schools policies and practices with a reflexive understanding that things will change.

Friedman (2012) and Levin's neoliberal framing of the world in which we're living and appropriate adaptation identifies new allies in the struggle for social justice for those interested in rural America. Rural citizens are not the only group who suffers from maldistribution, misrecognition, and misrepresentation. For example, Gig.U sends ultra-high-speed broadband only to innovation ecosystems, while celebrated Google Fiber and Comcast Internet Essentials treat low-income urbanites with a similar disdain as Friedman and Levin hold the last 5%. To achieve redistribution and recognition, both rural and urban groups must frame representation differently and see themselves as a coalition (at least on this issue) for broadband justice. In neoliberalism, the geographic boundaries between urban and rural spaces begin to disappear. Moreover, the school turnaround model distributed nationally through Race to the Top should unite impacted rural, small town, suburban, and urban groups in order to insist on reframing reading education toward participatory parity. These are not personal or even regional problems, but rather social issues requiring social movements for justice for all.

REFERENCES

Beede, D., & Neville, A. (2013, May). Broadband availability beyond the rural/urban divide. Broadband Brief # 2. *National Telecommunications and Information Administration; Economics and Statistics Administration.* Retrieved May 22, 2014, from http://www.ntia.doc.gov/files/ntia/publications/broadband_availability_rural_urban_june_2011_final.pdf

Bryk, A., Sebring, P., Allensworth, E., Luppescu, S., & Easton, J. (2010). *Organizing schools for improvement: Lessons from Chicago.* Cambridge, MA: Harvard Education Press.

Calfee, R. (2013). Knowledge, evidence and faith. In K. Goodman, R. Calfee, & Y. Goodman (Eds.), *Whose knowledge counts in government literacy policies?* New York, NY: Routledge.

de la Torre, M., & Gwynne, J. (2009, October). When schools close: Effects on displaced students in Chicago public schools. *Consortium on Chicago School Researach.* Retrieved June 20, 2014, from https://ccsr.uchicago.edu/sites/default/files/publications/CCSRSchoolClosings-Final.pdf

Dewey, J. (1897). The university elementary school: Studies and methods. *University Record, 1*, 42–47.

Engelmann. S. (2011). Critique and erasure: Responding to Eppley's "Reading mastery as pedagogy of erasure." *Journal of Research in Rural Education, 26*(15). Retrieved from http://jrre.vmhost.psu.edu/wp-content/uploads/2014/02/26-15.pdf

Eppley, K., & Corbett, M. (2012). I'll see that when I believe it: A dialogue on epistemological difference and rural literacies. *The Journal of Research in Rural Education, 27*(1), 1–9.

Federal Communications Commission. (2010). *Connecting America. The National Broadband Plan.* http://www.broadband.gov/plan/

Fraser, N. (2005). Reframing justice in a globalizing world. *New Left Review, 36*, 69–88.

Fraser, N. (2009). *Scales of justice: Reimagining political space in a globalizing world.* New York, NY: Columbia University.

Friedman, T. (2012, January 3). So much fun. So irrelevant. *New York Times.* Retrieved May 22, 2014, from http://www.nytimes.com/2012/01/04/opinion/friedman-so-much-fun-so-irrelevant.html

Gamse, B., Bonlay, B., Fountain, A., Unlu, F., Maree, K., McCall, T., & McCormack, R. (2011). Reading first implementation study 2008–2009. *U.S. Department of Education.* Retrieved December 19, 2013, from http://www2.ed.gov/about/offices/list/opepd/ppss/reports.html#reading

Gee, J. (2003). *What video games have to teach us about learning and literacy.* New York, NY: Palgrave.

Heath, S. B. (1984). *Ways with words.* New York, NY: Cambridge Unversity Press.

Howley, A., & Howley, C. (2000). The transformative challenge of rural context. *The Journal of Educational Foundations, 14*(4), 73–85.

Hull, G., & Schultz, K. (2001). Literacy and learning our of school: A review of theory and research. *Review of Educational Research, 71*, 575–611.

Hull, G. A., & Moje, E. B. (2010). What is the development of literacy the development of? Understanding Language Initiative. *Stanford University.* Retrieved July 22, 2013, from http://ell.stanford.edu/sites/default/files/pdf/academic-papers/05-Hull%20%26%20Moje%20CC%20Paper%20FINAL.pdf

Lemert, C. (2008). *Social things: A introduction to the sociological life* (4th ed.). Lanham, MD: Rowman & Littlefield.

Levin, B. (2014, March 19). *Surprises, lessons, and still in beta.* Paper delivered at the Information Technology and Innovation Foundation Forum, Washington DC. Retrieved May 22, 2014, from http://www.gig-u.org/cms/assets/uploads/2012/12/Thoughts-on-4th-Anniversary-of-Plan_FINAL-v2.pdf

Luke, A., & Freebody, P. (1999, August). Further notes on the four resources model. *Reading Online.* Retrieved September 24, 2013, from http://www.readingonline.org/research/lukefreebody.html

McDonald, J., & Klein, E. (2003). Networking for teacher learning. *Teachers College Record, 105*, 1606–1621.

Moll, L. (1994). Literacy research in community and classroom: A sociocultural approach. In R. B. Ruddell, M. R. Ruddell, & H. Singer (Eds.), *Theoretical models and processes of reading* (4th ed., pp. 179–207). Newark, DE: International Reading Association.

Moore, D. (2012, February). Chicago's democratically-led elementary schools far outperform Chicago's turnaround schools. Chicago, IL: Design for Change. Retrieved February 20, 2014, from http://www.designsforchange.org/democracy_vs_turnarounds.pdf

National Center for Education Evaluation and Regional Assistance (2014, April). A focused look at rural schools receiving school improvement grants. *Institute of Education Sciences.* Retrieved June 20, 2014, from http://ies.ed.gov/ncee/pubs/20144013/pdf/20144013.pdf

Powell, D., Higgins, H., Aran, R., & Freed, A. (2009). Impact of No Child Left Behind on curriculum and instruction in rural schools. *The Rural Educator, 31*(1), 19–28.

Shannon, P. (2007). *Reading against democracy: The broken promises of reading instruction.* Portsmouth, NH: Heinemann.

Shannon, P. (2013). *Closer readings of the Common Core.* Portsmouth, NH: Heinemann.

Smith, A. (1776). Inquiry into the nature and causes of the wealth of nations. *Library of Economics and Liberty.* Retrieved May 22, 2014, from http://www.econlib.org/library/Smith/smWN.html

Stockard, J. (2011). Increasing reading skills in rural areas: An analysis of three school districts. *Journal of Research in Rural Education, 26*(8), 1–19. Retrieved from http://jrre.vmhost.psu.edu/wp-content/uploads/2014/02/26-8.pdf

Street, B. (1984). *Literacy in theory and practice.* Cambridge, UK: Cambridge University Press.

Trujillo, T., & Renee, M. (2012, October). Democratic school turnarounds: Pursuing equity and learning from evidence. *National Education Policy Center.* Retrieved June 20, 2014, from http://greatlakescenter.org/docs/Policy_Briefs/Research-Based-Options/02-Trujillo_Turnarounds-PB.pdf

Wertsch, J. (1991). *Voices of the mind.* Cambridge, MA: Harvard University Press.

PART II

IMPLICATIONS OF LOCAL POLICY AND PRACTICE IN RURAL SCHOOLS

CHAPTER 5

IT TAKES A COMMUNITY

Preparing Teachers for Rural African American Early Childhood Students

Janeula M. Burt and Daniel Boyd

ABSTRACT

The intended outcomes of national legislation often can impose significant obstacles or unintended impacts on rural school districts. For example, district leaders have be able to think and plan in more creative ways to attract, recruit, and retain highly qualified teachers who also will be able to meet the challenges of rural teaching environments. The purpose of this case study was to illustrate how rural school district leaders used internally developed strategies and built upon the cultural capital of the rural community to meet the challenges of NCLB and improve the long-term achievement outcomes for African American preschoolers.

Background

Faced with limited candidate pools, rural school leaders have to look inwardly or be creative when it comes to the professional development training of rural teachers and teacher candidates. "Grow your own" or "nurture your own" type programs and strategies are designed to encourage and support community-based

Educational Opportunity in Rural Contexts: The Politics of Place, pages 77–105.

recruitment and retention of teachers in order to address current or potential teacher shortages (Hammer, Hughes, McClure, Reeves, & Salgado, 2005; McCullough & Johnson, 2007). The challenges in finding or training potential teachers are exacerbated by lack of student access to teacher education or preparation, certification, and professional development opportunities in rural communities. While the intent and purpose of No Child Left Behind's highly qualified teacher requirements were well intentioned, the legislation imposed a more negative effect and significant impact on rural school districts. Unequal resources, inadequate numbers of teachers, geographical challenges, shifting student demographics, and limited school choice options are several of the issues that are making it difficult for rural schools to keep pace with their suburban and urban counterparts. Therefore, it is up to rural school leaders to examine and define strategies, resources, and initiatives that can meet the challenge of finding, preparing, placing, and retaining highly qualified teachers in rural communities (McCullough & Johnson, 2007).

In addition to finding ways to meet the requirement of being *highly qualified* teachers, rural school leaders also are charged with attracting, recruiting, and retaining teachers who also will be successful in teaching in rural teacher districts. Therefore, in addition to the *No Child Left Behind Act of 2001, 2002* (NCLB) requirements, rural school leaders also must be able to recruit teachers who have, or are able to acquire a level of *cultural competence*, or the ability to understand children's relationships between the rural community and the context of the larger world around them (Eppley, 2009; Morgan & Reel, 2003; Whitebook, 2003). Residents in rural communities often define their identity, or who they are, through their connections to or foundations within their rural community. In other words, the needs and expectations of rural residents are a reflection of the local circumstances and contexts that surround them (Eppley, 2009). Therefore, "rurality" is seen as social and cultural constructs, where there is a distinction between both "inhabitancy" and "residency." The implication for the notion of rurality is that there is a deep connection to "place," which is more than just a backdrop to a rural person's life (Eppley, 2009). Place, or the connection to the community, is a key component of rural living.

> The ideal rural teacher is someone who is comfortable with the rural way of life and capable of wearing many hats; that is, certified to teach multiple subjects or grade levels, prepared to supervise several extracurricular activities, and able to teach students of differing ability levels within a single classroom. (McClure, Redfield, & Hammer, 2003)

Purpose of Study

Unfortunately, there is limited empirical research available on whether teachers with bachelor's degrees or specific training in early childhood education or development translate to better-quality preschool programs (Whitebook, 2003). Which means that the research on the impact of how highly qualified teachers effect rural, predominately African American early childhood program is even more negligible. The purpose of this study was twofold: (a) to examine the unique issues and strategies that were implemented by a predominately African American rural school district in order to meet the NCLB highly qualified teacher, early childhood requirement; and (b) to examine the post-NCLB impact and outcomes of having varying levels of highly qualified preschool teachers within predominately African American rural classrooms.

At the end of 20th century, informal and formal preschool educators were not required to have more than a high school education. However, with NCLB (2001, 2002) and other state policies, the bar has been raised, with preschool education teachers being required to be not only certified in early childhood education but also to be working toward postsecondary degrees. Therefore, post-NCLB, there has been a renewed interest in and attention to standards and certification, a new interest and spotlight also has been focused on early childhood education.

When faced with the challenge of trying to implement the ensuing NCLB requirements for highly qualified preschool teachers, the superintendent and Director of Head Start of a rural, southeastern school district took a proactive and creative approach. Rather than waiting for preschool teachers to find training, school district leaders facilitated preschool teacher training by providing the opportunity and the resources to attain the credentials necessary to meet the criteria of being a "highly qualified" early childhood educator. After providing these rural, preschool teachers with the resources needed to meet the highly qualified teacher criteria, district leaders also found that the student achievement scores of the preschool students who were taught by the "highly qualified" teachers not only increased but also sustained over time. The purpose of this chapter to illustrate how rural school leaders can use internal strategies to help meet the challenges of NCLB.

Federal Legislation: A Brief Overview

Elementary and Secondary Education Act.

For over 40 years, there has been a growing body of research directed at how best to address social, educational, and economic inequities in the United States. Fueled by the social and economic upheavals of the1960s, the *War on Poverty* was initiated to help to decrease the disparities in income, social status, education, and such that existed between various historically disenfranchised groups within the United States. Also known as the *Great Society Legislation*, policymakers enacted several American economy-driven and social status–related legislative acts, policies, departments, and programs, which included the *Civil Rights Act* (1964), *Food Stamp Act* (1964), *Elementary and Secondary Education Act* (1965), *Higher Education Act* (1965), *Medicare* and *Medicare* programs (1965), *Head Start* (1965), and several other urban renewal, rural recovery, and job-training programs (Germany, 2010):

> Wanting to do more than ameliorate the symptoms of poverty, policymakers sought reform in a wide range of areas that included education, housing, health, employment, civic participation, and psychological disposition. Antipoverty planners tried to provide poor people access to the American "good life" by offering them a "hand-up" rather than a "handout." A full attack on poverty, therefore, came to require local action and individual initiative. (p. 5)

Initiated in 1965 by the U.S. Department of Education, the overall goal of the Elementary and Secondary Education Act (ESEA) has been to improve the educational opportunities for children in poverty. ESEA funding was designed to be designated to individual students rather than individual schools or school districts. In other words, ESEA federal funds were designed to be distributed through state education agencies (SEAs) to local education agencies (LEAs) or school districts based upon the number (or proportion) of students in poverty within each school, thereby giving local schools and districts the ability to improve the educational outcomes of their most "needy" students. Embedded within the ESEA legislation was an evaluation component that was designed to help education stakeholders quantify the effect and impact of these federal dollars: "The 1965 ESEA emphasized standardized testing as a means to address poverty. By 1983, teacher quality was seen as an important factor in student achievement" (Eppley, 2009, p. 5). Therefore, it was within ESEA (and its Titles I–IX) that standardized tests would set the standards, or criteria, that schools would have to meet in order to receive ESEA-related funding for students in poverty (Eppley, 2009).

Similarly, after the publication of *A Nation at Risk* (1983), policymakers again began to examine the effectiveness of intended educational reform efforts such as ESEA, noting that teacher preparation programs were not providing enough core (e.g. reading, math, science, etc.) content-related coursework (Eppley, 2009):

> While the report was a continuation of themes identifiable in *ESEA* and the *Higher Education Act*, *A Nation at Risk* more clearly links deficits in teaching and the intellect of teachers themselves to the educational crisis described in the document. (p. 5)

Teachers, who lacked discipline-related knowledge, taught unstructured or non-standardized curriculum, and failed to demand rigor in the classroom were blamed for the perceived deficiencies of American students, and as a result were placing the nation and its resources "at risk" (Eppley, 2009). For the first time, "high quality teaching" was defined as content-matter-knowledge dependent as well as context independent (Eppley, 2009).

Although ESEA and its subsequent iterations were aimed at leveling the economic parity between communities and schools, despite supplemental federal funds, school funding disparities still existed in the 1990s (Eppley, 2009). The sentiment of the time was driven by a notion of a market-based model, or that economic competition was the key to not only economic development but also educational enhancement. The *Goals 2000 Educate America Act of 1994* continued to push for the higher achievement of not just students in poverty, but of *all*

U.S. students (Eppley, 2009). It was through *Goals 2000* that policymakers called for "'continued improvement of (teachers') professional skills,' specifically citing a need for teacher to obtain 'additional knowledge and skills needed to teach challenging subject matter' enabling them to teach increasingly diverse students and prepare 'all' students for the next century" (Eppley, 2009, p. 6). In 1998, *ESEA*'s reauthorization continued to push for "standards-based" testing and "accountability" and to show gains in student achievement among poor and disadvantaged students among schools who were receiving federal monies. Additionally, the concept of improving teacher quality also was more clearly defined within the *Goals 2000* legislation iterations (1994, 1998).

The *No Child Left Behind Act of 2001, 2002* (NCLB) federal legislation was passed as a part of the Elementary and Secondary Education Act (ESEA). Of the many significant reform-related requirements, one of the most important challenges within NCLB was that, by the end of the 2005–2006 school year, all teachers in core academic subject areas must be "highly qualified." According to Secretary of Education Margaret Spellings (2005), there was evidence that the highly qualified teacher requirement had contributed to increases in reading and math scores as well as a decrease in the achievement gaps between African Americans, Hispanics, and White 9-year-old students. However, how do highly qualified early childhood teachers contribute to not only increased student achievement but also sustained student achievement over time?

Overall, the *Elementary and Secondary Education Act* was designed to address the educational needs of school-aged children (K–12), particularly those students who are in impoverished or disadvantaged circumstances. Over the several iterations of the *ESEA* legislation history (1965–present), education research and policy has continued to advocate the connection between "highly qualified teachers," "accountability," and "higher student achievement." The nexus of these three concepts continues to influence national goals and outcomes in education.

Head Start Overview and Context

While the U.S. Department of Education has targeted policies, programs, and resources to address the *War on Poverty* through education (e.g., *ESEA*), the U.S. Department of Health and Human Services (HHS) paralleled and addressed the issue of social, economic, and educational inequities through programs such as *Head Start* (1965):

> The large research base demonstrating the benefits of high-quality preschool education for disadvantaged children, as well as cost-benefit analyses showing high rates of return, suggest a strategy of first serving those who "need it most" and are least able to purchase it on their own. (Ackerman, Barnett, Hawkinson, Brown, & McGonigle, 2009, p. 1)

And as states seek to improve student's short- and long-term educational outcomes, many choose to provide access to preschool education programs. However, many preschool programs are reserved only for those children are who most at risk of school failure (Ackerman et al., 2009).

For the past 40 years, Head Start programs have been enhancing the preschool educational experiences of low-income children throughout the United States. Overall, the primary goal of Head Start programs are intended to build short-term solutions that will have long-term positive effects for children and families (Garces, Thomas, & Currie, 2002). Unlike day care or nursery school programs, Head Start programs not only provide free, oftentimes full-day childcare for disadvantaged preschool children, it also provides a structured, research-based education program and provides access to quality health care, nutrition, and other social services to participants and their families (Garces et al., 2002). Research (Garces et al., 2002) has shown that children who attended Head Start are more likely to complete high school and to attend college than their siblings who did not attend, and they are more likely have higher earnings.

Mission of the Head Start Program

Administered through the office of Administration for Children and Families of the U.S. Department of Health and Human Services, Head Start was designed to promote school readiness by enhancing the social and cognitive development of children through the provision of educational, health, nutritional, social, and other services to enrolled children and families. Head Start is the largest national comprehensive early childhood education (ECE) and family development program administered in the United States. In 2001, Head Start was being funded at nearly $5 million and was serving nearly one million children and families (Garces et al., 2002). Although Head Start initially was designed to serve the needs of 3- and 4-year-olds, in 1995, the Early Head Start program was established in order to serve children from birth to three years of age in recognition of the mounting evidence that the earliest years matter a great deal to children's growth and development (HHS, 2003, 2007). The child-centered focus of the Head Start programs have the overall goal of increasing the social competence of young children in low-income households (HHS, 2003, 2007):

> By "social competence," is meant the child's everyday effectiveness in dealing with both his (or her) present environment and later responsibilities in school life. Social competence takes into account the interrelatedness of social, emotional, cognitive, and physical development. (p. 1)

In order to support the overall goal of improving social competence, Head Start programs encourage their centers to commit to a core set of values and commitments, which include:

- Establish a supportive learning environment for children, parents, and staff, in which the processes of enhancing awareness, refining skills, and increasing understanding are valued and promoted;

- Recognize that the members of the Head Start community—children, families, and staff—have roots in many cultures. Head Start families and staff, working together as a team, can effectively promote respectful, sensitive, and proactive approaches to diversity issues;
- Understand that the empowerment of families occurs when program governance is a responsibility shared by families, governing bodies, and staff, and when the ideas and opinions of families are heard and respected;
- Embrace a comprehensive vision of health for children, families, and staff, which assures that basic health needs are met, encourages practices that prevent future illnesses and injuries, and promotes positive, culturally relevant health behaviors that enhance lifelong well-being;
- Respect the importance of all aspects of an individual's development, including social, emotional, cognitive, and physical growth;
- Build a community in which each child and adult is treated as an individual, while at the same time, a sense of belonging to the group is reinforced;
- Foster relationships with the larger community so that families and staff are respected and served by a network of community agencies in partnership with one another; and
- Develop a continuum of care, education, and services that allows stable, uninterrupted support to families and children during and after their Head Start.

Head Start Program Description

Unlike traditional public schools, Head Start programs are provided grants by HHS, in order to fund local public and private nonprofit and for-profit agencies, which provide comprehensive child development services to economically disadvantaged children and families, with a special emphasis on helping preschoolers develop the early reading, math, and technology skills that they will need in order to be successful in public school. Head Start programs are designed to engage parents in their children's learning and help them in making progress toward their educational, literacy, and employment goals. Significant emphasis is placed on the involvement of parents in the administration of local Head Start programs. Head Start programs promote school readiness by enhancing the social and cognitive development of children through the provision of educational, health, nutritional, social, and other services to enrolled children and families.

Head Start grantees and delegate agencies work together in order to provide a range of individualized services in the areas of education and early childhood development, medical, dental, mental health, nutrition, and family involvement. Additionally, the program is continuing to help centers to strive for providing responsive and appropriate services that are unique to each child and family's developmental, ethnic, cultural, social, and linguistic heritage and experience.

The spirit and intent of the Head Start is to "level the playing field" through the implementation of early intervention strategies designed to remedy deficiencies that continue to hinder the development of disadvantaged children as they begin the schooling process. Head Start addresses the academic, physical, and social issues being faced by low-income children. Administered at the local level, hundreds of Head Start programs use federal program to maintain a nurturing learning environment, provide nutritious food, and empower parents through conferences and home visits to enhance the learning opportunity for economically disadvantaged preschoolers. One of the central tenets of the Head Start program requires active monitoring of each child's medical, dental, and mental health referrals and follow-ups (HHS, 2003, 2007).

Head Start originally started as a summer school program then later became a half-day preschool program, which included a 90-minute home-site visit, and later became a full-day, early education program (Garces et al., 2002; Soriano, Duenas, & LeBlanc, 2006). Head Start programs determine whether to administer services through a center-based or home-based model, or through a combination of both. Center-based programs may be in a classroom operated directly by Head Start or through a partnership with a childcare center that complies with the Head Start Program Performance Standards (Hamm, 2006).

> In 1998, Congress mandated that half of all center-based Head Start teachers nationwide obtain at least an A.A. [Associate Arts degree] by September 2003. Head Start programs met that mandate, and the number of teachers with degrees and credentials continued to increase in 2005, with 69% of teachers holding an A.A. or higher. Thirty-one percent of teachers had a B.A., 33% had an A.A., and 5% had a graduate degree. (Hamm, 2006, p. 7)

Head Start mandated that by 2008, at least 50% of classrooms would be required to have teachers who had a bachelor's degree with training in early childhood education (Whitebook, 2003). And although the empirical evidence of the impact of teacher background and teacher quality and student achievement is limited, the research suggests that teachers with baccalaureate degrees, with specialized training in early childhood education, leads to better short- and long-term education outcomes for children (Whitebrook, 2003). However, finding the resources that would be necessary to create a pool of highly qualified rural preschool teachers would be a challenge for rural education stakeholders. With the legislative requirements for highly qualified teachers, Head Start administrators were faced with resolving cost implications with already limited resources that would be hampered by (a) concerns about the current preschool workforce's ability to meet the highly qualified teacher requirement, (b) assuring that the preschool workforce is adequately diverse both linguistically and culturally, (c) making sure that the postsecondary community will have the capacity and resources to handle the demand for preparing highly qualified preschool teachers, and (d) finding the financial resources to fairly and adequately compensate a long-underpaid field within the workforce (Whitebrook, 2003).

State-Level Responses to Early Childhood Education

Although the goal and purpose of Head Start programs are to address the educational and health needs of disadvantaged and poor children and families, many state policymakers saw the need to address or supplement the school readiness of preschool children through state-funded early childhood education programs. The long- and short-term success of children who attend high-quality preschool education programs has been demonstrated through numerous rigorous research studies (Barnett, Jung, Wong, Cook, & Lamy, 2007; Goodman & Sianesi, 2005; Graces, Shores, Zaslow, Brown, Aufsceeser, & Bell, 2006; Stebbins & Scott, 2007; Whitebrook, 2003): "While Head Start maintains a common set of standards for all of its programs, variations in state pre-K standards occur at the state level and even at the community level" (Stebbins & Scott, 2007).

While on an abstract level the benefits of providing early childhood education to disadvantaged programs is beneficial, whether the funding is at the state or federal levels, "when the public funds programs for the poor rather than for everyone, the majority of voters may be unwilling to pay for a high-quality program for a small portion of the population, despite its relatively low total cost." (Ackerman et al., 2009, p. 2) Meanwhile, there has been a growing body of research that high-quality preschool education brings about substantial and significant gains for not only disadvantaged children but also for all students above and below the poverty line (Ackerman et al., 2009; Barnett et al., 2007; Manguson, Meyers, Ruhm, & Waldfogel, 2004; Stone, 2006):

> While the school readiness gap is greatest for disadvantaged children, middle-income children are frequently ill-prepared to do well in kindergarten and beyond. This is evidenced by the fact that middle-income children also experience unreasonably high rates of grade retention and failure to graduate from high school. The percentage of disadvantaged children who experience these outcomes is admittedly higher, but because the rest of the population is so much larger, the potential benefits and savings to education budgets are quite substantial. In short, although targeting may appear reasonable at the outset, it is problematic in many respects. Offering high-quality preschool education to all children is more likely to make a major impact on the school failure problem by reaching all those at risk of grade retention, dropout, and other academic problems. The initial cost of such a program is higher, but the increase in returns from improving the quality of services to disadvantaged children, while also adding returns for other children, can more than justify the added costs. (Ackerman et al., 2009, p. 3)

The emergence of state funded early childhood education programs began to appear as early as 1980, again, in response to addressing statewide school readiness needs of preschool children entering public schools (Ackerman et al., 2009; Barnett et al., 2007; Stone, 2006). For example, in 2006, it was estimated that anywhere from 38 to 41 states were funding and implementing preschool education programs and serving nearly 1 million children (Ackerman et al., 2009;

Stone, 2006; Wong et al., 2007). Nationally, the numbers of children participating in state-funded preschool programs have surpassed the number of students enrolled in Head Start programs children (Akerman et al., 2009). Like Head Start programs, the goal of state-funded preschool programs is to prepare preschool students for kindergarten and beyond through various programs and activities that promote the positive social, cognitive, behavioral, mental, and educational outcomes of preschool children (Ackerman et al., 2009; Barnett et al., 2007; Goodman & Sianesi, 2005; Graces et al., 2006; Stebbins & Scott, 2007; Wong & Cook, 2007).

One of the differences between early childhood programs such as Head Start and state-funded prekindergarten programs is that SEAs provide Head Start with federal funds with the stipulation that LEAs coordinate with health-related agencies. State-funded early childhood programs are funded directly by the state and can not only cooperate with local human services departments but also may partner with federally funded Head Start programs (Stone, 2006; Wong & Cook, 2007). However, one of the most significant differences between state- and federally funded early childhood programs is that many states require that pre-K programs meet higher standards of quality, which are often aligned with state standards for regular public school standards (e.g., teacher qualifications, curriculum standards, pedagogy requirements, teacher-student ratios, and classroom environment expectations) (Ackerman et al., 2009; Barnett et al., 2005; Graces et al., 2006; Goodman & Sianesi, 2005; Stebbins & Scott, 2007; Stone, 2006; Wong & Cook, 2007; Wong et al., 2007).

Costs of State Funded Pre-K Programs

Despite the social, moral, legislative, and educational support and attention that early childhood education has received, the most challenging obstacle to expanding the availability of and access to preschool education programs are fiscal constraints (Stone, 2006): "High-quality, public pre-K programs cannot be created solely through better use and coordination of federal funds. State policymakers must allocate substantial and sustainable state funds that can be increased over time" (Stone, 2006, p. 2). Early childhood programs are outside of what we consider to be publicly funded schooling (e.g., grades K–12). Therefore, funding for preschool programs typically is scant and often inconsistent, with services that are constrained to limited numbers of children. Consequently, state and local education policymakers and stakeholders are forced to be creative when it comes to developing funding or revenue streams for early childhood education programs within their states and school districts.

The ways in which states fund early childhood education programs has a direct impact on the school readiness and eventually the education impact and outcomes of each state. And although there are several ways in which preschool programs are funded within states, "most states allocate their portion of pre-K funding out of general state revenues" (Stone, 2006, p. 4). However, policymakers and stakeholders must be mindful that whatever the funding formula or stream, the strategy must be at limited risk for budget cuts or economic downturns. Therefore, many SEAs and LEAs have developed diverse funding formulas that combine federal, state, and local funds to supplement state preschool programs. "Earmarking special revenue sources for pre-k often enjoys more public support than a general tax increase, and funding can be structured to prohibit diversion of dedicated monies to other public programs" (Stone, 2006, p. 6). In addition to complementing federal funds for early childhood education programs (e.g., Title I, Head Start, etc.), there are several ways in which states are supplementing the funding of statewide preschool programs. For example, funding sources may include lottery and gaming revenues, tobacco settlement money, and excise taxes.

Lottery and gaming revenues.

While the state of Georgia was among the first states to enact legislation that offered universal early childhood education for 4-year-olds, limited program funding has restricted the number of children that the preschool program can support (Stone, 2006; Wong & Cook, 2007). For example, Georgia's universal preschool program is entirely funded using state lottery funds. Unlike state tax funding sources, regressive-based funding such as lottery and other gaming funds cannot provide a predictable, stable, secure, or interest-bearing stream of money (Stone, 2006). In other words, states that fund preschool programs using lottery monies are dependent on whether or not people play the lottery, citizens are who typically from low-income circumstances.

Excise taxes and tobacco settlement money.

Also known as "sin taxes," excise taxes are the taxes that are levied upon goods such as cigarettes and liquor. In 1998, the state of California passed the Children and Families First Act, which added a 50-cent tax to every pack of cigarette sold. In 2004, over $590 million were raised through this excise tax, which was earmarked to focus on the school readiness of children from the prenatal months to 5-year-olds (Stone, 2006). School readiness–related programs supported by state excise taxes include children's health, preschool education, parent and family support, and "building an integrated early childhood system" (Stone, 2006, p. 10). Meanwhile, only two states (Louisiana and Kansas) have reported using tobacco settlement dollars to supplement early childhood education programs (Stone, 2006). In 2004, "Louisiana used $1.5 million in tobacco settlement money to supplement its $58 million pre-K program." (Stone, 2006, p. 10) While Kansas supplemented its $58 million statewide preschool program with $1.5 million in tobacco settlement money (Stone, 2006).

State-Funded Early Childhood Programs

In its 2004 study of state-funded early childhood education programs, the National Institute for Early Education Research (NIEER) assessed how well states were meeting criteria believed to promote high-quality preschool programs (Wong & Cook, 2007). According to Wong and Cook (2007), NIEER measures included requirements related to:

- Teacher education and training;
- Minimum staff-child ratios and classroom sizes;
- Comprehensive early learning standards;
- Provisions for meals, vision, hearing, and health screenings;
- Teacher-parent conferences;
- Referrals to external social services; and
- State monitoring of preschool programs through site visits, questionnaires, and surveys.

Again, due to varying state requirements (e.g., participants, teachers, curriculum, standards, etc.), it is difficult to make cross-comparisons or generalize the outcomes of state-funded early childhood programs. However, a significant amount of qualitative and quantitative results are demonstrating significant effects and impacts of these statewide educational opportunities for preschool children (Ackerman et al., 2009; Stone, 2006; Wong & Cook, 2007). Federally funded Head Start preschool programs are nationally consistent and standardized. However, although primarily funded by state funds, statewide preschool programs can differ in some of the following ways:

- Supplementing federal funding for existing Head Start programs that restrict eligibility to low-income students;
- Limiting programs to public school providers only;
- Offering either half-day, work-day, or full-day schedules;
- Restricting preschool availability to 4-year-olds only; and
- Providing "wrap around" social services such as healthcare and parenting classes or educational services only. (Stone, 2006)

The state of Michigan offers a universal preschool program in which at least half of the students must be at least 4 years old, exhibit at least one (of 25) educational risk factor, and meet an income eligibility criterion. Unlike Head Start, Michigan's statewide program required that *all* preschool teachers have a baccalaureate and that the staff-to-child ratio be 1:8 or less than 18 children (Wong & Cook, 2007). Established in 1980 as a pilot program, in 1998, the state of Oklahoma was the second state (after Georgia) to offer state-funded, voluntary, universal preschool education to all 4-year-olds (Wong & Cook, 2007). In 2004–2005, nearly 65% of all 4-year olds (approximately 30,180) were enrolled in the statewide preschool program (Wong & Cook, 2007).

In Oklahoma, the state-funded pre-K program used a comprehensive curriculum standards framework, and had a preferred staff-child ratio of 1:10. Regardless of the setting, all pre-K teachers were required to have a bachelor's degree and a certificate in early childhood learning. Also, since most children were being served in public schools, districts also could collaborate with private childcare or Head Start centers to provide services (Wong & Cook, 2009).

> Most children were served in public schools, though districts could also collaborate with private childcare or Head Start centers to provide services. Regardless of setting, all pre-K teachers were required to have a bachelor's degree and a certificate in early childhood learning. . . . Oklahoma had comprehensive curriculum standards and limited the staff-child ratio to 1:10, with a maximum class size of 20. (p. 13)

While the implementation of state-funded early childhood programs varies from state to state, rigorous studies (Ackerman et al., 2009; Barnett et al., 2005; Barnett et al., 2007; Goodman & Sianesi, 2005; Graces et al., 2006; Stebbins & Scott, 2007; Stone, 2006) have demonstrated statistically significant outcomes as well as moderate effect sizes in the short- and long-term outcomes of both disadvantaged and other student participants. However, what is also notable about state-funded early childhood education programs is that what constitutes a high-quality preschool program is often purposely and strategically aligned with statewide public school requirements such as highly qualified teachers and curriculum standards.

Rural Education

Nearly a third of all public schools are located in rural communities, with nearly a fifth of all public school students attending rural schools (Alliance for Excellent Education; 2010; Eppley, 2009; McClure et al., 2003; National Rural Education Summit, 2008). There are rural schools and school districts in every state (Johnson & Strange, 2007). For example, while Delaware is one of the nation's *least* rural states, its rural communities are among some of the most impoverished. However, similar to other rural communities, educational attainment among rural community members in the state of Delaware is extremely low, with fewer than 6 in 10 rural students graduating from high school, which is the third-worst rate in the nation (Johnson & Strange, 2007). Students in high-poverty rural districts have a 66% greater chance that he or she will not be taught by a fully certified teacher than students in low-poverty districts. For example, in 30 high-poverty rural districts in North Carolina, almost one of every seven teachers was not fully certified (McCullough & Johnson, 2007).

Whether it is an urban, suburban, or rural school district, recruiting and retaining highly qualified teachers presented very different, unique, and significant challenges for rural school districts (McCullough & Johnson, 2007; McClure et al., 2003). Geographic seclusion, small district size, low teacher salaries, distance from student residences to schools, limited resources, and social isolation often are some of the top issues cited for why rural schools and districts have a difficult time recruiting, placing, and retaining teachers, particularly in high need areas and other unique and special contexts (McClure, Redfield, & Hammer, 2003; McCullough &

Johnson, 2007; NCLB, 2001, 2002). Also, schools in rural areas serve the needs of their students and communities in ways different than those of schools in urban and suburban school districts. For example, "rural school districts are often the largest single employer in their area and rural schools serve as the social, recreational, and cultural foundation of their communities" (NEA, 2010). However, despite the size of the rural school district and community, rural and small schools compose over 40% of the nation's public school students, they only receive about 22% of federal education funds (NEA, 2010).

While NCLB has shined a new spotlight on highly qualified Kindergarten through grade-12 teachers, what is not as widely known is that the highly qualified teacher requirement also applied to early childhood educators. For example, in 1998, preschool teachers needed to be working toward an associate's degree or certification (CDA) in early childhood education. Previous to 1998, informal and formal preschool educators were not required to have more than a high school education. However, in 2002, the bar was raised for early childhood educators, with pre-school education teachers being required to not only specialize or have specific training in early childhood education, but also to have earned a bachelor's degree by the year 2013 (NCLB, 2001, 2002). Unfortunately, attracting teacher candidates from urban or suburban environments to low-economic and high-need rural settings was already an insurmountable task for rural school leaders. Therefore, the introduction of the NCLB highly qualified teacher (HQT) requirement made the challenge of hiring rural highly qualified teachers even more taxing for rural communities.

Unequal resources, inadequate numbers of teachers, geographical challenges, shifting student demographics, and limited school choice options are several of the issues that are making it difficult for rural schools to keep pace with their suburban and urban counterparts. The challenges in finding or training potential teachers in rural communities are exacerbated by lack of student access to teacher education or preparation, certification, and professional development opportunities. While the intent and purpose of NCLB's HQT requirements are well intentioned, the legislation may have unintentionally imposed a more negative effect and impact on rural school districts. Therefore, it is up to rural school leaders to examine and define strategies, resources, and initiatives that can meet the challenge of finding, preparing, placing, and retaining highly qualified teachers in rural communities (McCullough & Johnson, 2007). Faced with an already limited candidate pool, rural school leaders had to look inward or be creative when it came to recruiting potential teacher candidates. "Grow your own" or "nurture your own" type programs and strategies are designed to encourage and support community-based recruitment and retention of teachers in order to address current or potential teacher shortages (Hammer, Hughes, McClure, Reeves, & Salgado, 2005; McCullough & Johnson, 2007).

In examining the impact of teacher background and quality, researchers (Barnett, 2003; Bowman, Donovan & Burns, 2001; Howes & Brown, 2000; Whitebook, 2003) have suggested that having BA-level teachers in preschool classrooms with specialized training in early childhood education can lead to better outcomes for preschoolers. Unfortunately for rural school districts and in many states, "recommending a BA in ECE or a similar standard would result in a significant raising of standards for teachers in early childhood settings, and such a suggestion can therefore trigger considerable debate" (Whitebook, 2003, p. 1). Among rural school administrators, the challenges of staffing preschool programs with highly qualified teachers with adequate training in early childhood education and development would be more than a difficult task to accomplish (Schwartzbeck & Prince, 2003).

According to the *No Child Left Behind* legislation (2001), the close of the 2005–2006 school year was the deadline for public schools to ensure that all classroom teachers met the "highly qualified teacher" criteria: (a) be fully certified by the state in which they are teaching; (b) hold at least a bachelor's degree; and (c) demonstrate subject-matter competence in each of the core academic subjects that they teach (McClure et al., 2003; Schwartzbeck & Prince, 2003). Consequentially, it has been the task of state and school leaders who are able to think and plan in creative ways to attract, recruit, and retain highly qualified teachers who not only will be able to meet the HTQ requirements, but also who will be able to meet the challenges of teaching in a rural community .

Again, the mandatory highly qualified preschool teacher requirement would potentially pose significant unanticipated and unique challenges for rural LEAs and school leaders. For example, (a) the interest and willingness of the early childhood and childcare workforce to seek higher education; (b) the capacity of postsecondary programs to prepare an often underprepared workforce; (c) the cognitive and pedagogical ability of the current workforce to meet the ensuing teacher quality standards; (d) the time and resources needed to complete an associates or bachelor's degree program; (e) the availability of and the distance between a rural school district and an accredited early childhood teacher preparation program; and (f) the capacity of the LEA, the field, or the school district to meet the financial strain of a more highly educated preschool educator workforce would be among many of the unforeseen problems that local school leaders would have to face.

Rural, Highly Qualified Preschool Teachers

> To help each child prepare for successful employment and productive citizenship in the 21st century, all teachers must know their subject areas deeply, understand how children learn and be able to use that knowledge to teach well, use modern learning technologies effectively, and work closely with their colleagues to create rich learning environments. (NCTAF, 2002, p. 13)

In addition to meeting the requirements of what it means to be a highly qualified teacher, successful rural teachers also must have, or be able to acquire a level of *cultural competence*, or the ability to understand children's relationships between the rural community and the context of the larger world around them (Eppley, 2009; Morgan & Reel, 2003). However, it is critical to point out that what constitutes a "highly qualified" rural (or urban, suburban, etc.) teacher is a very complex and multifarious issue (Eppley, 2009).

Although few would argue that having highly qualified teachers in rural classrooms would have positive outcomes. However, "definitions and criteria for teaching credentials are based on norms that do not necessarily take notions of 'rural' into account." (Eppley, 2009, p. 7) Unfortunately, under NCLB legislation, "school or community fit," or teacher understanding of how "place" or rural environments impact student learning and educational outcomes, is not a criterion or variable for which LEAs can make teacher hiring decisions: "School administrators are forced to put aside what they know about the qualities of strong rural teachers" (Eppley, 2009, p. 7) in favor of the generic qualifications that place all teachers, with the proper credentials, as highly qualified for all school or community contexts.

One of the many positive attributes for recruiting rural teachers through grow-your-own or local recruiting efforts is that most rural teachers report that rural communities are good places to live and work (Alliance for Excellent Education, 2010; McCullough & Johnson, 2007; Hammer et al., 2005). Rural residents often define their identity or who they are through their connection to or foundation within their rural community. In other words, the needs and expectations of rural communities are a reflection of the circumstances and contexts that surround them (Eppley, 2009). Therefore, connection to the community is a key component to rural living.

Additionally, rural teachers report that rural communities are supportive, tight-knit communities with more simplistic lifestyle, and access to natural landscape beauty (Alliance for Excellent Education, 2010). Rural teachers "generally report a high level of job satisfaction, greater autonomy, and more direct influence over school policy" (Alliance for Excellent Education, 2010, p. 26). Teachers in rural communities also reported feeling safer in their schools than their urban and suburban counterparts (Provasnik et al., 2007). Public school teachers in rural communities also reported fewer serious student behavioral problems compared to public school teachers nationally. Again, the small, close-knit nature of a rural community gives the opportunity for teachers to not only know their students, but also family members well (Provasnik et al., 2007).

Overall, rural teachers tend to settle into small and rural districts and stay for extraordinarily long periods, making teacher retention in rural school districts greater than in other schools (Monk, 2007). Many teachers who grew up in or near a rural community spend their entire career in the same school, which can be both good and bad (Monk, 2007). Teachers who teach in rural schools do so either by choice or because they cannot get work elsewhere. Conversely, district and school administrators in rural districts tend to seek teachers who are highly talented and genuinely interested in teaching in rural schools. However, it is unclear how many highly qualified teachers and teacher candidates fall into the latter category.

Methods of Inquiry

In this single case study, "Mingo County School District" (MCSD) is a rural school district located in the southeastern region of the country. When faced with the challenge of trying to implement the NCLB requirements for highly qualified preschool teachers, the superintendent and Director of Head Start of this rural district took a proactive and creative approach. Rather than waiting for preschool teachers to find training, school district leaders facilitated preschool teacher training by providing the opportunity and the resources to attain the credentials necessary to meet the criteria of being a "highly qualified" early childhood educator not only in order to fulfill NCLB requirements but more importantly to address the needs of this rural school community. The purpose of this case study was to illustrate how rural school leaders can use internally developed strategies, such as drawing from the cultural capital (Swartz, 1998; Winkle-Wagner, 2010) of the rural community, to help meet the challenges of NCLB and improve the long-term achievement outcomes for African American preschoolers.

Description of School District

Mingo County is a rural, agricultural county located approximately 30 miles south of the third-largest urban center within the state. Located in the southeastern section of the state, Mingo County covers approximately 700 square miles in area and is populated with approximately 13,000 citizens, which is significant because, like many rural districts, some of the schools within the district are located as far away as about 30 miles from school district offices.

Approximately 80% of the Mingo County population is African American, while approximately 20% is White (non-Hispanic). The median income for Mingo County is approximately $22,000, and the number of citizens within the county holding at least a bachelor's degree is approximately 16%. Rural children are significantly less likely than nonrural children to have parents with a bachelor's degree (Zaslow, Brown, & Aufseeser, 2005). Although in 2007 the average state unemployment rate was approximately 3%, the average unemployment rate for Mingo County was over four times the state average (13%).

The single largest employer within Mingo County is the school district itself. The second-largest employer is a truck stop, which is located on a major highway that runs through the county. Therefore, like many rural citizens, Mingo County residents must travel significant distances outside of the county to work. There are no national grocery store chains or retail stores located within the county, and there are only two gas stations. Similarly, there are no healthcare or legal services providers located within the county.

The Mingo County School District is composed of approximately 2,415 students, and has a teacher-student ratio of approximately 1:15. Although 20% of the population is White, 99% of the Mingo County School District student population is African American, while only approximately 1% is White. Approximately 95% of the student population is eligible for free or reduced-price lunch. The district's per-pupil expenditure is approximately $7,297. The district contains a total of seven schools, three elementary schools, two middle schools, and two secondary schools.

Early Childhood Education Program Opportunities

In 2000, the superintendent initiated a communitywide school district plan which included not only curriculum and textbook upgrades, but also the building and renovation of school facilities. The Mingo County Head Start (MCHS) program classrooms are physically located within each of the elementary schools. Locating Head Start classes within the public school buildings has allowed the LEA and community members to leverage the resources that make it more convenient for parents to have their preschool and school-aged children in central locations. Having the Head Start program located within each of the elementary schools also has reduced the transportation costs for both the LEA and Head Start programs. LEA and MCHS administrators consistently assess the program offerings and parameters at other programs within the school district.

The Mingo County School District is one of three school districts within the state that is the administrator of record for the Mingo County Head Start Program. The Mingo County School District has been overseeing the Head Start program in Mingo County since 1966. According to Early Childhood Longitudinal Study-Kindergarten Cohort (ECLS-K[1]) data (2005), on average, only approximately 14% of rural African American children participate in Head Start programs (Zaslow et al., 2005). Although most early childhood education students are enrolled in the Mingo County Head Start program (85%), approximately 15% of preschool students enter kindergarten from either two local center- or home-based preschool programs.

There are two other center-based early childhood education programs located within Mingo County: a state-funded, faith-based program and a state-funded preschool program. Both programs are designed to serve Mingo County children from the ages of 0 to 5 years old. However, they tend to lose students in the 3–5-year-old range because they are eligible for the district's Head Start program, which has access to more resources. The final early childhood opportunity available for Mingo County citizens includes noncenter-based programs such as local babysitters, relatives, and parents. Some 56% of Black rural preschoolers were more likely to participate in multiple childcare arrangements in the year before kindergarten (Zaslow et al., 2005).

Another plus for parents who participated in these alternative preschool center-based programs was that both operated during the hours of 6:00 a.m.–6:00 p.m.

for working parents. Although the MCHS program initially served pre-K students 4 days a week, after a parent-needs survey, MCHS increased program services from 4 to 5 days. In 2006, MCHS program staff members assessed the possibility of increasing the hours of operation from 7:30 a.m. to 3:00 p.m. to 6:00 a.m. to 6:00 p.m. in order to meet the work schedule needs of parents. Similar to the geographic challenges of parents in finding viable local employment, access to high-quality early childhood experiences were not necessarily tied to cost but rather to location and access to reliable transportation.

Mingo County Head Start Program (MCHS)

The Mingo County Head Start (MCHS) program typically serves approximately 300 children between the ages of 3 and 5 years old. At the beginning of the 2006–2007 school year, approximately 289 of the students enrolled in the Head Start program were African American and approximately six students were White. However, in October 2006, four of the six White students left the Mingo County Head Start program. Approximately 85% of eligible Mingo County children participate in the Head Start program, the remaining 15% participate in church- or home-based opportunities. As the administrator for the Head Start program, the LEA also has the opportunity to share academic and other school district resources for the benefit of children from birth to age 4.

As required by the Head Start program, the district's program focuses on the emotional, social, health, nutritional, academic, and psychological needs of Mingo County early childhood students. As a result, the Mingo County Head Start program provides academic and social services such as mental health; family services/resources; parent workshops, services, and resources; and food services and nutrition. Unfortunately, unlike in urban communities, the challenge of providing access to the necessary Head Start resources in rural communities rests upon the creativity of LEA and Head Start administrators. Therefore, rather than relying on the expectation that parents will have the time or the resources available to follow through on the health-related requirements, Mingo County LEA and Head Start Administrators pool resources to create schedules and provide transportation for all MCHS health services. The Head Start program also partners with health providers to offer onsite services to MCHS participants.

The Mingo County Head Start Program is overseen by the federally mandated Mingo County Head Start Policy Council (MCHSPS). The MCHSPC is composed of primarily of parents (of current students), teachers, community members, and administrative staff. Each member of the council serves for a maximum of 3 years. Similar to a district board of education, council members must approve all policies, programs, curriculum, and human resource issues.

Early Childhood Education Professional Development Training Opportunities

Mingo County is located an average of approximately 30–75 "rural" miles away from the closest institution of higher education. An understanding of "rural miles" is essential because in rural communities, it is not unusual for roadways to be unpaved or in need of repair, have limited arteries to major thoroughfares, have limited lighting, and so on. Additional rural transportation challenges also may include access to reliable vehicles, limited numbers of vehicles per household, lack of public transportation, and conflicts between the work schedules of working adults.

In 1998, the Head Start program coordinator and the MCHS decided to exceed Head Start program requirements and require that not only 100% (rather than 50%) of teachers have at least an associate's degree but also that the program would provide transportation to and from the school district to the postsecondary training as well as money for books. Mingo County Head Start teachers who participated in the teacher education program took early childhood development and education courses as a cohort group from a local 2-year state technical college located in the closest urban city. The selected postsecondary institution offers associates degrees, certificates, and specialized training certificates in early childhood care and education. Using the strategy of a purposeful cohort group gave this group of early childhood educators an opportunity to collectively prepare, study, and apply their rural preschool experiences with classmates who could contextualize childhood development and education with rural African American preschoolers.

As a result of the strategic and proactive vision and implementation of the LEA, the MCHS professional development cohort participants completed study and attained associates degrees with an emphasis on early childhood education. As of October 2006, there were four Head Start teachers who were seeking to complete their bachelor's degrees at a rural historically Black college and an urban historically Black university. Both institutions frequently partner with the LEA to conduct teacher training in early childhood education. Since Mingo County schools receive preschoolers from outside of the MCHS program (e.g., center and noncenter-based programs) LEA and MCHS administrators also provide early childhood development and education training for non-MCHS preschool programs and teachers.

Promising Practices for Retaining Highly Qualified Rural Preschool Teachers

Recognizing that Mingo County schools, particularly preschools, would be presented with unique and challenging circumstances with regard to meeting the challenges of NCLB requirements, school administrators anticipated and proactively used strategies and approaches that built upon the cultural capital of their rural location, rather than waiting for suggestions for how to overcome potential obstacles. For example, rural school leaders leveraged local, state, and federal resources to give teachers access to certification-required coursework (e.g., Head Start vans, LEA/Head Start professional development funds, etc.). As a result of this collaboration of resources, 100% of all Mingo County Head Start teachers have at least an associate's degree, and several Head Start teaches have either attained or are in the process of attaining their bachelor's degrees.

One of the unintended consequences of a more educated preschool staff was that many were drawn away from preschool classrooms by higher regular education programs. Therefore, in order to address one of the compensation issues faced by rural preschool teachers, LEA administrators began to supplement the fringe benefits of Head Start teachers by enabling preschool teachers to collect unemployment insurance during the summer months. As noted in earlier research (Whitebrook, 2003), increasing the salary of a previously underpaid profession (preschool educators) will continue to be a challenge that rural school districts would have difficulty meeting, particularly within the already low and limited salaries of regular K–12 teachers. Allowing MCHS teachers to supplement their salaries with unemployment benefits was a strategy that helped LEA administrators keep highly qualified preschool teachers in the classroom.

While Mingo County demographically possesses many of the characteristics that could place children at risk of educational failure, participation in high-quality educational opportunities not only levels the playing field for potentially at-risk students, it also provides high-achieving students with opportunities to excel. Therefore, using Head Start and other early childhood assessments, LEA and MCHS administrators use assessment scores to place MCHS students who score high on academic assessments the opportunity to take classes with the Mingo County Kindergarten students.

Data Sources and Evidence

Again, the Head Start program is designed to promote school readiness and healthy development among underserved preschool children. As a Head Start program grantee, the Mingo County school district administers the largest early childhood program in the county, serving the academic, social, and health needs of nearly 300 African American preschool students.

In 2003, federal government officials announced their intention to require that every 4- and 5-year-old participating in the Head Start program would be tested in literacy, math, and language skills at the beginning and at the end of each program year to assess the progress of Head Start students (GAO, 2005). The biennial compilation of preschool student assessment data would be collected and sent to the National Reporting System (NRS), which would allow school leaders and teachers to be able to see how LEA preschoolers compared to the national averages. The NRS was originally developed to help meet a long-standing need for systematic information on how well specific Head Start programs were helping preschoolers to learn. During the 2003–2004 school year, over 400,000 Head Start students were assessed in the areas of literacy, math, and language skill development (GAO, 2005). From 2003 until 2007, CCPSD participated in the NRS assessment reporting.

From 1997 to 2009, MCSD began implementing HighReach Learning Curriculum, a state-approved early childhood curricula. The HighReach Learning curriculum provides early childhood curriculum programs and teacher resource materials for ages 16 months through kindergarten. Teacher resources include puppet and activity books, emergency kits, and learning cassettes. As a curriculum package, HigherReach includes criterion-referenced assessment tools which are primarily focused on assessing the progress of preschoolers within the age range of 36–60 months (3–5 years old). The HighReach early childhood curriculum and assessments are aligned with early childhood standards and are designed to assess not only current competencies but also to emphasize emergent skills with diverse learners and take into consideration the necessary precursor skills which are fundamental to school readiness. HighReach assessments are administered three times per year (e.g., beginning, middle, and end). Also, preschool teachers are encouraged to make decisions using data from generated reports in order to set child development goals, individualize instruction, and plan for groups of children on an ongoing basis.

Results

Data from the National Reporting System assessment noted that from 2003 to 2007, preschoolers participating in the MCSD Head Start program performed significantly higher than the national average in the areas of math, literacy, and language skills. Meanwhile, in an examination of three years of HighReach assessment data (2006–2009), it was determined that the preschool students who had teachers who were "highly qualified" or who had attained a BA performed significantly higher than the students whose teachers were not considered to be highly qualified.

Scholarly Significance of the Study

> Rural areas in the South are viewed as being in a period of transition, a period in which the education and skill levels of the labor force are becoming increasingly critical to the welfare of rural residents and rural communities. (Mulkey, 2010, p. 2)

There is limited empirical evidence to support or address the needs and outcomes of rural communities in general or rural African American communities specifically (Mulkey, 2010). The outcomes of this study demonstrate that having highly qualified teachers in rural, predominately African American early childhood classrooms has positive and long-term effects on student achievement. However, what is not accounted for is the importance of recruiting and retaining highly effective preschool educators in hard-to-staff rural communities. While it is difficult to make causal connections between the impact of teacher qualifications and student achievement (Whitebook, 2003), it is still helpful to be able to examine the longitudinal effects of a more highly qualified early childhood teaching workforce.

Methodology

This study was conducted in order to examine the effectiveness of early childhood teachers who had received a Bachelor of Science versus early childhood educators who did not have a bachelor's degree. Teacher effectiveness was measured as it related to student achievement over time. In other words, the student achievement of early childhood or Head Start participants was measured through longitudinal data collected through the HighReach Learning Progress Reporting and Evaluation Program.

A total of 17 Head Start teachers were eligible to participate in the study. However, of the 17 teachers, only 6 had earned a Bachelors of Science degree, while 11 of the teachers had not earned a BS. Head Start teachers were selected for the study using a systematic sampling procedure in which teachers were divided into non-BS and BS categories and listed in alphabetical order. Non-BS teachers who fell in the first, fourth, and eighth positions on the list were selected for the sample of the non-BS teachers. Teachers who fell in the first, third, and fifth position on the list of BS teachers were selected for the BS teacher sample. In other words, the sample consisted of six rural Head Start teachers, three teachers with a Bachelor of Science, and three without a bachelor's degrees.

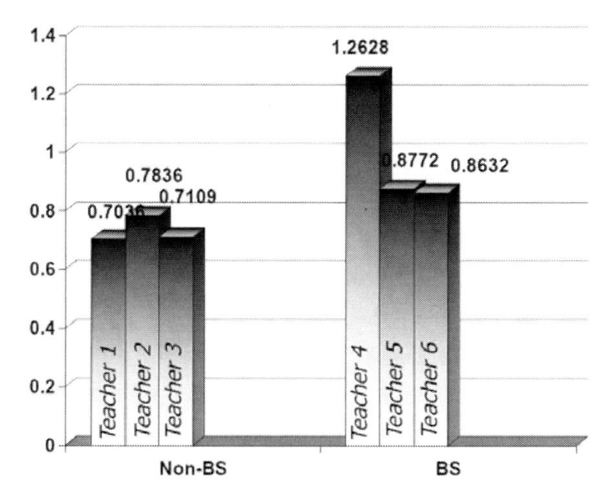

FIGURE 5.1. Mingo County Mean Scores of BS and Non-BS Head Start Teachers-Language Arts

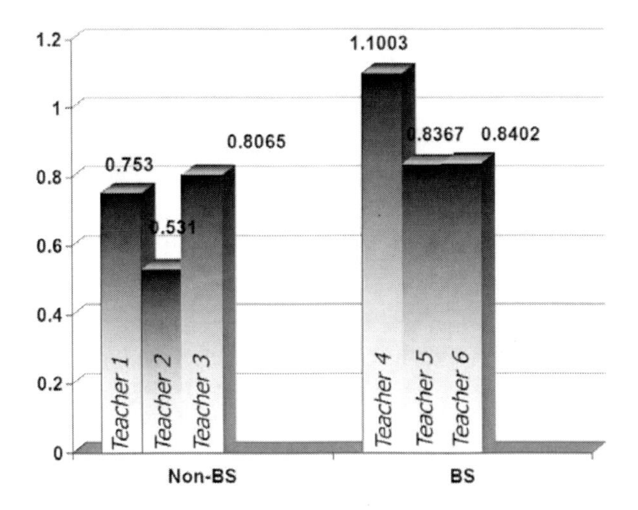

FIGURE 5.2. Mingo County Mean Scores of BS and Non-BS Head Start Teachers-Mathematics

Data from the HighReach Learning Progress Reporting and Evaluation Program (2006–2007, 2007–2008, and 2008–2009) were analyzed for 319 former Head Start students who had received instruction from one of the six teachers in the study. Differences in pre- and postassessment scores among students were analyzed using independent t-tests. In other words, longitudinal pre- and postassessment scores were assessed for BS and non-BS teachers. Mean scores for both language arts and mathematics were analyzed based upon teacher category (e.g., BS or non-BS). The language arts scores for the students who were taught by teachers who had received a Bachelor of Science degree scored significantly higher ($p < .001$) than the non-BS teachers (see Figure 5.1).
Similarly, the students who received math instruction from the BS teachers also scored statistically significantly higher ($p < .001$) than those students who received math instruction from non-BS Head Start teachers (see Figure 5.2).

CONCLUSIONS

In understanding how to best meet the educational needs of rural students, there is also a need to understand the unique needs of rural teachers. Over 90% of teachers with bachelor's degrees in Mingo County Public School live outside of the rural community, while, over 90% of the Head Start teachers not only work but also live in Mingo County. While the MCPS Head Start teachers may have the cultural competence to be able to help rural African American preschool children, in addition to meeting the "highly qualified" criteria, MCPS Head Start teachers also needed to be able to be able to connect to and understand the larger world outside of their rural community. The relational and interactional styles, as well as the social protocols (Kea, 2009) of rural community members can vary greatly from urban and suburban environments. Therefore, understanding and acknowledging the cultural capital of small-town, close-knit, fictive-kin relationships among rural community (Kea, 2009) teachers is important in helping them gain "highly qualified" teacher status.

As a rural school district, it was the goal of the MCPS district leadership to have *all* Head Start teachers be "highly qualified" and to have a minimum of a bachelor's degree. Therefore, rather than waiting for teachers to seek and complete their degrees, administrators took a proactive stance by providing funding, resources, and the time to complete their degree programs through a district planned cohort-based group. The cohort-based model was built upon a rural cultural understanding and context where the preschool teachers were able to navigate their postsecondary experiences as a cohesive unit or "family" rather than individually. Additionally, district leaders provide professional development using the data from HighReach and other prescriptive data (e.g., disaggregated HighReach assessment scores, teacher needs assessments, and teacher observations) to enhance and remediate the skillsets of Mingo County Head Start teachers. District administrators also partnered with local universities to meet the needs of teaching staff (i.e., hours of courses, online assistance, etc.) and encouraged teaching staff to explore online courses or universities that were accredited and approved by the state for licensure. Again, rather than drawing from a deficit-based lens of what the district lacked, in an effort to provide classroom coverage for teachers, district staff increased the number of classroom volunteers. And finally, the Mingo County School district leaders used American Recovery Reinvestment Act (ARRA) Quality Improvement Funds (P.L. 111-5) to provide tuition assistance for MCPS Head Start teachers. Quality Improvement federal funds were designed to help school districts such as MCPS, to increase Head Start teacher compensation, enhance staff qualifications, and provide education and professional development that enables teachers to be fully competent to meet Head Start standards.

Over the past 40 years, the effectiveness of the Head Start and other high-quality early childhood education programs has been questioned and studied, with varying results. Generally, in theory as well as in practice, Head Start is perceived to be an effective school readiness tool for disadvantaged preschool children (Zill, Resnick, Kim, O'Donnell, & Sorongon, 2003). Short-term benefits of high-quality preschool programs include increased cognitive outcomes for students. Long-term benefits include increased academic achievement, which includes a greater likelihood that Head Start students will graduate from high school (Graces et al., 2006; Zill et al., 2003). However, what has most recently been called into question has been the strength or "evidence base" for Head Start program evaluation and research.

NCLB (2001, 2002) and other legislation has increased the teacher quality and professional development requirement standards for all teachers, including, for the first time—preschool educators. Although the rise in the educational attainment of Head Start teachers is perceived to have a significant effect, the significantly low Head Start teacher salaries is leading to another unanticipated problem—teacher shortages. Higher salaries and better benefits have caused significant numbers of to seek employment within the local school district. State teacher certification credentialing have given Head Start teachers, who are now being certified in early childhood education, are now able to transfer to a more high paying to a more steady employment opportunity (state vs. grant funds). However, for some school districts, as fast as early childhood teachers receive their degree and certification, is as fast as they are leaving preschool for public school programs.

As with many grant-based programs, the strength or effectiveness of the Head Start program is only as good or effective as the program implementation. Head Start programs can be administered by local entities such as local government agencies, non-profit organizations, regional partnerships, private childcare facilities, community organizations, or local school districts. Community members, local advisory groups, Head Start staff, and parents play a critical role in the ensuring that federal program guidelines and policies are properly implemented (HHS, 2003). Local agencies are required to establish effective systems and procedures for the Head Start program, financial, and human resources management (HHS, 2003). For example, as the local grantee, one school district is able to increase services to Head Start participants by sharing the cost of transportation, classroom maintenance, professional development, and school nutrition with the local education agency. Similarly, in addition, having Head Start classrooms located within the elementary school building is also helpful for Head Start and elementary school teachers in aligning not only professional development but also curriculum.

NOTE

1. ECLS-K data contains a national sample of early childhood education students. In other words, the data do not contain the entire universe, but rather a random sampling of preschool students (center- and non-center-based programs). Therefore, it should be noted that the subsample of African American preschool students contains negligible numbers of early childhood education African American participants.

REFERENCES

Ackerman, D. J., Barnett, W. S., Hawkinson, L. E., Brown, K., & McGonigle, E. A. (March, 2009). Providing preschool education for all 4-year Olds: Lessons from six state journeys. Preschool Policy Brief, Issue 18. *National Institute for Early Education Research.* Retrieved July 11, 2010, from http://nieer.org/resources/policybriefs/19.pdf

Barnett, W. S. (2003). Better teachers, better preschools: Student achievement linked to teacher qualifications. *Preschool Policy Matters, 2.* New Brunswick, NJ: NIEER.

Barnett, W. S., Jung, K., Wong, V., Cook, T., & Lamy, C. (October, 2007). Effects of five state pre-kindergarten programs on early learning. *National Institute for Early Education Research.* Retrieved December 11, 2007, from http://nieer.org/pdf/Multi-State1007.pdf

Bowman, B., Donovan, M. S., & Burns, S. (Eds.). (2001). *Eager to learn: Educating our preschoolers.* National Research Council, Committee on Early Childhood Pedagogy. Washington, DC: National Academies Press.

Eppley, K. (2009). Rural schools and the highly qualified teacher provision of No Child Left Behind: A critical policy analysis. *Journal of Research in Rural Education, 24*(4), 1–11.

Germany, K. B. (2007). *New Orleans after the promises: Poverty, citizenship, and the search for the great society*. University of Georgia Press.

Germany, K. B. (2010). *War on poverty.* University of Virginia. Retrieved on August 5, 2010, http://www.faculty.virginia.edu/sixties/readings/war%20on%20poverty%20 entry%20poverty%20encyclopedia.pdf

Goodman, A., & Sianesi, B. (2005, December). *Early education and children's outcomes: How long do the impacts last? Fiscal Studies, 26*(4), 513–548.

Graces, C., Shores, E. F., Zaslow, M., Brown, B., Aufseeser, D., & Bell, L. (2006). *Rural disparities in baseline data of early childhood longitudinal study: A chartbook.* Retrieved August 4, 2008 from http://www.ruralec.msstate.edu/reports/ecls-frontmatter.pdf

Hamm, K. (August, 2006). *More than meets the eye: Head Start programs, participants, families, and staff in 2005.* Center for Law and Policy. A Policy Brief. ERIC Document Reproduction Service No. ED494132. Retrieved July 4, 2007, http://eric.ed.gov/?q=ED494132&id=ED494132

Hammer, P. C., Hughes, G., McClure, C., Reeves, C., & Salgado, D. (2005). *Rural teacher recruitment and retention practices: A review of the research literature, national survey of rural superintendents, and case studies of programs in Virginia.* Charleston, WV: Edvantia.

Howes, C., & Brown, J. (2000). Improving child care quality: A guide for Proposition 10. commissions. In N. Halfon, E. Shulman, M. Shannon, & M. Hochstein (Eds.), *Building community systems for young children.* Los Angeles: UCLA Center for Healthier Children, Families, and Communities.

Johnson, J. & Strange, M. (2007). *Why rural matters 2007: The realities of rural education growth.* Arlington, VA: The Rural School and Community Trust. (ERIC Document Reproduction Service No. ED498859)

Kea, C. (2009). Connecting rural African American families with differentiated home learning instruction for their preschoolers. *Rural Special Education Quarterly, 28(4).*

Manguson, K. A., Meyers, M. K., Ruhm, C. J., & Waldfogel, J. (2004). Inequality in preschool education and school Readiness. *American Educational Research Journal, 41*(1), 115–157.

McClure, C. T., Redfield, D., & Hammer, P. C. (2003, December). *Recruiting and retaining high-quality teachers in rural areas*. Charleston, WV: AEL Policy Briefs.

McCullough, P., & Johnson, J. (2007). *Quality teachers: Issues, challenges, and solutions for North Carolina's most overlooked rural communities.* Arlington, VA: The Rural School and Community Trust. (ERIC Document Reproduction Service No. ED497982)

Morgan, L. L., & Reel, S. (Spring, 2003). Developing cultural competence in rural nursing. *Online Journal of Rural Nursing and Health Care, 3*(1), 28–37.

Mulkey, D. (2010). Education in the rural South: Policy issues and research needs. *Southern Rural Development Center.* Retrieved June 15, 2010, http://srdc.msstate.edu/publications/archive/167.pdf

National Rural Education Policy Agenda (NREPA). (Summer 2009). *The rural school and community trust. Curriculum and teaching subcommittee.* National Rural Education Association Convention. October, 2008. Tuskegee, AL.

NCTAF. (August, 2002). *Unraveling the "teacher shortage" problem: Teacher retention is the key.* The National Commission On Teaching and America's Future. Washington, DC.

National Education Association. (2010). *Rural schools.* Retrieved from http://www.nea.org/home/16358.htm

No Child Left Behind (NCLB) Act of 2001, Pub. L. No. 107-110, § 115, Stat. 1425 (2002).

Schwartzbeck, T. D., & Prince, C. D. (2003, December 19). How are rural districts meeting the teacher quality requirements of No Child Left Behind? *Appalachia Educational Laboratory.* Retrieved from http://aasa.org/uploadedFiles/Policy_and_Advocacy/files/RuralTeacherQualityStudy.pdf

Provasnik, S., Kewal-Ramani, A., McLaughlin Coleman, M., Gilbertson, L., Herring, W., & Qingshu, X. (July, 2007). *Status of education in rural America.* U. S. Department of Education. NCES 2007-040. http://nces.ed.gov/pubs2007/2007040.pdf

Soriano, D., Duenas, M., & LeBlanc, P. (2006, August). *The short-term and long-term effects of Head Start education and No Child Left Behind.* Paper presented at the Association of Teacher Educators, Philadelphia, PA.

Stebbins, H., & Scott, L. C. (2007, January). *Better outcomes for all: Promoting partnerships between Head Start and state pre-k.* Washington, DC: Pre-K Now and the Cener for Law and Social Policy (CLASP).

Stone, D. (February, 2006). *Funding the Future: States' approaches to pre-k finance.* Washington, DC: Appleseed and Pre[K]now.

Swartz, D. (1998). *Culture and power: The sociology of Pierre Bourdieu.* Chicago, IL: University of Chicago Press.

U.S. Department of Health and Human Services (HHS). (2003). *Head Start program performance standards and other regulations.* Washington, DC: Office of the Administration for Children and Families. Administration on Children, Youth and Families; Head Start Bureau.

U.S. Department of Health and Human Services (HHS). (2007). *About Head Start.* Office of the Administration for Children and Families. Administration on Children, Youth and Families; Head Start Bureau. Retrieved July 4, 2007, from http://www.acf.hhs.gov/programs/hsb/about/index.htm

United States Government Accounting Office (GAO). (February, 2005). *Head start: Comprehensive approach to identifying and addressing risks could help prevent grantee financial management weaknesses.* Report to Congressional Requestors. GAO-05-176.

United States. National Commission on Excellence in Education. (1983). *A nation at risk: The imperative for educational reform. A report to the Nation and the Secretary of Education.* United States Department of Education. Washington, DC: The Commission.

Whitebook, M. (2003). *Early education quality: Higher teacher qualifications for better learning environments: A review of the literature*. Berkeley: University of California, Institute of Industrial Relations, Center for the Study of Child Care Employment.

Winkle-Wagner, R. (2010). *Cultural capital: The promises and pitfalls in education research*. ASHE Higher Education Report Series. San Francisco, CA: Jossey-Bass.

Wong, V., Cook, T. D., Barnett, W. S., & Jung, K. (2007, June). An effectiveness-based evaluation of five state pre-kindergarten programs using regression-discontinuity. *National Institute for Early Education Research*. Retrieved December 11, 2006, from http://nieer.org/resources/research/EvaluationFiveStates.pdf

Zaslow, M., Brown, B., & Aufseeser, D. (2005, March). *Preliminary rural analysis of the early childhood longitudinal study-Kindergarten cohort*. Rural Early Childhood Brief, Number 2. National Center for Rural Early Childhood Learning Initiatives. Mississippi State University.

Zill, N., Resnick, G., Kim, K., O'Donnell, K., & Sorongon, A. (2003). *Head Start faces 2003: A whole-child perspective on program performance*. Washington, DC: U.S. Department of Health and Human Services (HHS). Office of the Administration for Children and Families.

CHAPTER 6

A NEW NARRATIVE ON RURAL EDUCATION

How One High School Takes on 21st Century Challenges

Stephen Kotok, Erica L. Kryst and Annelise Hagedorn

Secretary of Education Arne Duncan used an appearance at the 2013 Rural Education National Forum to tout a "New Narrative of Rural Education." In his speech, he detailed many challenges for rural schools and described examples he found contrary to the "old" narrative that rural schools are incapable of having innovative curriculum or rigorous STEM education. For many rural school leaders, Secretary Duncan provided neither a new nor complete narrative on rural education. Over the last few decades, most leaders in rural districts have been actively and creatively negotiating the dual challenge of readying students for postsecondary options while also considering how they can develop the long-term welfare of the local community (Carr & Kefalas, 2009; Hektner, 1995; McDonough, Gildersleeve, & Jarsky, 2010; Schafft, Alter, & Bridger, 2006). Of course, these rural school leaders must often balance these goals amidst high poverty (Irving, Meece, Byun, Farmer, & Hutchins, 2011), declining economies (Hines, 2002), shrinking populations (Schafft et al., 2006), and attracting and retaining qualified teach-

Educational Opportunity in Rural Contexts: The Politics of Place, pages 107–122.

ers (Monk, 2007). We were interested in how school and district leaders manage these competing challenges and opportunities in a way that promotes academic achievement for all students while also strengthening the community.

Thus, this case study examines how one rural school district in Western Pennsylvania, Brockway Area School District (BASD) and its high school, Brockway Area Jr./Sr. High School (BJSHS) navigate these various 21st century challenges. In addition to the aforementioned obstacles, BASD must also deal with other challenges unique to Pennsylvania, including the presence of the Marcellus Shale industry (Schafft, Kotok, & Biddle, 2013) and favorable cyber charter school laws that allow rural students to exit their home districts with local tax dollars in hand (DeJarnatt, 2014). On the other hand, Brockway benefits from a relatively stable economy, close proximity to colleges, and the presence and support of community members with prominence beyond Brockway.

Our study draws in part on Carr and Kefalas' (2009) framework of "stayers," "achievers," "seekers," and "leavers" to analyze how Brockway district and school officials negotiate the dual challenge of readying students for postsecondary options while also considering how they can make Brockway a desirable place for young professionals to settle. While our study is far more limited in its scope than the work of Carr and Kefalas, we found it a useful lens through which to consider how school and district leaders conceptualize their ideas and the goals pertaining to secondary education. According to the BASD superintendent, the district is "first and foremost" concerned that their students are "going to be successful no matter where they are." Yet, through the process of promoting better opportunities, the district and community create conditions that will also retain and attract some young families to the area. Despite the uniqueness of Brockway, we think the philosophy and policies of its school leaders can provide other rural school leaders with creative ideas for how to simultaneously prepare students for successful postsecondary lives without sacrificing the future of the local community. Finally, the chapter concludes with some discussion of how decisions in Brockway may limit some students' opportunities and the extent that this self-described "forward-thinking school" model would work in other rural communities.

Literature Review

Students in rural communities face a unique set of challenges as they position themselves for lives beyond secondary education, and rural school districts play a pivotal role in shaping both the options available to students and the decisions they make. While more rural students are completing high school than ever before, the number of rural students enrolling in higher education remains low compared to students from urban and suburban settings (Byun, Meece, & Irvin, 2012; NCES, 2007; Schafft & Jackson, 2010). Additionally, in the United States, rural students are less likely to attend 4-year, private, or highly selective institutions (Koricich, 2014).

Teachers, parents, and other influential adults play a pivotal role in deciding who is destined to achieve academically and ultimately leave rural areas, and ignoring those who have been labeled as low achievers (Carr & Kefalas, 2009). According to Carr and Kefalas (2009), in order for students to consider leaving their home communities, they must be "pushed, prodded, and cultivated to do [so], whereas staying just sort of happens" (p. 9). The achievers, stayers, seekers, and returners, as defined by Carr and Kefalas, all receive different kinds of attention and energy from the adults in their communities, and this impacts who will stay and take jobs in the community and who will leave to pursue education and other career opportunities. The returners come back for a variety of reasons such as family or disenchantment with urban areas rather than as a function of their former teachers encouraging their return (Carr & Kefalas, 2009). Yet other scholars suggest that adults in rural schools sometimes reinforced student plans of returning after college (Alleman & Holly, 2013).

While parents, teachers, and community members play a significant role in shaping rural youths' postsecondary paths, their level of knowledge and experience with higher education and careers outside of the local area varies greatly (Carr & Kefalas, 2009; Byun et al., 2012). In the United States, there are fewer rural parents with higher education degrees, and in rural settings parents are less likely to expect their children to earn a bachelor's degree (NCES, 2007). Here it is important to note that there is also a strong relationship between parental educational achievement and its influence on students' educational aspirations (Ley, Nelson, & Beltyuova, 1996). Additionally, for rural students, connections to family can impact their higher education aspirations and often delay their pursuit of higher education (Hardre, Sullivan, & Crowson, 2009) and indeed, rural students tend to have slightly lower aspirations to pursue higher education than those in urban settings (Ley et al., 1996).

School size and engagement can also impact students' educational outcomes. In rural areas, a greater proportion of students attend very small schools as compared to students in urban and suburban areas (NCES, 2007; Khattri, Riley, & Kane, 1997). Although smaller school size often limits course and extracurricular offerings (Anderson & Chang, 2011; Graham, 2009), small schools can also benefit rural students. Specifically, small rural schools are credited with creating "a positive school climate, an orderly environment, a high level of student-faculty engagement, and better school-community relations" (Khattri et al., 1997; see also Kearney, 1994). Teacher and student connections also impact educational aspirations. In their research on rural students' educational aspirations, Hardre et al. (2009) observed that, compared to larger urban and suburban schools, rural teachers are more connected to their student population and are better able to create learning spaces that motivate students. Teachers in rural settings were even found to be more motivating than peers groups (Hardre et al., 2009). Through these relationships, teachers can have a significant impact on the choices rural students make.

The rural community can also influence students' educational outcomes (Alleman & Holly, 2013; Bauch, 2001). Community-school support for students flows from both informal social capital networks (Coleman, 1988) as well as formal partnerships with nonprofits or businesses (Bauch, 2001). Informal community support occurs in a variety of forms such as extended family, part-time jobs, or affiliation with a church group. Although rural districts tend to have fewer absolute resources than urban communities, students in rural schools profit greatly from these ties (Alleman & Holly, 2013). Some of the symbiotic relationships between schools and rural communities involve job shadowing programs, scholarship funds, and drug abuse curriculums. Importantly, these informal and formal networks not only promote increased academic outcomes but also provide benefits vital to the maintenance of the community itself.

Brockway Background

Brockway, Pennsylvania, is a small rural community with a rich manufacturing history. It is located approximately 100 miles northeast of Pittsburgh and about 75 miles northwest of Pennsylvania State University's central campus. Just 30 years ago, Brockway was home to a Fortune 500 company, Brockway Glass, which provided the community with a steady flow of decent-paying manufacturing jobs. In 1985, Brockway Glass moved its corporate headquarters to Florida and was bought out by rival, Owens-Illinois Inc. for almost $750 million 2 years later (Associated Press, 1987). Although Owens-Illinois continues to maintain a plant in Brockway, the nearby town of Clarion (35 miles west of Brockway) was devastated when Owens-Illinois shut down that town's plant, resulting in the loss of over 400 jobs and a critical tax base (Fuoco, 2010). Thus, the threat of a multinational company such as Owens-Illinois closing its doors remains a constant fear for the community of Brockway.

However, Brockway is advantaged in several key ways that make it less susceptible to immediate economic devastation in the event of the glass factory closing. According to the American Communities Survey (2010), Brockway has virtually no residents involved in agriculture and a sizeable population employed in health care, education, social services, and retail. However, like much of rural America, manufacturing remains the largest employer in Brockway as well as Jefferson County (Schafft, 2006). While glass manufacturing remains important, there is also a large locally owned metal plant and other small factories. Brockway resident Peter Varischetti owns the metal factory along with several other entities across Pennsylvania and New York, including a minority ownership of the Pittsburgh Steelers national football team.

The metal company along with the entire community has also benefited from the emergence of a booming natural gas industry. The natural gas is extracted from Marcellus Shale, found in high concentrations in certain regions of Pennsylvania and extracted through a process commonly called fracking. According to McLaughlin, Martin, Gunsallus, Brasier, and Davis (2012), more than half of

Jefferson County (where Brockway is located) is in the core of the Marcellus Shale formation, but there has only been moderate drilling activity in the area. In addition to the actual drilling of natural gas, fracking creates "spinoff" jobs in the manufacturing and service industries (D. Hawkins, personal communication, March 27, 2014). Like the coal industry, this may leave towns such as Brockway vulnerable to the "boom and bust" cycle if the town fails to diversify economically. Dan Hawkins, the BASD Superintendent, was very aware of this potential issue and although he viewed the Marcellus Shale as "a net positive" for the community, he felt a responsibility to prepare students academically for other occupations or at least develop skills that were transferable to other fields.

Despite Brockway's small size, they currently hold a large voice in legislative issues with the President pro tempore of the Pennsylvania Senate, Joseph Scarnatti, being from and representing Brockway. Both Scarnatti and Varischetti have remained active in promoting education in Brockway and statewide. Varischetti serves as a board chair for the area Catholic schools as well as the BASD foundation, and he was named by Senator Scarnatti as a trustee for the University of Pittsburgh. Although Brockway has several financial and political advantages over other rural communities, BASD still faces several challenges common to rural communities, namely, how to prepare students for postsecondary options and distributing resources in a way that helps motivate and support all students (Bauch, 2001).

Methods

We selected Brockway with two other schools for a larger comparative case study that examines how rural high schools in Pennsylvania prepare students for postsecondary options. The sample was stratified so as to include a school located in each of the three census-defined rural areas (fringe, distant, and remote). Brockway is classified as distant rural.[1] We determined that Brockway was a particularly compelling individual case study in terms of its relative advantage and the creative ways in which it utilizes community resources.

In order to better understand the challenges, opportunities, and strategies at BASD, we utilized complementary mixed methods mainly relying on interviews with school and district leaders (Krathwohl, 2009). Prior to visiting Brockway, we compiled various economic data from the U.S. Census American Community Survey and educational data from Pennsylvania Department of Education as well as a short survey completed by the school principal. We met and interviewed the guidance counselor and the principal at BJSHS, as well as the district superintendent. The guidance counselor, Jessi Donlin, was relatively new to BJSHS and Brockway itself, though she grew up in western Pennsylvania. Principal Denise Carlini is a self-described "hometown girl," who has been a special education teacher, assistant principal, and principal in BASD for over 30 years. Superintendent Dan Hawkins was appointed superintendent of BASD 5 years ago. He had worked as a principal in a nearby high school and has lived in western Pennsylvania throughout his life. Interviews were semistructured and lasted between 45 and 60 minutes. After transcribing the initial interviews, we conducted follow-up phone interviews with the principal and superintendent. Open coding was used to identify themes across the interview data. In order to ensure the validity of our findings, triangulation was used, with researchers coding each transcript individually: separately, identifying themes, and then together, discussing themes that were consistent across each analysis.

Success at Brockway

Although demographically, Brockway is fairly typical of rural districts in Pennsylvania, Brockway differs in key financial and academic indicators. Like many rural communities, Brockway remains virtually all White. Approximately 40% of Brockway students are considered low income in that they receive free or reduced lunch, a number almost identical to the statewide average and similar to other rural districts in Pennsylvania. Brockway provides special education services for around 10% of its students—a rate slightly lower than the state average. According to the Pennsylvania Department of Education, approximately two thirds of school districts had higher regular education per-pupil spending, while more than 9 out of 10 districts in the state had higher per-pupil spending for special education students for the 2012–2013 academic year. Even when comparing only rural districts, Brockway spent less on students than the majority of other districts.

Despite the lack of per-pupil funding, Brockway demonstrates average or above-average academic results on several measures. Principal Carlini proudly proclaimed, "For 10 years, we made Adequate Yearly Progress. Nobody else in the area . . . did that." Still, several students fail to meet the proficient criteria set forth by the state. In both 2011 and 2012, eleventh graders scored only around the state average on math, reading, and science tests. However, notably, the 2012 scores of low-income students at the school exceeded state averages for low-income students by at least 15 percentage points in math, reading, and science. That same year, 92% of students graduated high school—a number that exceeds the state average by about 10 percentage points. The graduation rate for low-income students in Brockway also exceeded the state average for low-income students by 10 percentage points. Of course, given the myriad factors contributing to student achievement and attainment, these indicators do not necessarily indicate that BJSHS performs better or worse than other rural schools. Still, we think these measures—especially the success of low-income students—suggest BJSHS provides a quality education for most of their students. In order to better understand how school leaders at BJSHS view the quality of their school, we relied on our interviews. The four main themes that emerged included rigor or relevance, maintaining student motivation, teacher quality, and community outreach.

Rigor or Relevance: Tracks and Course Offerings

Superintendent Hawkins said that "relevant and rigorous are part of my conversation with faculty at all times . . . and I think they are starting to get it." Indeed, we found evidence that this idea permeated the school leadership, as the phrase came up in our conversations with Principal Carlini as well. Our study did not delve deep enough into curriculum or classrooms to accurately measure the level of rigor, but we were able to make a few conclusions based on our data. According to the school leadership, there are two main tracks for high school students: college preparatory (60%) and academic/technical preparatory (40%). Within these tracks, there are about 40 students who attend a regional vocational school, and there are students who are part of an informal honors track. We were interested in this process of tracking regarding two different dynamics: the process of how students ended up in each track and what types of advanced courses were available for the college prep students.

These two tracks seemingly map onto the achievers and stayers typology. While the school lacked exact data, they estimated that almost all of the college prep students enrolled in a 2- or 4-year college. Moreover, the explicit aim of the academic-technical track was to prepare students to transition straight into the workforce. Counselor Donlin explained that the college prep kids tended to be "your more ambitious, hard-working" students with "maybe a little bit more support at home—you know that the parents really talk to them, and they have that support, and financial support as well because that's a big thing for some of our kids." Since the choice on which track to pursue represented a watershed moment in a student's future, Counselor Donlin said she encouraged most students to take the college prep track "if they even have the slightest hint of thinking about going to college, don't shut the door on themselves. Take the college prep, see how it goes." Ultimately, there seemed to be a feeling that not all students needed to attend college or complete college prep courses to be successful after high school. Superintendent Hawkins expressed some frustration that the vocational school has "the same academic expectations for those kids as I think they do the academic kids." Yet he also conveyed a slightly contradictory expectation that students needed to take advanced "courses that you're capable of regardless of your destination."

Compared to nonrural schools, rural schools tend to have less advanced courses and less advanced placement courses (Anderson & Chang, 2011). Nationally, about half of rural students attend schools with less than three Advanced Placement Courses (Graham, 2009). These deficits are often justified due to practical constraints such as small schools, lack of qualified teachers, and low need/low interest. However, small private and suburban schools deal with similar challenges so it is not a foregone conclusion that rural schools cannot offer more rigorous courses. Superintendent Hawkins explained, "There was [only] one AP class when I got here . . . because they had [GPA] weight on the AP, but it was almost an insignificant amount." Currently, Brockway offers five advanced placement courses, three of which are in the math department. One of his strategies for increasing enrollment was to incentivize it by offering more points toward grade point average (i.e., 4 points for a B). This allowed the achievers to compete with other applicants when applying to universities. Still, Principal Carlini cautioned that they were "gonna take a break and not add anymore" as enrollment had stagnated and teachers were spread too thin.

Something for Everybody: Maintaining Student Motivation

Superintendent Hawkins described a concerted effort to instill a connection between the school and students. Both the guidance counselor and the principal supported the superintendent's approach for increasing student motivation. According to Principal Carlini, "We want every student to be involved in some way in school life other than just coming and sitting in your classes." They estimated that over three-fourths of students were involved in some sort of extracurricular activities such as sports or band. While this participation indeed reflects a high level of involvement, the school leaders never discussed why some students decided not to participate. Nonetheless, this high involvement was impressive, especially in an age when adolescents often gravitate to after-school jobs and informal social gatherings rather than school activities.

For rural schools in Pennsylvania, technology has been double-edged. Technology allows schools to offer increased, diverse content, but it has also enabled a cyber school movement that weakens the role of rural school as the central institution in the community. As stated previously, Pennsylvania has more cyber charter schools at 16 than any other state, with the number of enrolled students totaling approximately 35,000 (DeJarnatt, 2013). Cyber school operators promised to save districts money since the sending district reimburses only around 80% of tuition. Yet it only saves districts money if they send enough students to cut a teacher or move a full-time teacher to part-time, and the academic performance of these schools lags far behind that of Brockway (CREDO, 2011). Superintendent Hawkins did not want to cut back on teachers or course offerings, so one of his first actions on the job was to seek out the cyber school students and convince them to return. In essence, he negotiated with students on what would keep them coming to the district schools.

Many of these flexible solutions for former cyber students involved a blended learning model where students used online software provided by PLATO Learning and attended the physical high school only part-time. The district used high-interest courses such as CAD-3D Printing or music to attract them away from full-time cyber programs, and many ended up attending full-time after first attending on a limited basis. Today, the district estimates the number of K–12 students within the district attending cyber charter schools is only "two or three." Although the software for the part-time students diverts classroom resources, it also allows BASD to offer a diversity of courses for all of the students. The district currently offers 27 courses via digital platforms including advanced and special interest classes. Evaluating the quality of these courses fell out of the scope of our study, but the idea of offering such courses reflects creativity in cultivating student motivation and sustaining the rural area school as a central institution for the community.

Retaining High-Quality Teachers

Despite technological advances for providing instruction, the school leaders at Brockway knew the success of its students relied heavily on their ability to attract and retain strong teachers. Although we did not conduct formal observations of the classrooms, the principal and superintendent both voiced pride regarding the faculty. All three interviewees highlighted the fact that in the past four years, Brockway has had two finalists for Pennsylvania Teacher of the Year—one of whom won last year and went on to be one of the four finalists for National Teacher of Year. The chemistry teacher, who had been nominated in 2011, has taught at BJSHS for 18 years. Both the principal and superintendent credited him with encouraging several students to seek engineering-related careers. According to Superintendent Hawkins, the chemistry teacher is "on top of his game, so the kids cling to chemistry." The long-time popularity of science and engineering found at BAJSHS stand in opposition to Secretary Duncan's suggestion that rural schools neglect these fields.

The 11th-grade English/technology teacher who won the award for Pennsylvania Teacher of the Year was actually a BJSHS alumnus who had been teaching there for 7 years. According to Carr and Kefalas' typology (2009), the English/technology teacher was a "returner." Superintendent Hawkins felt that students enjoyed his classes because they were rigorous, but extremely creative in pedagogy and integration of technology. Notably, he provided a great example of how one can obtain a degree, return to the community, and still achieve your dreams. We expect this success story resonated with the community as they planned their future lives.

According to the principal, "the number of teachers who leave the Brockway School District for another teaching position is almost zero percent. The majority of those hired at Brockway stay until retirement." At least a quarter of the teachers as well as the principal originally came from the Brockway area. Though Superintendent Hawkins admits the salaries were low compared to urban districts, a district job at Brockway was considered a very desirable job. In addition to a "very supportive community, Board of Education, and administration," Principal Carlini explained that the school "stay[s] current with our technology, encourage[s] staff to be creative and do[es] exciting projects, and establish[es] partnerships with civic organizations and colleges/universities, thus affording our students and staff additional choices and opportunities normally not available to small rural school districts." It is possible that it is these nonmonetary benefits that allow a place such as Brockway to retain a National Teacher of the Year finalist for almost 10 years.

Forming Partnerships in Brockway and Beyond

Brockway JSHS benefits from local partnerships and educational initiatives created in the Brockway community. Given the low level of per-pupil funding for BASD students, the superintendent views external funding as a key ingredient for creating and sustaining new academic programs. These community partnerships have included the establishment of a local foundation focused on educational initiatives in the area and the growth of local higher education opportunities. The Brockway JSHS principal classified the community support as "phenomenal," citing that "from people that leave money for scholarships through their estates . . . it's just a very close-knit community and the relationship with their schools and our students."

One local initiative that demonstrates the community's commitment to education is the establishment of the Brockway Foundation. With the help of Peter Varischetti, Superintendent Hawkins founded the organization as a means through which to raise money for educational programs through individuals, corporations, and estates. In its first year, the foundation provided funding for 42 students to take dual-enrollment classes with area colleges and also brought local artists in to work with elementary and secondary students. According to Superintendent Hawkins, 20% of the foundation funding can be spent on whatever the school wants to spend it on, provided that it is not spent on anything remedial. The focus of the funding is therefore on improvements to the schools, technology advancements, and increasing educational opportunities available to students.

Principal Carlini noted the merits of the foundation and the increased opportunities it enables BASD to offer to students, including the availability of educational testing, such as the PSAT. Prior to the foundation, only about one third of sophomores took the PSAT, but because of the foundation, all sophomores will take the PSAT this year. Additionally, the foundation provides funding for dual-enrollment courses for students with Butler County Community College, located in Brockway; The Pennsylvania State University campus at Dubois; and Mount Aloysius College located in Cresson, Pennsylvania. According to the JSHS guidance counselor, students can take these courses in the spring and the fall, and they can take many kinds of different classes. The Brockway Foundation covers the cost of these classes, and the guidance counselor believes the classes are "really beneficial to our students." Moreover, Superintendent Hawkins hopes to see dual enrollment increase in the future, particularly because the cost is covered.

Advancing students' access to technology is also an important goal for Superintendent Hawkins, and the support of the foundation has allowed students to have access to cutting-edge classes and equipment. Through a partnership with the Siemens Corporation, Brockway will soon be getting state of the art 3-D printers for use in the redesigned CAD/Engineering class that will be offered in the

JSHS. Siemens donated the software, while the foundation will provide the financial support for the printers. According to these school administrators, these types of advances would not be possible without the support of the Brockway Foundation and its benefactors.

Butler County Community College (BC3), located in Brockway in one of the old Owens-Illinois Glass buildings, is itself a community enterprise. According to Superintendent Hawkins, the college, which opened last fall, was the result of the efforts of "politicians and people in town that have some money and all of our expertise put together." As a result of their hard work and political connections, the state provided a $500,000 grant to build the new campus. This community initiative enables students to take dual-enrollment courses during high school and also provides a place in the community where students can enroll in 2-year degree programs. Superintendent Hawkins is on the advisory board for the college and believes that the presence of this college in the community has made a difference, specifically for students who might not have pursued higher education. According to Superintendent Hawkins, "We also have some of our high school kids that are graduating that might not have gone to a 4-year school, starting at Butler next year." From the superintendent's perspective, the presence of this college has made a difference both for students currently completing secondary education, and beyond. Although BASD primarily viewed BC3 as a vehicle for its students, the college also injects valuable resources back into the community, namely, job opportunities or continuing education for adults.

In addition to BC3, Brockway also recently opened the Brockway Center for the Arts and Technology (BCAT) in 2013. According to Principal Carlini, this local facility offers free certificate programs in areas like pharmacy technician, medical assistant, as well as art programs. BCAT is funded by the Manchester Bidwell Corporation from Pittsburgh. The primary audience for their programs includes high school students interested in the arts, unemployed workers, and underemployed workers. The goal of BCAT's programs is to provide individuals with training for careers in the Brockway area (brockwaycat.org). The JSHS guidance counselor takes students on tours of both BC3 and BCAT to show them educational options in the area they can pursue while still high school students.

It's important to note Superintendent Hawkins' involvement in initiatives that are relevant not only to students enrolled in BASD. He is also invested in the opportunities available to students' upon graduation from secondary education, and the support of the community and involvement of local benefactors has allowed him to implement some successful programs.

Discussion: Success With Limits

Taking into consideration the educational initiatives and community support present in the Brockway community, the school district has an advantage in many ways compared to other rural districts. However, the students and district still face challenges, including student and parent buy-in to college preparation opportunities, a strong tracking system, and getting students to remain or return to Brockway. There are also unique qualities present in this community that may not be replicable in other rural districts.

Although Brockway seems to be relatively advantaged compared to some rural districts, Superintendent Hawkins realizes that "one of the biggest problems we have in rural areas is bringing our smart kids back." As evidenced in the literature, this is a problem that plagues many rural school districts (Carr & Kefalas, 2009). There are many reasons that rural students choose not to stay in rural areas upon completing secondary education. In Brockway, Superintendent Hawkins believes that "our kids don't come back to Brockway because there's nothing for them to do. And there isn't." He cites that a bowling alley or movie theater are just some of the amenities not available in this rural community. However, the recent additions of BC3 and BCAT are likely to enhance social and cultural opportunities for young people.

Like other rural communities, local employment opportunities are limited and diminishing in Brockway. Principal Carlini explained the industry options available for students, including work at the glass factory and a powdered metals company, and limited employment in the natural gas industry. However, she explains that "not everybody can work at McDonald's or wherever; you know there's only so many jobs." Jobs in this community are limited; however Superintendent Hawkins is hopeful that more opportunities can be created for students. He has aspirations for forming partnerships with local companies to help not only fund students' college education but also bring those students back to work for the company that funded them. The JSHS guidance counselor also shared some of the school initiatives implemented to promote students staying in the community, including tours of local educational facilities. These types of initiatives, she hopes, will bring students back to Brockway and also encourage them to set educational goals.

Considering the challenges faced by these administrators in encouraging students to stay or return to the community, they also want to see their students be successful. Superintendent Hawkins hopes that

> they are going to be successful no matter where they are, and if they are, hopefully they can regenerate that success back here in Brockway and they don't forget where they came from. But first and foremost that they're successful in whatever career they have.

So while encouraging students to stay in Brockway is a priority, administrators also see the reality presented to students who stay, and ultimately hope students can be successful. Given the strength of the educational initiatives present in this community, strong corporate partnerships, and support from teachers and staff, it is still a challenge for this Brockway to "bring a smart kid back to the community" (Superintendent Hawkins).

Tracking is another aspect of the Brockway school district that influences not only the paths students choose but the paths available to rural students; and it represents a potential barrier to students pursuing higher education. Superintendent Hawkins is supportive of tracking and having different academic expectations for kids: "You teach them enough English and enough writing for them to fill out a work order and to understand that . . . and that's where I think they should be." The administrators at Brockway strongly believe that student placement reflects a combination of high expectations from the school alongside student interests and aspirations. However, in interviewing only school leaders and not students or parents, we were limited in our ability to gauge the extent to which some students (i.e., low-income) were discouraged from pursuing higher tracks. It is worth considering what might occur if BASD abandoned tracking.

Parental involvement and motivation in the educational process were also identified as a challenge at the JSHS. Fostering relationships with parents was identified repeatedly as one of the main ways through which students will be encouraged to pursue educational opportunities both during and beyond high school, including enrollment in dual-enrollment courses. Lack of parental involvement was named as one of the reasons for low enrollment in dual-enrollment courses and other free educational programs offered at Brockway. Principal Carlini attributed some lack of involvement on the part of parents to them being "clueless" about what their children want to do and what their children are actually doing at school. For Counselor Donlin, parental support is key to students pursuing higher education: "Support base is a big one. The parents that are involved and look at their child's schedule for next year when they bring them home and things like that." Engagement in the entire educational process and promoting higher education is a challenge at Brockway, as it is in other rural schools.

Brockway's model for promoting and encouraging student achievement obviously relies on several components. The unique support found in the Brockway community allows the school to set high goals for the future development of the school and its programs. It also exposes students to many educational opportunities that they might not have experienced without the Brockway Foundation or BC3 and BCAT. However, whether or not this model is replicable in other districts remains to be seen. According to Superintendent Hawkins, "You always have to put the right people on the right seat on the right bus" in order to successfully change and advance a district, as he has done since arriving at Brockway 5 years ago. He cites the support and autonomy given to him by the school board as a key factor in the successful institutionalization of his academic programs. He also recognizes that the support of the community has been a major factor in his success, as well as being "creative fiscally." These factors make Brockway a unique case.

The relative harmony among the superintendent, school board, and community has created ideal conditions in which to create and implement educational change. The presence of local benefactors, additional funding sources, and teacher retention and quality, also contribute to Brockway's uniqueness and success. With all of these pieces in place, Brockway has an advantage; however it is difficult to see all of these factors coming together in other rural districts, especially considering the vast differences between rural communities.

CONCLUSION

When Secretary Duncan spoke about his new narrative on rural education, he alluded to successful models similar to Brockway as the anomaly. He also conceptualized the role of rural students as what they could provide for the nonrural globalized community rather than how they might also benefit their community. School leaders in Brockway realize the need to respond to this changing local and global economy, but we argue that fueling this economic growth does not have to come at the expense of Brockway itself. Similar to the Iowa principal highlighted in Carr and Kefalas's (2009) study, Brockway school leaders ultimately sought to provide a rigorous education for the highest achieving and most motivated students while offering a relevant preparation for stayers. The BASD greatly benefited from a supportive community and some extremely well-connected community members. As a result, the town symbolically transformed the "old" factory into a "new" community college. Although BASD leaders conceptualized these resources for what they could do for students, the resources also allow a town such as Brockway to remain vibrant and viable in the 21st century. In other words, the new narrative on rural education tells a slightly different story than that told by Secretary Duncan.

NOTE

1. According to the U.S. Census, distant rural indicates a "territory that is more than 5 miles but less than or equal to 25 miles from an urbanized area, as well as rural territory that is more than 2.5 miles but less than or equal to 10 miles from an urban cluster."

REFERENCES

Alleman, N. F., & Holly, L. N. (2013). Multiple points of contact: Promoting rural postsecondary preparation through school-community partnerships. *The Rural Educator, 34*(2), 1.

Anderson, R., & Chang, B. (2011). Mathematics course-taking in rural high schools. *Journal of Research in Rural Education, 26*(1). Retrieved from http://jrre.vmhost.psu.edu/wp-content/uploads/2014/02/26-1.pdf

Associated Press. (1987, September 18). Owens-Illinois may buy Brockway for $744 million. *Los Angeles Times.* Retrieved from http://articles.latimes.com/1987-09-18/business/fi-5744_1_owens-illinois

Bauch, P. A. (2001). School-community partnerships in rural schools: Leadership, renewal, and a sense of place. *Peabody Journal of Education, 76*(2), 204–221.

Byun, S. Y., Meece, J., & Irvin, M. (2012). Rural-nonrural disparities in postsecondary education attainment revisited. *American Educational Research Journal, 49*(3), 412–437.

Carr, P. J., & Kefalas, M. J. (2009) *Hollowing out the middle: The rural brain drain and what is means for America.* Boston, MA: Beacon.

Center for Research on Education Outcomes (CREDO). (2011, April). *Charter school performance in Pennsylvania.* Stanford, CA: CREDO. Retrieved from http://credo.stanford.edu/reports/PA%20State%20Report_20110404_FINAL.pdf

Coleman, J. S. (1988). Social capital in the creation of human capital. *American Journal of Sociology, 94*, 95–120.

DeJarnatt, S. (2013, Fall). Keep following the money: Financial accountability and governance of cyber charter schools. *Urban Lawyer, 45*(4), 915–951.

Duncan, A. (2013, October 31). The new narrative of rural education. *U.S. Department of Education.* Retrieved from http://www.ed.gov/news/speeches/new-narrative-rural-education

Fucoa, D. A. (2010, June 2010). For Clarion, plant's closing an economic, emotional loss. *Pittsburgh Post Gazette.* Retrieved from http://www.post-gazette.com/business/businessnews/2010/06/13/For-Clarion-plant-s-closing-an-economic-emotional-loss/stories/201006130211

Graham, S. (2009). *Students in rural schools have limited access to advanced mathematics courses.* Issue Brief No. 7. Retrieved from http://scholars.unh.edu/cgi/viewcontent.cgi?article=1088&context=carsey

Hardre, P., Sullivan, D., & Crowson, H. (2009). Student characteristics and motivation in rural high schools. *Journal of Research in Rural Education, 24*(16), 1–19.

Hektner, J. (1994). When moving up implies moving out: Rural adolescent conflict in the transition to adulthood. *Journal of Research in Rural Education, 11*(1), 3–14.

Hines, P. L. (2002). Transforming the rural school counselor. *Theory Into Practice, 41*(3), 192–201.

Irvin, M. J., Byun, S. Y., Meece, J. L., Farmer, T. W., & Hutchins, B. C. (2011). Educational barriers of rural youth: Relation of individual and contextual difference variables. *Journal of Career Assessment, 33*(2), 87–111.

Kearney, J. (1994). *The advantage of small rural schools: Final report to the Idaho Rural School Association.* Boise: Idaho Rural School Association.

Khattri, N., Riley, K., & Kane, M. (1997). Students at risk in poor, rural areas: A review of the research. *Journal of Research in Rural Education, 13*(2), 79–100.

Koricich, A. (2014). The effects of rurality on college access and choice. *Proceedings from AERA 2014.* Philadelphia, PA.

Krathwohl, D. R. (2009). *Methods of education and social science research: The logic of methods.* Long Grove, IL: Waveland.

Ley, J., Nelson, S., & Beltyukova, S. (1996). Congruence of aspirations of rural youth with expectations held by parents and school staff. *Journal of Research in Rural Education, 12*(3), 133–141.

McDonough, P. M. Gildersleeve, R. E., & Jarsky, K. M. (2010). The golden age of rural college access: How higher education can respond to the rural life. In K. A.Schafft & A. Y. Jackson (Eds.), *Rural education for the 21st century: Identity, place, and community in a globalizing world.* University Park: The Pennsylvania University Press.

McLaughlin, D. K., Martin, M. A., Gunsallus, A. L., Brasier, K., & Davis, K. D. (2012, August). *Does Marcellus Shale natural gas extraction contribute to increasing inequality among Pennsylvania's families and communities?* Paper presented at the Annual Meeting of the Rural Sociological Society, Chicago, IL.

Monk, D. H. (2007). Recruiting and retaining high quality teachers in rural areas. *The Future of Children, 17*(1).

National Center for Education Statistics (NCES). (2007). *Status of education in rural America.* (NCES Publication No. 2007-040). Washington, DC: U.S. Department of Education.

Schafft, K. A. (2006). Poverty, residential mobility and student transiency within a rural New York school district. *Rural Sociology, 71*(2), 212–231.

Schafft, K. A., Alter, T. R., & Bridger, J. (2006). Bringing the community along: A case study of a school district's information technology rural development initiative. *The Journal of Research in Rural Education, 21*(8), 110.

Schafft, K. A., & Jackson, A. Y. (2010). *Rural education for the twenty-first century: Identity, place, and community in a globalizing world.* University Park, PA: Penn State Press.

Schafft K. A., Kotok, S., & Biddle, C. (2013). *Marcellus Shale gas development and the impacts on Pennsylvania schools and education.* Report submitted to the Center for Rural Pennsylvania, Harrisburg, PA.

United States Census Bureau (2010). *American Community Survey.* Retrieved from https://www.census.gov/programs-surveys/acs/

CHAPTER 7

THE POLITICAL ECONOMY OF RURAL APPALACHIAN SCHOOL ACHIEVEMENT

Craig B. Howley, Caitlin W. Howley, and Wesley A. Kuemmel

The contemporary use of student achievement as a tool to advance education reform provides ample reason why rural Appalachians might be said to be ambivalent about formal schooling (Woodrum, 2004). This chapter (a) connects the history of the Appalachian "resource curse" (Douglas & Walker, 2013) to the early phase of the region's industrialized schooling, (b) suggests how "high modernism" (Scott, 1998) underwrote Appalachian achievement deficiency, with particular reference to West Virginia, and (c) plots the issues for the policy future of Appalachian schooling in a neoliberal context, including some unpopular realism about alternatives.

Mass schooling is historically a key institution for reorganizing society and for legitimating the related ideology—in previous regimes, the related ideology was nationalism and the ideal of the nation-state itself (e.g., Blacker, 2013; Cremin, 1980; Hobsbawm, 1992; Weber, 1976); in particular the liberal democracies created by the revolution in France and the war for colonial independence in British North America. Those regimes understood that it was essential to school the

Educational Opportunity in Rural Contexts: The Politics of Place, pages 123–153.

public to its hoped-for role as citizens (Cremin, 1980; Weber, 1976). But so had Frederick the Great in Prussia. It was a different, Enlightening era.

However, today, as the State privatizes formerly public systems of schooling, and as its spokespersons articulate and impose particular templates for leadership and pedagogy, neoliberalism (e.g., via lobbying and other vectors) steers schooling as it chooses (Blacker, 2013). Even the American Supreme Court agrees: corporations are people and their money has the right to speak. This is what the rule of law looks like under neoliberal rules.

Neoliberalism has been working for quite some time toward this end in the realms of policy, research, and practice (Howley & Howley, 2015; Ravitch, 2013). Make no mistake, neoliberalism is reorganizing all segments of the former profession of "education." In the future, even more than in the recent past, the only place true education will transpire is outside of the mass schooling sanctioned (but no longer operated) by the State. At least this is what education philosopher David Blacker (2013) thinks. Our analysis is a sort of assessment of his hypothesis as it applies to Appalachia.

Rectifying the Terms

Let us first clarify what we mean by *neoliberalism*. It is an ideology—the ideology of globalization.[1] Neoliberalism explains, justifies, and defends the purposes and commitments of postindustrial wealth accumulation and (most importantly) the use of capital to generate wealth: arguing, deploying, and imposing the associated rights, privileges, and purposes through political, military, financial, and cultural vectors (lobbying, warring, media publishing, scientific research, and—notably for us—schooling).

What is "political economy" in our title? Before there was economics, there was political economy; politics was understood as intrinsically bound to what we now sever from it, that is "economics." Think of political economy, then as *economics with the power turned back on.* Citizens, and not only experts, are presumed to possess the capacity to understand and to critique the political economy.

Of course, these days as soon as one does *turn the power back on* in social science analysis, the empowered analysts find themselves slotted into the realm of critical theory—and dismissed on that basis. Thus, we resist the characterization because we like to think of our outlook on *all things school* more as very old-school sociology in the spirit of Marx, Weber, and Durkheim, but completely lacking the grand aspirations to create equally grand and consistent theory (for another contemporary example, see Bickel, 2013). Like critical theorists (and like C. Wright Mills in particular), we recognize, however, not only economics and sociology and history and the natural sciences and even mathematics, but also "the education sciences," *as political domains*, intellectual realms though they be, that find themselves carved out, invaded, and contested—altered for good and ill and in many ways—*by power*. We are in any case examining political-economic power as it has deformed schooling, livelihood, and life-ways in Appalachia. It is exactly the sort of deformation and evacuation of meaning that Habermas said the *system-world* sucked out of everyday life (Habermas, 1987). But we see ourselves no more as critical theorists than Karl Marx himself could see himself a Marxist.[2] With Michel Foucault and James Scott, moreover, we find that power pushes both ways, and even then, in the end, it seems that hegemony must have a center that cannot hold. It seems a sort of defensible version of hope.

What about "achievement?" For us achievement is not mostly a test score, though quite unlike many colleagues and comrades, we do find that really good standardized (even-norm-referenced) tests exist and might be put to good use for students. They seldom are, one must admit.[3] Why? Mass schooling too commonly betrays true, and even *decent*, education in almost any place that is not filthy rich in the United States (policy stacks the decks; we are decidedly not blaming educators here). In other words, with "educational achievement" we are not pursuing an analysis about testing, although it of course figures in below.

Motivated at the Periphery

The very commonness of this well-known betrayal is the dilemma we treat here *as it transpires in Appalachia*—where we have lived for much of our lives. One inspiration for this analysis comes from rural education sociologist Alan J. DeYoung, who once observed that "the ascendance of American public education is primarily a story of how city needs and interests turned into state and then national ones" (2002, p. 2). Neither rural nor Appalachian needs or interests figure notably in the contemporary neoliberal move.

Indeed, as metropolitan concerns "globalize" at the political-economic core, so do curricular and pedagogical practices—always and forever hectored by state and national accountability regimes and by corporate philanthropists (e.g., see Kovacs, 2011; Malczewski, 2002). These impositions of neoliberal practice attend little to local purposes at the political-economic periphery (e.g., in Appalachia): indeed, the profession itself ignores local purposes and conceptions (Howley, Pickett, Brown, & Kay, 2011). Purposes have been decided for them, and their localities, and the profession has by and large accepted the arrogation of purpose to politicians and neoliberal functionaries. School consolidations (Howley, Johnson, & Petrie, 2011; Streifel, Foldesy & Holman, 1991) offer one material confirmation of the historically long acquiescence that has worked to undermine even the idea of rural community across Appalachia. The contemporary message from the metropolitan core of neoliberalized purpose, then, is an intensification of the message that emerged during the key period of Appalachian exploitation—that Appalachian locals cannot be trusted to raise their children and especially not to fulfill the purposes now imagined for them. We conclude, with many others, that such an assessment reflects reality, however harsh a judgment and a reality it may seem to many others.

APPALACHIAN POLITICAL ECONOMY IN HISTORICAL PERSPECTIVE

Appalachia's "resource curse" is a phrase that means the region is rich in natural resources but its people are, ironically, poorer on average than those in less resource-rich areas (Douglas & Walker, 2013); this (harsh) reality seems a conundrum. In this section, we briefly discuss (a) Appalachia before the arrival of the resource curse, (b) the emergence of the resource curse following the Civil War, and (c) how the paradox of mineral wealth in the midst of poverty shaped the development of industrial schooling in this rural and (still comparatively) remote region.

Note that *Appalachia* is a social construction; its boundaries shift and meander, across a variety of formalized State or academic definitions and throughout popular imaginings. Most broadly, "Appalachia" covers a geographical space from Mississippi to New York running alongside the mountain range. But what is called *Central Appalachia*—southwestern Virginia, West Virginia, and eastern Kentucky—is at the heart of the region's resource curse, and its experience can be characterized as one of exploitation, impoverishment, cultural stereotyping and marginalization, and ill-fated and misguided outside attempts at rescue (missionary zeal).

Reasons for the Appalachian resource curse are multiple, including industry manipulation of State policy and legislation to protect the interests of natural resource extraction (e.g., coal, timber); economic instability arising from cycles of economic boom and bust; low tax bases arising from sweetheart deals that limit corporate taxes; and the export of profits to the often out-of-state owners of industry (Eller, 2008). But even before the coal and timber were discovered and accursed, Appalachia represented a rural frontier to be exploited in the manner of all frontiers (Barbier, 2011).

Before the Resource Curse

The Appalachian Plateau remained unglaciated through the ice age, creating a habitat for vast numbers of animals and plants and an ideal place for Paleolithic humans to thrive; occupation has been ongoing for perhaps 10,000 years. First contact between the Indians of Appalachia and Europeans did not occur until relatively recently, however. In 1671, Thomas Batts and Robert Fallam searched in vain for a passage to Asia, and then in 1673–1674, two other Englishmen, James Needham and Gabriel Arthur, penetrated the Appalachian frontier. This excursion was meant, in fact, to establish trade between the Indians of Appalachia and the colonists; from first contact interest in Appalachia centered on taking possession of its natural resources (Briceland, 1987; Davis, 2000).

The topography of Central Appalachia determined its early history. Road building through the rugged terrain was expensive, and rivers offered only limited navigability. Access to the far reaches of Appalachia awaited the penetration of railroads. This want of easy transport and the challenging topography suited Appalachia to traditional subsistence living on small family farms. The farms also enjoyed some limited outside commerce. Ironically, many such farms struggled as Appalachia monetized; a cycle of low monetary productivity led farmers to seek wage employment in the mines, if only to pay increasing land taxes, which were driven by outside investment in coal mining and land speculation (Cook, 2000). Appalachians could no longer afford their residence. Contemporary city residents enjoy the similar experience of gentrification.

The Coming of the Curse

Considering the age of the mountains from which the region derives its name, the era of Appalachian coal mining has been brief. Industrial efforts began in the years after the Civil War, when railroads first enabled large-scale transport from the coalfields to industrial centers, first in the United States, and then to eastern docks for global export. Popular conceptions of the region as isolated and pre-modern are belied by its post-bellum rapid industrialization (Lewis, 2013). Large coal companies headquartered elsewhere acquired land and mineral rights throughout West Virginia, eastern Kentucky, eastern Tennessee, and southwestern Virginia between 1870 and 1930, and then established mining operations. Coal companies also founded company towns—privately held entities rather than public jurisdictions—which offered some services (e.g., hospitals, schools) not otherwise available. But company stores also famously entangled miners and their families in debt to their employers; and miners were often paid in scrip, negotiable at the company store but nowhere else. Coal towns also became increasingly diverse; local residents were heavily recruited for new mining operations, but eventually rural Southern blacks and European immigrants were also imported. Meanwhile, other industries followed, including textile mills and furniture factories, often in company towns near railways and rivers (Shannon, 2006).

Work in these new industries was difficult and dangerous, and corporations colluded with federal and state authorities—and local elites—to keep mining communities politically and economically weak. Money talks and cheap energy is big money; hence, political collusion (aka corruption) remains a theme here as elsewhere in the United States (where such "speech" is approved and encouraged by law). Thus, despite a vigorous labor history, legislators, businessmen, and judges consistently fail to protect their livelihood, safety, and (of course) environment (Shannon, 2006); natural resource extraction is not an environmental movement.

Since the 1930s, at the peak of extraction, Appalachia has experienced general economic decline. Overproduction of coal led to lower prices; brief booms, such as during World War II, were offset by longer cycles of decline; new fuel sources (e.g., natural gas, diesel) increasingly replaced coal; coal seams were depleted and mines closed; and dramatic technological developments sharply reduced the number of miners needed to extract coal. Union strength crumbled as miners left the mines (Eller, 2008). Although the extraction of natural resources (coal, oil, gas, and timber) yielded enormous wealth for corporate operators, it has impoverished residents of Central Appalachia. As noted above, corporations dominated the political economy, and they have systematically disabled community and governance. Three additional conditions have systematized the dominance. First, even establishing ownership of land in Appalachia has long been problematic. Vast tracts were granted to former soldiers as payment for their efforts in the colonial war of independence, but many tracts were never even visited by grantees, and so a succession of pioneering squatters muddied any possibility of proving who owned what (Cook, 2000). This cloudy state of affairs led to abuses by absentee landowners and speculation by interests outside the region. Even when sufficient title could be established by a pre-coal Appalachian,[4] there was no guarantee that ownership also included control of what lay *beneath* his land. The use of broad form deeds by speculators, in which landowners retained nominal title to the surface of their land, but which gave mineral rights' grantees the right to extract coal or other materials *by any means,* ruined many families and their land. This is a history of land grabbing (also a feature of the frontier mentality; cf. Barbier, 2011; Williams, 1969). In any case, the grabbing has been in place since the 18th century, so that 90% of private land in some West Virginia counties is owned by outside interests (Cook, 2000).

A second condition is export of wealth. Corporate owners understandably did not reinvest resource-extraction wealth in the region's public services. It would have been contrary to the interests of extraction—an impoverished population in a prostrate civil society was exactly what was wanted. Appalachians have seen the profits from extractive industries depart the region, often leaving behind little more than environmental scars, industrial hulks, and communities rendered unsustainable by cycles of economic boom and bust. Today there are few miners to offer organized resistance, and the extraction and dispossession continue more intensely than ever (e.g., mining by exploding entire mountains and filling entire valleys with "overburden").

A third condition is the corporate political influence, previously noted. In the coalfields, elections could be absurdities; for instance, a miner, dependent on the coal operator for his livelihood and often his home and hearth, would be given a list of owner-approved candidates, which he would then give to another coal company employee, who would then fill in the ballot for the miner, all of it proceeding under the watchful eyes of a police force paid by the coal company (Lee, 1969). One scholar (Cole, 1998) argues that the establishment of the West Virginia State Police was a result of the corporate realization that local sheriffs and their "gun thugs" were incapable of maintaining order—the status quo—in the coalfields. That 1919 decision was prescient, for in 1921 some 10,000 organized miners faced off 3,000 "lawmen" in Logan County. Such disorder was not permissible—obviously. Even offices meant to benefit workers were perverted. In West Virginia, for example, the first commissioner of the newly created State Workmen's

Compensation Fund was Lee Ott, a coal operator. During his 14 years in office, he led the fund into insolvency by failing to pursue payments due the fund by fellow coal operators. Ott's replacement increased assessments but met stiff resistance from coal operators. Eventually, coal interests were able to pass legislation abolishing the commissioner's office—and immediately created the office headed by a new commissioner friendlier to extractive interests (Lee, 1969).

Today, relative to the nation as a whole, Appalachia remains impoverished. Per capita personal income in the United States in 2009 was $36,306, compared to $29,702 across Appalachia and $24,578 in Central Appalachia. Per capita market income (personal income less transfer payments) was 25% lower than the nation in Appalachia in 2009, and 47% lower in Central Appalachia (Appalachia Regional Commission, 2011). And whereas 14.1% of Americans lived below the federal poverty line between 2007 and 2011, 16.1% of Appalachians did so, with rates as high as 23.5% in Central Appalachia (Pollard & Jacobsen, 2013).

Located in the southern tip of West Virginia, McDowell County is a notable example of the paradox of the resource curse at work, and its effect on the people there is startling. For generations, McDowell produced some of the finest metallurgical coal for America's steel industry, and the county population grew from under 2,000 in 1865 to a peak of 100,000 in 1950 (U.S. Census Bureau, 1995, 1996). Reflecting the regional boom-and-bust cycle, changes in coal mining reduced McDowell's population to just over 20,000 by 2013 (U.S. Census Bureau, 2014). The locality had nothing to show for a century or more of furious extraction. It was a place to be stripped clean and then abandoned in the name of the national interest (sponsoring industrialization and winning or losing devastating 20th century wars). Entire company towns were sold or abandoned altogether, schools were consolidated, and whole communities were left without basic necessities such as drinking water and sewage treatment.

The McDowell story is like that of many coal counties in Appalachia, and the story reflects a peculiarly American view that the hinterlands are a reservoir of natural resources to be harvested to exhaustion—*national sacrifice zones*[5] (Eller, 2008; Orr, 2009). Whatever comes next, in this view, *it is not in the national interest.*

Industrial Schooling

The urban Common School Movement conveniently arrived in Appalachia in the late 19th century as a diverse workforce assembled to mine the coal and timber the hills. The movement sought to compel primary schooling everywhere, but particularly for immigrant children it claimed needed assimilation and moral education (Katz, 1968; Shaw, DeYoung & Rademacher, 2005; Teets, 2006). Seeking more stable, family-oriented miners, some mining companies constructed schools, bought supplies, contracted with teachers—and charged miners an education fee (Eller, 1982). Settlement schools, inspired by Jane Addams' Chicago Hull House, were also established by Christian missionaries. These institutions claimed an interest in preserving Appalachian culture, as well as educating both children and adults, but they often replaced actual local or regional culture instruction with a sanitized and romanticized version—for instance, supplanting banjo instruction with instruction in the nonnative dulcimer. Settlement schools were often (and not surprisingly) supported by coal companies, so the schooling tended to suppress, not to encourage, dissent or critique (Teets, 2006).[6]

By the late nineteenth century, all states had enacted compulsory school attendance laws and provided legislatively for a system of public schools. However, Appalachian communities often resisted such efforts, believing that families and churches were the appropriate sites for their children's instruction. Moreover, they did not see life as requiring more than a basic schooling; it was only after the more complete industrialization of Appalachia (ca. 1920–1940) that secondary schooling became more firmly established across the region's rural communities (DeYoung, 2002; Shaw et al., 2005).

Given the remoteness of rural Appalachian communities, many were indeed able to avoid the introduction of State-run formal schooling altogether until the early 20th century. Even after public schools were actually established throughout the region, local districts and residents clashed with state education officials over curriculum lives (DeYoung, 1995a; Shaw et al., 2005). But education professionals claimed (then and now) that Appalachian school systems were not effective in preparing students for a national "progress" (today, of course, they are ineffective at cultivating "global competitiveness").

The secondary school movement, gaining momentum in the 1920s, sought to include occupational training in the belief that the national economy increasingly required a more industrially skilled labor force. The industrial schooling that emerged in rural Appalachia was also linked to federal and philanthropic efforts to "modernize" the region, with much critique of Appalachians as ignorant, unsophisticated, and in need of inculcation in the norms of the nation cursing it as a national sacrifice zone (Whisnant, 1980). Although efforts were made to ensure that schooling reflected the lifeworld of Appalachian families and communities, such efforts have always been marginalized (as the history of settlement schools illustrates), and the education profession and the rising power of state education agencies increasingly reorganized school systems for efficiency (an important a principle given the corporate export of resource-extraction wealth). The political economy can be seen as requiring meager funding, lock-step grade levels, standardized and bland curriculum, and evolving restrictive content standards. It also necessitated centralized control of school systems, closure of small community schools, and consolidated high schools as large as could be imposed (DeYoung, 1995a, 1995b; Teets, 2006).

In addition to inuring Appalachian youth to a bland, standardized, and centralized schooling, some schools, led and staffed by local elites who often linked their interests to corporate interests, served as "cultural bridges," fostering in students the norms and illusions prevalent in the fabricated national ethos (Eller, 2000;

Hennen, 1996). In this fabricated ethos, rural Appalachians were and are misrepresented as "backward," wild, and both stubbornly and unaccountably resistant to the modernist project. Schools too often have devoted effort to compensatory instruction in non-Appalachian speech patterns, middle-class manners, and, of course, the value of schooling to prepare for an economically productive life in an industrialized or digitized nation (DeYoung, 1995a; Pendarvis, 2014).

Given the dynamics of the resource course, the compensatory effort has not—and cannot—succeed (Teets, 2006). Success of this sort would be counterproductive in a national sacrifice zone (wherever located). The resources available hardly match the rhetoric—only a minority will get the message, and only a minority arrives at school prepared to receive it. The disparity of lofty rhetoric and meager funding follows a well-beaten path that keeps local communities decentered—gently simmering in discontent, divided and comparatively powerless (Eller, 2009; Gaventa, 1980). A predictable result is a steady depopulation of rural Appalachia, particularly by those who have assimilated the fabricated national norms to a sufficient degree to pursue mastery outside the region.

ACHIEVEMENT AND THE DYNAMICS OF SCHOOL CLOSURE IN RURAL APPALACHIA

Next we examine the history and meaning of school consolidation in West Virginia. Here, tested achievement is a central issue. The lesson is applicable across American schooling in general, but the underlying dynamics related to managing a national sacrifice zone for the benefit of a national political economy are specific to schooling in rural Central Appalachia.

Mass schooling is an odd institution.[7] In the modern world, the education profession itself confounds schooling, training, and education under one term: *education*—education sciences, education research, educational attainment, secondary education, preschool education, and (indeed) the education profession. One is an educator, not a schooler. In schooling, a true or even decent education remains inaccessible to a great many who are in fact merely *massed* (another meaning of "schooled").

We make an uncommon and unhappy argument to this effect in the discussion that follows—one that locates the storied threats to school learning across Appalachia in state policy, with school consolidation in West Virginia the exemplar. The struggle for education in Appalachia illustrates the oddness of schooling most aptly, particularly with respect to schooling's tragic nature as a manipulation of the literal masses by the power of capital working fist-and-glove with the State.

High Modernism and Consolidation, Phase One

For this phase of the analysis, we adopt the term "high modernism" from political theorist James Scott (1998). "Modern," of course, means contemporary, current, up-to-date. In the industrially revolutionized world, being modern earns acceptance—it is a mark of worth (Lasch, 1991). Modern*ism* is the cultural and political ideology that establishes such worth as a necessary feature of technical rationality (science and reason, applied instrumentally to get something done). The industrial revolution, one might say, established the necessity of modernism-the-ideology. This legacy originates in the 19th century.

High modernism is the maturing version of the ideology evident in the 20th century. According to Scott, "What are new [in high modernism] are the administrative technology and social knowledge that make it plausible to imagine organizing an entire society in ways that only the barracks or the monastery had been organized before" (1998, p. 378). In other words, high modernism enables functionaries of "the State" (i.e., nations, federated units, provinces) not only to believe they know best, but without a thought to "modernize" everywhere and everyone.[8]

In some places in the United States, the Great Depression provided an unusual opportunity to accelerate the modernization of schooling. The Depression subverted public schooling to the point of closure in many rural American communities (Teets, 2006), but the effects of the Depression were arguably most extreme in resource-cursed places like Central Appalachia. West Virginia schools stopped operating altogether in some communities (Hughes, 1992).

When schools cease to function in such uncommon circumstances, it is disturbing. But if hundreds of schools were permanently to cease functioning as a result of official decisions, the closures can, under the press of high modernism, seem even commonplace and even (to allies of the powerful) beneficial.

The Backstory of Best Practice

How can this be? Let us explain how, before we give the further details of the phase-one consolidation in West Virginia, 1932–1933. When state government acts to close schools in line with professional views of "best practice," the closures will routinely be read as wise by influential members of the public (which does not include "backward" local communities that lose schools, of course). This circumstance would have prevailed among educators and policymakers in West Virginia during the Depression. After all, early in the century such leaders as Columbia University's Ellwood Cubberley (1914) had set consolidation to county borders as the management strategy needed for maximum efficiency and effectiveness throughout the then-still-mostly-rural nation: cities had done it, rural zones needed to do so as well. It was "best practice,"[9] and it remained conventional wisdom circa 1932; indeed, it persisted as such nationally through the 1980s, and in West Virginia up through the present moment, as we report below. So much for how.

An Offer They Couldn't Refuse

Now for the Depression-era details. In 1932, West Virginia schooling took place in 419 districts (many were single-school rural districts), but in 1933, with one legislative act, the state established the 55 districts still in existence today, all of them co-terminous with county lines.[10] West Virginia did it deftly in one Act, but other states in the region followed more erratically (Kentucky, Tennessee, Virginia, and even Ohio in some of its Appalachian counties). West Virginia's only competitors in this "success" were America's colonially administered territories; today as a result, the state of Hawaii operates a single district, as does Puerto Rico (which remains a colony). The similarity is not coincidental or accidental, but it is convenient—all three domains (West Virginia, Hawaii, and Puerto Rico) exhibit a strong colonial legacy.

So what did the best practice of consolidation in West Virginia achieve *in practice*? During the consolidation of 419 districts into 55, the state *also* closed 600 one-room schools and 34 high schools: "Enrollment [simultaneously] increased approximately 10,000 [though] there were 1,026 fewer teachers. The $615,000 saved in teachers' salaries did not, however, equal the [additional] cost of transportation" (Hughes, 1992, p. 25). Note that increased enrollment at this time would likely have stemmed from lack of jobs for the young and the rapid growth of high school attendance. Employment of adolescents 16–18 years of age had been common before the Depression, especially in anthracite mining (Hindman, 2002).

So if one compares the original problem (25% loss of revenue; some schools temporarily not functioning) to the solution (local district governance eliminated, hundreds of schools permanently closed, fewer teachers for more students, increased unemployment among teachers, and higher costs and taxpayer burden in a famously impoverished state), one recognizes a "solution" that is rather worse than the original problem. Subsequent reality, in short, falsified best practice by a very wide margin, exactly as Scott's theory suggests—high modernist solutions impose new problems, and, as in this case, sometimes worse ones. Worse, that is, from the perspective of the common good. This result is consistent with Scott's view of high modernism. In his view, rulers cannot read local realities in any adequate way, but they are *all* nonetheless armed with notions of "best practice" and the hubris to impose the requisite measures.[11] The issue for power is who benefits—in this case, it was not the public.

Underwriting Deficiency with Consolidation, Phase Two

West Virginia retained its reputation as a rough cultural backwater in need of still more modernization. Presidential candidate John Kennedy's visit during the 1960 election brought the state and the region to national attention, and his election helped create the Appalachian Regional Commission, with its mission of modernizing the region still more systematically (Whisnant, 1980). Modern schools were a priority, and the Commission understandably endorsed the still-prevailing best practice, and consolidation provided an opportunity to build modern schools (Whisnant, 1980). All of this newness and alleged betterment transpired during what our West Virginia colleague Robert Bickel (2013) dubs "the era of the Social Contract."[12] The argued intent was to provide better service and more equal opportunity—great public good was imagined and proclaimed.

As one of the nation's most rurally populated states, in the grip of the predations of fossil-fuel extraction, and with high rates of impoverishment, however, local communities in rural West Virginia have always lacked access to capital for school-building to the standards increasingly prescribed for them by the state. There, by the 1980s, and at the edge of a conservative restoration with the ascendency of the Reagan presidency (the end of Bickel's "era of the Social Contract"), many schools had aged appreciably. Simultaneously, however, West Virginia elected its first Republican governor in a long time—Arch Moore. By the end of the decade, the Moore administration was overtaken by fiscal scandal (Moore pled guilty), the coal industry was depressed, and what little local debt capacity for school construction had existed no longer did (DeYoung & Howley, 1992). In this crisis, voters chose conservative democrat Gaston Caperton as governor in 1988; his crisis was more than economic—it was a crisis of legitimation (Habermas, 1973). Could the center hold? It usually does, but the public always needs convincing.

The phase-two consolidation thus began quickly, eventually involving the closure of hundreds of schools, though there was talk of consolidating county districts as well (DeYoung & Howley, 1992).[13] An editorial writer for the liberal-slanted and Caperton-supporting *Charleston Gazette* made the best-practice argument once again:

> I believe that the case of consolidation is overwhelming. Without it, West Virginia will continue to operate schools too small and too poor to teach classes that are mandatory if our kids are to keep up with the rest of the country. . . . Consolidation has to come. Otherwise public education will bankrupt the state. . . . Closing a school stirs primitive fears. Communities claim their existence is at stake. (Marsh, 1992, p. 6A)

Marsh's statement repeated the high-modernist cant, but it represents well what the state maintained then and now, despite very strong public resistance organized statewide by Linda Martin and the West Virginia Challenge organization (Eyre & Finn, 2002).

At the time of the crisis and subsequent closings (which sponsored a school-construction boom), a sea-change occurred in research knowledge about school size. Whereas decades of previous "best-practice" work had focused on the improvements to schooling inputs (new construction, curricular specialization, professionalization, motorized transport), the famed Coleman report (Coleman et al., 1966) refocused concern for "best practice" on outcomes. Don Marsh (1992) and the local elite, of course, were more focused on appearances (and not on inputs or outcomes); their concern was catching up (not for *keeping up,* which was never an option) "with the rest of the country." Appearances clearly trumped substance; resolving a crisis of legitimation is a matter of public perception, of forcing public acknowledgment of the State's legitimacy. The more insistent and consistent the

State is in asserting its authority in just this realm, and whatever the cost, the better for such a demonstration. There were many such costs, all of them immaterial to the State (and to its Caperton regime).

In the matter of substance, however, the new research suggested that consolidations would impose achievement costs on West Virginia students, since the point was to create much larger schools. Briefly, a robust line of study demonstrated that larger school size was detrimental to the tested achievement of students in impoverished communities (e.g., Bickel & Howley, 2000; Coladarci, 2006; Friedkin & Necochea, 1988; Huang & Howley, 1993; Howley, 1996).[14] The West Virginia Challenge opposition publicized the findings widely to little avail—the consolidations continued for over a decade. But there were other costs, including (as in the previous phase) financial costs as demonstrated in the award-winning journalism of Eyre and Finn (2002). The long-term ill effects of losing a school in an already stressed community had, of course, been well covered in rural education research (e.g., DeYoung, 1995b; Lyson, 2002; Peshkin, 1982). So the costs were heavy. They did not matter to the State or to Caperton (who was subsequently president of the College Board from 1999 to 2012).[15]

What did appear to matter was the continued cultivation of a powerless public, and the just-enumerated costs to the common good are, in fact and once again, beneficial to that durable purpose. The claim is not a cynical one. Scott (1998) names among the conditions needed to sponsor the worst blunders of high-modernist "reforms" *a prostrate civil society*:

> [One] that lacks the capacity to resist these plans. War, revolution, and economic collapse often radically weaken civil society as well as make the populace more receptive to a new dispensation. *Late colonial rule*, with its social engineering aspirations and ability to run roughshod over popular opposition, occasionally met this last condition. (Scott, 1998, p. 5; emphasis added)

West Virginia does suffer late colonial rule—a State, whatever the party taking charge of the government, ready to do whatever might be needed to ensure continued resource extraction, including a perpetually less effective system of State schooling. Clearly, the public *had* objected, but the state continued with its policies (DeYoung & Howley, 1992; Howley, 1996). And now West Virginia ranks at the very bottom of the listed statistically significant differences on the National Assessment of Student Progress (NAEP, 2014). We do not claim causality, just consistency.[16]

Schooling for Loss and Depression

The region's schools are another sort of extractive industry. Many of the "best and brightest" from local elites (and admittedly a few others) *are* supported, *do* thrive academically, and *do* depart for higher education and "brilliant" careers elsewhere (DeYoung, 1995b; Duncan, 1999; Howley, Howley, & Johnson, 2014). Not everyone leaves, of course, but leaving is very widely encouraged. In some places we have studied and others where we have worked, teachers explicitly tell young people to leave—to do well, go to college, and never return (e.g., Carr & Kefalas, 2009; DeYoung, 1995b; Howley et al., 2014). Seemingly good reasons surround these teachers, as the McDowell County example that we consider shortly will suggest.

In any case, such students seem to be the winners in a badly rigged game. They succeed; whereas the rest seem almost purposely confined to the local lives in a very economically unpromising zone according to sociologist Zygmunt Bauman:

> The dimension along which those "high up" and "low down" are plotted in a society of consumers, is their *degree of mobility*—their freedom to choose where to be. One difference . . . is that the first may leave the second behind—but not vice versa. (1998, p. 86)

Nonetheless, even these approved successful students (largely from local elites) and those they leave behind *each* lose something via bad schooling and unhappy bargains: generative connection to their homes and cultures.

One West Virginia study (Howley, Harmon, & Leopold, 1996) in fact found that very talented West Virginia students were both more likely to aspire to leave the state and more attached to their local community than other students (see also Hektner, 1995, for similar results in rural Illinois, and Howley & Hambrick, 2014 across several states). A sense of loss, in fact, pervades the experience of nearly all rural people, who are almost universally trained (not mostly by their schooling) to believe that what is good and valuable in life is located elsewhere, especially in world-class cities (Burnell, 2003; Berry, 1970; Carr & Kefalas, 2009; Corbett, 2007; Williams, 1973). In economically destitute "resource-extraction" zones, the lie is abundantly easy to believe: destitution surrounds one and invades one. It is abundantly evident.

Indeed, the loss, depression, and misery are so very abundant that the *New York Times* is from time to time compelled to report Appalachian misery, often from West Virginia. Here is what the world heard from this respected source in 2014:

> [McDowell County] produced more coal than any other county in West Virginia, but it got almost none of the wealth back as local investment. Of West Virginia's 55 counties, McDowell has the lowest median household income, $22,000; the worst childhood obesity rate; and the highest teenage birthrate. It is also reeling from prescription drug abuse. The death rate from overdoses is more than eight times the national average. Of the 115 babies born in 2011 at Welch Community Hospital, over 40 had been exposed to drugs. Largely as a consequence of the drug scourge, a problem widespread in rural America, the incarceration rate in West Virginia is one of the highest in the country. "Whole families have been wiped out in this county: mother, father, children," said Sheriff Martin B. West. "These are good people, good families," Sheriff West, an evangelical pastor, said of his lifelong neighbors. "But they get involved with drugs, and the next thing you know they're getting arrested." (Gabriel, 2014, p. A1)

The cited article commemorated the 50th anniversary of the start of yet another lost and misguided American war (the one on poverty). The difficulty is not that the reporting is *wrong*, but that it affirms such places as wastelands that are indeed best abandoned. Bauman observes,

> The spectacle of disasters, as presented by the media, also support and reinforce the ordinary, daily ethical indifference in another way, apart from unloading the accumulated supplies of moral sentiments. Their long-term effect is that "the developed part of the world surrounds itself with a sanitary belt of uncommitment . . . all information coming from 'out there' are pictures of . . . murders, drugs, looting, contagious diseases, refugees, and hunger; this is, of something threatening to us."[17] (1998, p. 75)

Bauman is writing of the third world—now called "developing"—and so the characterization is perfectly apt for the *Times*'s reportage on Appalachia. *Times* readers east of the Delaware, *be afraid*—degenerates live in your air-conditioning!

CONNECTING THE DOTS: HUMAN CAPITAL DEVELOPMENT AS NEOLIBERAL RESOURCE CURSE

In this section we extrapolate some lessons about achievement and policy based partly on the presentation thus far, and partly on a sober prospective outlook on the future. The past is miserable, at least as we have analyzed it. The prospect for the future of the political economy that created the Appalachian construct is, at best, not promising (Blacker, 2013). We have much to explain, and some modest counsel to offer.

Bauman (1998) argued for a disconnection between the wealth creation of the neoliberalized developed world and the misery of the developing world, with nearly 4 billion people then worldwide living in poverty (p. 73). He has a point, the reality of which manifested itself in 2008, as much wealth created by "casino capitalism" (e.g., Blacker, 2013) was then destroyed.[18] That sort of phantom wealth is by no means the only sort of wealth, nor the most fundamental (and important).

The Relevance of Schooling Rigor in National Sacrifice Zones

From the vantage of resourceful Appalachia, we understand that its "resources" really do, in real-time-material-reality underwrite life as the developed world knows it: air-conditioning, elevators, strip malls, iPhones, electric lighting, and hot water (running water, too). Paper wealth is one sort of thing; actual wood, oil, meat, and vegetables constitute very much another sort. The hubris of the capitalist information age built atop the capitalist industrial age is that its ideology can pretend that the fantastical sort of wealth is more real and more important than the second, material, sort of wealth. The falsity of this distinction is well known rurally.

Most Americans are nonetheless quite unaware that every calorie of food they consume *also* contains 10 calories of fossil-fuel energy (Martenson, 2013). Is this a problem? It obviously is when fossil fuels become scarcer and more expensive. Indeed, life as we know it in every aspect is exactly this dependent upon these cheap-energy resources.

The institution of schooling seldom acknowledges the falsity, however, though some or many teachers may. The institution itself is, after all, tasked (by the ideology of neoliberalism) to *prepare students for college and careers*, a phrase taken verbatim from the Common Core curriculum (Common Core, 2014). This wording is so commonplace as to seem both bland and unexceptional to most who hear it. It seems to mean almost nothing (e.g., *duh*), but it stakes out schooling as the province of capital itself, helping to create a world based not in reality but in fantasies of wealth (Berry, 1970; Orr, 1995). Economics (the science of capital) has for a long time (Becker, 1964) called knowledge and skill "human capital." In Becker's original formulation, the construct applied to skills and knowledge obtained in many ways, most of them informal and on-the-job. Today schooling is advertised as the primary route to acquiring such capital. Of course, public schools are said by those in charge to be failing in this mission (Berliner & Glass, 2014; Blacker, 2013; Emery, 2002; Ravitch, 2013).

It was not even an especially sad day in West Virginia, for instance, when a previous governor—a Democrat—made the following confession[19] (not likely understood as a confession by most listeners):

> "I am so proud of West Virginia for being chosen to lead the nation as we embrace 21st century learning skills," said Manchin. "I believe that 21st century education will strengthen what our educators are teaching in classrooms across the state. Accelerating technological change, rapidly accumulating knowledge, increasing global competition and rising workforce requirements make 21st century skills essential for success in the new millennium. (West Virginia Department of Education [WVDE], press release, November 14, 2005)

And in the same source, the state superintendent of schools offered another confession:

> Along with that, we must focus on ensuring that our children are prepared for tomorrow. We are responsible for producing students that can read and write but these students also must be able to analyze data, solve problems and communicate effectively. (WVDE press release, November 14, 2005)

Let us paraphrase these confessions to make them clear:

1. *The governor*: Big business will soon wipe Appalachia clean of "natural resources" in the national interest, including those students who can get with the program; and I am very proud to help this great national effort.

2. *The superintendent*: In the past we schoolers had not imagined students would need to think, but boy were we wrong; so thank goodness we have big business to help us now.[20]

We are not being unfair here, because they do not talk this way *at all* in the elite Eastern preparatory schools that train those who organize the Appalachian depredations and who direct financial betting on Appalachian resource extraction. Here is what we find at Phillips Exeter Academy (perhaps the most storied of America's very most elite prep schools): "Exeter is a life-changing experience, challenging and fun. It asks a great deal from every student: higher standards, greater expectations, and deeper engagement not only in the world of ideas, but also in the life of the community" (2014, para. 4).

The contrast is astonishing. The difference resembles the one Jean Anyon highlighted a generation ago between big-city schooling for the working class as compared to that for the affluent classes (Anyon, 1980). *Fun*? The world of *ideas* and the life of the *community*? These are the very dangerous engagements from which Appalachian *stayers* need to be permanently separated.

It is hard for us to imagine a more complete capitulation by state leaders to the nastiness to come in this century (which we explain shortly). The confessions of the West Virginia authorities (in a long line of such cant) represent exactly the spirit of education policy needed by the Exeter graduates to manage a national sacrifice zone. Educational achievement on this basis works perfectly to keep Appalachia open[21] for the sort of business to which it is best suited—the business of imposing the resource-curse (Douglas & Walker, 2013).

Fracking Appalachia

The TV series *Battlestar Galactica*—one of the many 21st century apocalyptic entertainments—slyly substituted the term "fracking" for a more familiar one, and it is very much as a double-entendre that we use it here. Appalachia has already been *fracked* several times over, but the recent fracking onslaught is necessarily conducted on an industrial scale not previously seen.

Hydraulic fracturing ("fracking") is a massive assault on geology in order to release deeply trapped, and previously inaccessible and certainly more expensive, gas and oil. The new effort may produce 20 or 100 years of fossil fuel,[22] more expensively, and with greater damage than previous cycles of rapine. The evident problem is that each "frack-job" site uses about 10 million gallons of "brine" (water laced with a cocktail of proprietary additives), delivered through horizontal channels bored thousands of feet deep (far beneath groundwater aquifers) from which the drillers pressurize the "brine" into shale formations along the bore route, fracturing shale layers and releasing the prized "resource" trapped therein.

An estimated 60,000–100,000 wells will be drilled in Appalachia (Schafft et al., 2013).[23] That's a full *cubic mile* of water to obtain, contaminate, transport to sites, inject, and then, as the contamination returns to the surface, *to dispose of.*[24] Disposal involves yet another cycle of transport and injection because the energy companies pump the "brine" (and its undisclosed components and unknown hazards) into abandoned wells (*shallow wells*) in conventional oil and gas fields—from where it can, and eventually must, contaminate local groundwater. At present the industry is injecting billions of gallons of water from Appalachian Pennsylvania into abandoned conventional oil wells in Appalachian Ohio (Schafft et al., 2013)—where fracking has also arrived (with about 800 wells drilled, and 400 producing at this writing, according to local news reports). We're fracked—again.

PREPARATION FOR THE NASTINESS TO COME

A variety of sources from liberal to conservative, from activist to scientific, and from the destitute to the wealthy understand that an economic regime of unlimited growth (which is the classical principle of *capital formation*) is already destroying the fitness of the planet even for its own purposes, possibly to create human misery on an unprecedented scale (Blacker, 2013; Daly, 1999; Meadows, Meadows, Randers, & Behrens, 1972). In our experience in the United States, many educators and citizens are unaware of the implications. David Blacker summarizes them objectively, and we quote him at length because he states the threat in everyday terms familiar to North Americans:

> Just a moment's glance at modern lifestyles is enough to appreciate what is at stake here. Living without cheap fossil fuel is obviously possible (human beings did it until a few hundred years ago) but it is no longer something most of us in the industrialized world can even really contemplate. . . . Just about all of one's activities are based upon fossil fuels: almost all the food we eat depends on petroleum-based fertilizer, mechanized agriculture and gas-driven transport, our water depends on the same in terms of motorized public works and even most of those with wells require electric pumps. Electricity, it should be remembered, is created in power plants that burn fossil fuels, mostly coal and natural gas. Our jobs and transportation systems are obviously petroleum-based. So are all of our modern institutions, including schools, prisons, hospitals, police and the military. Without this energy input, and even with it in a compromised and/or substantially more expensive form, modern life would be unthinkable. But it is running out and it is only a matter of time. The same can be said in mitigated form of other indispensable resources whose easy abundance can no longer be assumed, such as unsullied fresh and ocean water, usable topsoil and certain minerals needed (and not merely optional) for agriculture. (2013, pp. 39–40)

Let us be clear: this is the world enabled by the human destitution and the environmental rape of national sacrifice zones such as Appalachia.

What Is Needed but Cannot Be Done

What is needed is a transition to a steady-state economy (Daly, 1999), one that need not grow in size annually. Neither policymakers nor neoliberal economists (the adjective is largely unnecessary) can grasp this strange idea. The neoliberal economy in which we *are* stuck *does* need to grow annually, preferably a lot—more growth is always better on its terms. "The economy" (different from the political economy) is said to be *bad* ("a bad economy") when growth *slows*: and few who hear this news question the assumption that growth is desirable and necessary.[25] The end of growth forever is unimaginable.

It seems quite likely, however, that growth cannot continue (growth is different from development in the way that quantity is different from quality; cf. Daly, 1999). The possibility of a smooth transition to a steady-state *political economy* is, however, remote, according to some observers (e.g., Blacker, 2013; Daly, 1999; Kunstler, 2005), and we agree with them. The regime of wealth accumulation cannot easily plan or even entertain such a transition, and resistance to it, especially in the United States, may prove even more fierce than resistance to the facts about climate change—a resistance led, quite probably, by very well-financed campaigns of denial.

The global mode of trade and business depends on unlimited growth, and the 19th and 20th century marvels of industrialization and digitization have in fact enabled the growth. Profit, too, depends on unlimited growth. In existential terms (and practical ones too), unlimited growth is not actually possible on a limited planet—a truism known for nearly two generations (Meadows et al., 1972). This sort of consideration could hardly have been imagined in the 19th century, though Malthus seems to have possessed partial understanding (Weisman, 2013).

This theorizing is objective and well reasoned in comparison with that sort of ideology rightly called "lies in the head" (Eagleton, 1991). But Eagleton notes that such lies cannot by displaced by stating the real facts:

> Ideology cannot be substantially transformed by offering individuals true descriptions in place of false ones: it is not in this sense simply a *mistake*. . . . A transformation of our lived relations to reality could be secured only by a material change in that reality itself. To deny that ideology is primarily a matter of empirical representations, then, goes along with a materialist theory of how it operates, and of how it might be changed. At the same time, it is important not to react so violently . . . as to abstain from trying to put people right on matters of fact. (1991, p. 30)

Trying To Put People Right on Matters of Fact

The human consumption of cheap energy has forced climate change—dangerously. The industrial revolution (on the back of cheap energy) multiplied productivity, wealth (and poverty), and population. Cheap energy is running out. It looks like very hard times are coming. The ideology of neoliberalism is founded on an existential error; worse, it uses its power to deny the fact. Growth cannot continue indefinitely, nor for long absent the intervention of a benevolent, omnipotent, omniscient god; or a miraculous and timely technological *deus ex machina*—vain hopes that amount to the same thing.

We are skeptical of anyone convinced she or he is right, including ourselves. And we too hope (vainly) that "technology" might find a new source of cheap energy that would keep us warm, clean, transportable, and terminally entertained. We could do without the greed and hubris, but the global misery of the disasters predicted by Blacker (2013), Kunstler (2005), and Weisman (2013) is sharper than anything apparent in the 20th century. Even more centrist Conkin (2007) and Mathez (2009) are appalled at the prospect of the 21st century. Thus, we doubt that the "nastiness to come" can be averted, and we imagine that the dark age predicted by Jane Jacobs (2004) has already begun. Full-blown disaster of some sort, or multiple sorts, seems likely to us, and to many sober observers (e.g., Cohen, 1995; Conkin, 2007; Jacobs, 2004; Jacques, 2009; Mathez, 2009; Solomon, 2010). We surely hope that we and they are very wrong.

So, in future, as predicted from the past but intensified by 21st century conditions, rural regions anywhere on the planet with valuable products will see such goods appropriated more and more *easily*. The appropriation and extraction—backed by huge corporate interests globally and by State power nationally—will take place as authoritatively deemed necessary in accord with neoliberal ideology and national security. The contemporary fracking of Appalachia is a case in point. Local property owners suffer the illusion that they own such resources, but the "resources" do not really, and will not seem apparently, to belong to them for long when the rule of law combines with hubris and money in the name of national security (Scott, 1998). In fact, 39 states already permit "forced pooling," wherein holdout property owners are *compelled by law* to allow resource extraction from their land to contribute to a producing unit (Baca, 2011). On this front, at least, there should be no hope; the Appalachian history is very clear as we and many others have told it.

Rural Schooling for a Decent Appalachian Future

Although we admire the contemporary defenders of public schooling in the United States, we do not anticipate their defense can be successful. With David Mathews (1996), we view what is already in place not as public schooling, but as State schooling. Because money talks and corporations are people, the American State belongs to its corporate citizens;[26] educational leadership and purposes clearly reflect this (evident) fact. In Appalachia the truth is very clear: the region's history, the legacy of school consolidation and the collaboration of official education leaders show that schooling has not harbored public purpose for several generations at least—perhaps it never did—once Appalachia stopped being a frontier, it quickly became a principal national sacrifice zone for the American State, its successive governments, and in particular its successive business regimes.

Blacker (2013) thinks public schools are done for. We do not think they are; what is done is simply public schools as we thought we knew them, mistakenly. It's too late to mourn. State schools have concertedly *excluded* the public under professional leadership, thereby failing families, communities, students, and the public good overall. Many, many educators do their best, but the system is monumentally rigged against them, *especially* against them, we would add. The problem with public schools is decidedly *not* teacher quality but rather the State and its corporate citizens, who speak so much louder than its actual citizens. Except of course in the most affluent neighborhoods; there, they often speak with one voice and seem to be particularly effective. One must note that *those* schools are largely the ones advertised as excellent by neoliberal accountability regimes. Contrary to popular opinion, we find them the worst; not on technical grounds, but on the political-economic ones considered in this analysis.

Pessimism about schooling notwithstanding, we are actually *confident* that people will continue learning to decode the word, and with it, the world (cf. Freire & Macedo, 1987; Gutstein, 2006)—even and perhaps especially during disasters and dark ages (Jacobs, 2004). Such engagement may not be widespread then, but it is not widespread now either, under State-managed mass schooling.

As the neoliberal economic model falters, however, what we in America very clearly *are* losing is the American Dream. Many feel its loss already, but it is a dream for which we personally harbor little nostalgia. Electricity and running water? Absolutely. But fantasies of conquest and a god-given right to dominance are dangerous illusions we can all do much better without.

A Poor Attempt at Wise Counsel

We have usually been asked in scholarly work to supply recommendations, as if having thought about something or done it entitles us to tell others what to do. We have become wary of this invitation to the point of framing the still-requisite recommendations as the need to refrain from doing something. Under present conditions, doing no harm would be a bit miraculous itself.

It seems in the case of ineluctable nastiness in the near or mid-term future that the counsel must be to do *less* harm than one will see all around one. Even now, precisely this counsel makes sense to critics like Blacker (2013).

Doing *no* harm will be nearly impossible; for teachers and administrators, in view of the imposed neoliberal expectations, doing no harm now is supremely difficult. As teachers and administrators with (for the most part) partners and families, we need jobs like everyone else. In many rural Appalachian communities, we have done all we can to acquire these jobs, and they are very good jobs where we live.

For exactly this reason, of course, the neoliberal agenda is working hard to propagate fear among educators and even families and students (Woodrum, 2004). The greedy rush for resources in a collapsing fossil-fuel resource base is already on view in the fracking of Appalachia. Acid rain and invasive beetles are destroying the Appalachian hardwood forests. Coal mining employs fewer workers, does more damage, and is now nearly as cutthroat as it was in the 1920s (not by volume of human misery, of course, but in terms of ecological, profitability, and marketability issues). Imagine, though, an Appalachia with degraded highways, poor drinking water, intermittent electric power, and abandonment of all sorts of infrastructure—including State schools, but with simultaneous intensification of extractive resource operations: coal, oil, gas, timber, water; construction of many nuclear plans; and intensified dumping of east-coast waste streams (dumping is extraction in reverse). None of this is certain, but some claim it will transpire before too long if those we have cited above are partly correct. Predictions about the future are always mostly wrong, but the pervading cultural sensibility, alongside the neoliberal cant, is of something wicked this way come—something deserved by what humans have done.

In this grim light, the following counsel aims at making the Appalachian experience of schooling more decent in small and temporary ways starting right now or whenever it may be for you, dear Appalachian reader especially:

1. Grasp the facts (see above). The State is a neoliberal plot, not a liberal plot: *big difference*.
2. Stop being afraid. For the time being, you can always work at Walmart; and later you can hunt, forage, grow gardens, and cut wood.[27]
3. Teach against the grain. This possibility is enabled by 1 and 2. For now, do it in school. Later, you will not have schools to do it. Political-economic necessity will require it of you.
4. Engage the world of ideas and the life of the community; it is a proven way to teach against the grain in your world. Engage the community in the world of ideas, and you and they will be able to *stop listening and speak out of turn*. And to do what makes sense for a change.
5. Help someone else think like this. This is your vocation—keep it at, especially later on. You *are* the school in this manner. To hell with their standards.
6. Read more about the nastiness to come. The prospect is in the contemporary flow of ideas; you will not have to look far. Reading is how you grasp the facts and the inspiration for rebooting reality.

All of this is monumentally difficult in our own experience *already*. But it has always made sense to the teachers in our family; we have taught in Pennsylvania, New Jersey, and Texas, as well as West Virginia.

Lacking cheap energy and a healthy planet, we will experience the human condition more intensely, and with particular intensity here in Appalachia. Wait, watch, think, and keep acting and talking and teaching whatever arrives. No one knows exactly what is coming, but such a plight is simply the human condition unfolding.

Despite our attempted counsel, we suspect that Blacker's (2013) advice might be the most practical of all: Be stoic (not a contemporary American virtue); realize what is coming; love well those around you; exploit gaps and fissures for local good when possible; and do not feel guilty about missed chances and hedged bets. This is a difficult world, getting inevitably more difficult. Struggle is the name of the game. But so is solidarity.

NOTES

1. Globalization is a material phenomenon, arguably evident and touchable in the "real world" of everyday life: Walmart filled with cheap household goods from China; capital sent worldwide with the click of a mouse; tractors and cars made everywhere; high-tech goods made in China: all shaped by the prerogatives of capital-without-borders.
2. For the practical context of the relevant quip by Marx, see http://libcom.org/forums/thought/im-not-a-marxist. We try to be independent thinkers and critics (rearing cattle in the evening!). We are inevitably less good scholars and less good activists than either Marx or many of our critical-theory colleagues.
3. The current misapplication ("accountability testing") of grade-level tests with high floors and low ceilings to judge districts, schools, teachers, and students are a sort of psychometric and political crime. Those in power know better, can be legitimately expected to know better, but they pretend otherwise; and they expect the rest of us to turn a blind eye to their authoritatively feigned ignorance.
4. Caitlin and Craig are, however, descendents of early in-migrants to Appalachian Ohio, circa 1805. We are not sure, however, if the Davis brothers purchased land from speculators or if it was received as a postwar grant.
5. We explain this term in our subsequent discussion of hydraulic fracturing of oil shales.
6. We're not claiming that this schooling purposes distinguishes Appalachian from working-class schooling elsewhere. It is different from the schooling for the elite, however. They are and were encouraged to engage debate and sponsor critique (Anyon, 1980; Blacker, 2013; Ravitch, 2013).
7. Etymologically, "school" derives from the ancient Greek scholē, meaning "leisure" (OED, 1971). Mass schooling compels a kind of leisure very widely. This sort of mass discipline is effective at some things and less effective at others, depending on context.
8. Scott studied the phenomenon in southeast Asian societies (e.g., Scott, 1985) and has recently theorized it globally (Scott, 1998, 2012). He argues the hubris of any State's grand schemes to "improve the human

condition" (from the subtitle of *Seeing Like a State*, 1998). Such modernization, of course, is famously "uneven." For Scott, local resistance is the interesting influence on such unevenness. The State's policy analysts prefer to explain unevenness as structural in origin or as the backwardness of locals (e.g., see Whisnant, 1980).

9. We, with many others (e.g., Berliner & Glass, 2014; Bickel, 2013; Blacker, 2013; Ravitch, 2013; Scott, 2012) find that the early 20th century devotion to scientific management (Rice, 2013) remains "best practice" in policymaking—with the new consolidation of national, standards-based and scientifically branded curricula; reductionist accountability regimes; and massive privatization constituting substantial evidence for the finding.
10. Across West Virginia during the Depression, education revenue had declined 25%. Conveniently, the tax expert advising the governor concluded that exactly that sum would be saved through district consolidation (Hughes, 1992).
11. Scott's family, in fact, hails from West Virginia, and he spent youthful summers in very rural Sandyville (Yahn, 2014). In *Two Cheers for Anarchism,* Scott (2012) notably applies his perspective to schooling in the United States, with its national standards, its mandated use of "scientifically" branded curricula, and its punitive oversight of local realities.
12. Bickel means to indicate a political-economic regime focused on equality of opportunity, redistribution of resources, and the intention to meet all citizens' basic needs—purposes seen as legitimately underwritten by the State. Under today's ideology—neoliberalism—markets and not the State are understood as best positioned to accomplish all purposes. The public good is supposed to be an unintentional result of, well, marketing.
13. Phase-three consolidation, which could create huge regional districts of several counties, or which could adopt the one-district colonial model of Hawaii and Puerto Rico, remains possible or probable in the future. Across the conservative restoration, proposals to eliminate local school boards altogether have appeared regularly in policy discussions (see Emery, 2002, for a very fine dissertation on the neoliberal attack on the existence of local school boards).
14. As Bickel and Howley (2000) noted, this line of evidence involved many replications using statewide data (AL, AR, CA, GA, ME, MT, OH, TX, and WV). Four of these replications appeared, moreover, in the peer-reviewed professional literature.
15. One might argue that the American schooling elite rewarded the governor for his local service in West Virginia.
16. But to scratch the surface of the substantial prima facie evidence, in 1996 the WV NAEP scaled score in mathematics for all 8th-grade students was 265 and the national average was 271; in 2013 the state score was

274 and the national average was 283 (see http://nces.ed.gov/nationsreportcard/statecomparisons/). Standard scores are equal-interval scales and NAEP standard deviations vary between 30 and 40, depending on test and grade level (e.g., see http://nces.ed.gov/nationsreportcard/pubs/studies/2010456.asp). As an effect size in comparison to the national rise over this 18-year period, WV scores in 2013 were arguably lower than in 1996. This calculation is likely an overestimate, however, since the 1996 calculation did not permit accommodations for the disabled, as it did in 2013.

17. In this excerpt, Bauman is quoting, as indicated, from René Passet (original work not cited by Bauman and often incorrectly attributed; possibly from Passet's *L'illusion Néo-Libérale* (Passet, 2000).
18. A gaming system that Blacker (2013, p. 107) characterizes as "tails they win, heads we lose."
19. The press release quoted here announced the state's membership in the Partnership for 21st Century Skills; Kentucky is also a member (see http://www.p21.org/).
20. Superintendent Paine later became CEO of the 21st century Skills Partnership, where as of this writing he remains "Sr. Advisor," though he is now "Chief Academic Officer" of Engrade, an education publisher and technology firm, with offices in Santa Monica and New York City; Engrade was acquired by McGraw-Hill in February 2014. The Engrade homepage, as of this writing, shows the logo of Kanawha County Schools, largest in West Virginia.
21. Under the Manchin government, highway entry points into West Virginia sported the signage: "West Virginia: Open for Business." It was in the same spirit as the Kentucky signage: "Education Pays!"
22. Estimates vary widely (e.g., see McElroy & Lu, 2014; Schafft, Borlu, & Glenna, 2013). Yields near the end of a field's productive life will obviously be small. The high estimate, reflecting industry optimism, would have predictably useful political value in delaying political action for environmental concerns or changes required by a steady-state economy.
23. Other regions are being fracked as well, but so far the Appalachian Marcellus Shale region is seeing the most action and seems to harbor the most gas—most of the extraction involves gas released in the frack-induced fissuring.
24. 1 cubic mile = 1.01 x 1012 gallons; 107 gallons per well x 105 wells = 1012 gallons = 1 mi3 (see http://www.unitconversion.org/volume/cubic-miles-to-gallons-us-conversion.html).
25. Gross Domestic Product must get larger every year to ensure a "healthy economy"; if GDP growth rate is small or stagnates, "the economy" is understood to be bad or very bad; if GDP shrinks, the economy is said to be "depressed"; if GDP shrinks, deflation takes place—and today's debts

will be repaid in much more expensive dollars, not in less expensive dollars. GDP shrinkage destroys wealth, and it also destroys the usual investment opportunities. A world of expensive energy, inhabited by a very large population created with cheap energy, confronted with climate made worse by that cheap energy, and hooked on endless growth—this is the nastiness to come according to a great many sober observers. For a synopsis of the steady-state alternative, see http://post.nyssa.org/nyssa-news/2010/04/moving-toward-a-steadystate-economy.html.

26. Note that the actual franchise (right to vote) is immaterial to this sort of effective "citizenship." One corporation, one vote? That won't work.
27. Walmart is a major supporter of privatized schooling (Ravitch, 2013); Rich (2014) reports that the Walmart Foundation has supported 25% of all charter schools to the tune of $335 million. This is another fact: escape is supremely difficult. Guilt is counterproductive according to Blacker (2013); individual action is morally important, but, short of a changed material reality, cannot have a systemic effect.

REFERENCES

Anyon, J. (1980). Social class and the hidden curriculum of work. *Journal of Education, 162*(1), 67–92.

Appalachian Regional Commission. (2011). *Economic overview of Appalachia—2011*. Retrieved from http://www.arc.gov/images/appregion/Sept2011/EconomicOverviewSept2011.pdf

Baca, M. (2011, May 18). Forced pooling: When landowners can't say no to drilling. *ProPublica*. Retrieved from http://www.propublica.org/article/forced-pooling-when-landowners-cant-say-no-to-drilling

Barbier, E. (2011). *Scarcity and frontiers: How economies have developed through natural resource exploitation*. New York, NY: Cambridge University Press.

Bauman, Z. (1998). *Globalization: The human consequences*. New York, NY: Columbia University Press.

Becker, G. S. (1964). *Human capital: A theoretical and empirical analysis, with special reference to education*. New York, NY: National Bureau of Economic Research-Columbia University Press.

Berliner, D., & Glass, G. (2014). *Fifty myths and lies that threaten America's public schools: The real crisis in education*. New York, NY: Teachers College Press.

Berry, W. (1970). *The hidden wound*. San Francisco, CA: North Point Press.

Bickel, R. (2013). *Classical social theory in use: Interpretation and application for educators and other non-specialists*. Charlotte, NC: Information Age.

Bickel, R., & Howley, C. B. (2000, May). The influence of scale on school performance: A multilevel extension of the Matthew principle. *Education Policy Analysis Archives, 8*(22). Retrieved from http://epaa.asu.edu/ojs/article/viewFile/413/536

Blacker, D. (2013). *The falling rate of learning and the neoliberal endgame*. Winchester, UK: Zero Books.

Briceland, A. V. (1987) *Westward from Virginia: The exploration of the Virginia-Carolina frontier, 1650–1710*. Charlottesville, VA: University Press of Virginia.

Burnell, B. (2003). The real-world aspirations of work-bound rural students. *Journal of Research in Rural Education, 18*(2), 104–113.

Carr, P., & Kefalas, M. (2009). *Hollowing out the middle: The rural brain drain and what it means for America*. Boston, MA: Beacon Press.

Cohen, J. (1995). *How many people can the earth support?* New York, NY: Norton.

Coladarci, T. (2006, November 3). School size, student achievement, and the "power rating" of poverty: Substantive finding or statistical artifact? *Education Policy Analysis Archives, 14*(28). Retrieved from http://scholarcommons.usf.edu/cgi/viewcontent.cgi?article=1613&context=coedu_pub

Cole, M. T. (1998). *A comprehensive history of the West Virginia State Police, 1919–1979*. Retrieved from http://www.wvsp.gov/about/Pages/History.aspx

Coleman, J., Campbell, E., Hobson, C., McPartland, J., Weinfeld, F., & York, R. (1966). *Equality of educational opportunity*. Washington DC: National Center for Educational Statistics, Department of Health, Education, and Welfare. Retrieved from http://www.eric.ed.gov/ERICWebPortal/contentdelivery/servlet/ERICServlet?accno=ED012275

Common Core State Standards Initiative. (2014). [Homepage]. Retrieved from http://www.corestandards.org/

Conkin, P. (2007). *The state of the earth*. Lexington: University of Kentucky Press.

Cook, S. R. (2000). *Monacans and miners: Native American and coal mining communities in Appalachia*. Lincoln: University of Nebraska Press.

Corbett, M. (2007). *Learning to leave: The irony of schooling in a coastal community*. Halifax, Nova Scotia. Canada: Fernwood.

Cremin, L. A. (1980). *American education: The national experience, 1783–1876*. New York, NY: Harper & Row.

Cubberley, E. (1914). *Rural life and education: A study of the rural-school problem as a phase of the rural-life problem*. Boston, MA: Houghton Mifflin.

Daly, H. (1999). *Ecological economics and the ecology of economics*. Cheltenham, UK: Elgar.

Davis, D. E. (2000). *Where there are mountains: An environmental history of the southern Appalachians*. Athens: University of Georgia Press.

DeYoung, A. (1995a). Constructing and staffing the cultural bridge: The school as change agent in rural Appalachia. *Anthropology and Education Quarterly, 26*(2), 168–192.

DeYoung, A. (1995b). *The life and death of a rural American high school: Farewell, Little Kanawha*. New York, NY: Garland.

DeYoung, A. (2002, October). *Dilemmas of rural life and livelihood: Academics and community*. Working Paper 3. Athens, OH: Appalachian Collaborative Center for Learning, Assessment, and Instruction in Mathematics. Retrieved from http://files.eric.ed.gov/fulltext/ED471920.pdf

DeYoung, A., & Howley, C. (1992). The political economy of rural school consolidation. *Peabody Journal of Education, 67*(4), 63–89.

Douglas, S., & Walker, A. (2013). Coal mining and the resource curse in the eastern United States. *Social Science Research Network*. Retrieved from http://papers.ssrn.com/sol3/Delivery.cfm/SSRN_ID2385560_code59895.pdf?abstractid=2385560&mirid=1

Duncan, C. (1999). *Worlds apart: Why poverty persists in rural America*. New Haven, CT: Yale University Press.

Eagleton, T. (1991). *Ideology: An introduction*. London, UK: Verso.

Eller, R. (2008). *Uneven ground: Appalachia since 1945*. Lexington: University Press of Kentucky.

Emery, K. (2002). *The business roundtable and systemic reform: How corporate-engineered high-stakes testing has eliminated community participation in developing educational goals and policies* (Doctoral dissertation). University of California-Davis, Davis, CA. Retrieved from http://www.educationanddemocracy.org/Emery_dissertation.html

Eyre, E. & Finn, S. (2002, August–October). Closing costs: School consolidation in West Virginia. *Charleston Gazette*.

Freire, P., & Macedo, D. (1987). *Reading the world and the word*. Westport, CT: Bergin & Garvey.

Friedkin, N., & Necochea, J. (1988). School system size and performance: A contingency perspective. *Educational Evaluation and Policy Analysis, 10*(3), 237–249.

Gabriel, T. (2014, April 21). Fifty years into the war on poverty, hardship hits back. *New York Times*, p. A1.

Gaventa, J. (1980). *Power and powerlessness: Quiescence and rebellion in an Appalachian valley*. Urbana, IL: University of Illinois Press.

Gutstein, E. (2006). *Reading and writing the world with mathematics*. New York, NY: Routledge.

Habermas, J. (1973). *Legitimation crisis* (T. McCarthy, *Trans*.). London, UK: Heinemann.

Habermas, J. (1987). *The theory of communicative action. Vol. 2: Lifeworld and system: A critique of functionalist reason*. Boston, MA: Beacon Press.

Hektner, J. M. (1995). When moving up implies moving out: Rural adolescent conflict in the transition to adulthood. *Journal of Research in Rural Education, 11*(1), 3–14.

Hennen, J. (1996). *The Americanization of West Virginia: Creating a modern industrial state, 1916–1925*. Lexington, KY: University of Kentucky Press.

Hindman, H. (2002). *Child labor: An American history*. Armonk, NY: Sharpe.

Hobsbawm, E. (1992). *Nations and nationalism since 1780: Programme, myth, reality* (2nd ed.). New York, NY: Cambridge University Press.

Howley, C. B. (1996). Compounding disadvantage: The effects of school and district size on student achievement in West Virginia. *Journal of Research in Rural Education, 12*(1), 25–32.

Howley, C. W., & Hambrick, K. (2014). Getting there from here: Schooling and rural abandonment. In C. B. Howley, A. Howley, & J. Johnson (Eds.), *Dynamics of social class, race, and place in rural education*. Charlotte, NC: Information Age.

Howley, C. B., Harmon, H., & Leopold, G. (1996). Rural scholars or bright rednecks? Aspirations for a sense of place among rural youth in Appalachia. *Journal of Research in Rural Education, 12*(3), 150–160.

Howley, C. B., & Howley, C. W. (2015). Farming the poor: Cultivating profit at the schoolhouse door. In K. Sturges (Ed.), *Neoliberalizing educational reform: America's quest for profitable market-colonies and the undoing of public good* (pp. 23–52). Rotterdam, The Netherlands: Sense.

Howley, C. B., Howley, A., & Johnson, J. (Eds.). (2014). *Dynamics of social class, race, and place in rural education*. Charlotte, NC: Information Age.

Howley, C. B., Johnson, J., & Petrie, J. (2011, February 1). Consolidation of schools and districts: What the research says and what it means. *National Education Policy*

Center. Retrieved from http://nepc.colorado.edu/publication/consolidation-schools-districts

Howley, C., Pickett, D., Brown, P., & Kay, L. (2011). Loving and hating high school: Divided opinion among adults in a rural university town. *Critical Questions in Education, 2*(1), 28–43.

Huang, G., & Howley, C. B. (1993). Mitigating disadvantage: Effects of small-scale schooling on student achievement in Alaska. *Journal of Research in Rural Education, 9*(3), 137–149.

Hughes, M. (1992). *The "fair share dilemma": Property wealth, per pupil revenue and resident ability to support public elementary and secondary education in West Virginia, 1991–1992.* Charleston, WV: West Virginia Education Fund. Retrieved from ERIC database. (ED356119).

Jacobs, J. (2004). *Dark age ahead.* New York, NY: Random House.

Jacques, M. (2009). *When China rules the world: The rise of the middle kingdom and the end of the Western world.* London, UK: Allen Lane.

Katz, M. B. (1968). *The irony of early school reform: Educational innovation in mid-nineteenth century Massachusetts.* Cambridge, MA: Harvard University Press.

Kovacs, P. (Ed.). (2011). *The Gates Foundation and the future of U.S. "public" schools.* New York, NY: Routledge.

Kunstler, J. H. (2005). *The long emergency: Surviving the end of oil, climate change, and other converging catastrophes of the twenty-first century.* New York, NY: Grove Press.

Lasch, C. (1991). *The true and only heaven: Progress and its critics.* New York, NY: Norton.

Lee, H. B. (1969) *Bloodletting in Appalachia: The story of West Virginia's four major mine wars and other thrilling incidents of its coal fields.* Morgantown: West Virginia University Press.

Lewis, R. L. (2013). Appalachian myths and the legacy of coal. In M. Evans, R. Santelli, & H. George-Warren (Eds.), *The Appalachians: America's first and last frontier* (pp. 75–83). Morgantown: West Virginia University Press.

Lyson, T. (2002). What does a school mean to a community? Assessing the social and economic benefits of schools to rural villages in New York. *Journal of Research in Rural Education, 17*(3), 131–137.

Malczewski, J. M. (2002). *Northern philanthropists, the state, and rural Blacks: The implementation of education reform in North Carolina during the progressive era.* (Unpublished dissertation). Columbia University, New York, NY.

Marsh, D. (1992, February 14). The seductive myth of tiny schools. *Charleston Gazette,* p. 6A.

Martenson, C. (2013). The really, really big picture: There isn't going to be enough net energy for the economic growth we want [Web blog post]. *Post Carbon Institute.* Retrieved from http://www.postcarbon.org/blog-post/1402948-the-really-really-big-picture-there

Mathews, F. D. (1996). *Is there a public for public schools?* Dayton, OH: Kettering Foundation Press.

Mathez, E. (2009). *Climate change: The science of global warming and our energy future.* New York, NY: Columbia University Press.

McElroy, M., & Lu, X. (2014, January–February). Fracking's future: Natural gas, the economy, and America's energy future. *Harvard Magazine*. Retrieved from http://harvardmagazine.com/2013/01/frackings-future

Meadows, D., Meadows, G., Randers, J., & Behrens, W. (1972). *The limits to growth*. New York, NY: Universe Books.

National Assessment of Educational Progress (NAEP). (2014). NAEP state comparisons. *National Center for Educational Statistics*. Retrieved from http://nces.ed.gov/nationsreportcard/statecomparisons/

Orr, D. (1995). *Earth in mind: On education, environment, and the human prospect*. Washington, DC: Island Press.

Orr, D. (2009). *Down to the wire: Confronting climate collapse*. New York, NY: Oxford University Press.

Oxford English Dictionary (OED). (1971). *School*. Oxford, UK: Oxford University Press.

Passet, R. (2000). *L'illusion néo-libérale*. Paris, France: Fayard.

Pendarvis, E. (2014). Learnin' a mountain to fly: Appalachian dialects and language arts textbooks. In C. Howley, A. Howley, & J. Johnson (Eds.), *Dynamics of social class, race, and place in rural education* (pp. 297–324). Charlotte, NC: Information Age.

Peshkin, A. (1982). *The imperfect union*. Chicago, IL: University of Chicago Press.

Phillips Exeter Academy. (2014). *About us*. Retrieved from http://www.exeter.edu/about_us/171.aspx

Pollard, K., & Jacobsen, L. A. (2013). The Appalachian region: A data overview from the 2007-2011 American Community Survey Chartbook. *Appalachian Regional Commission*. Retrieved from http://www.arc.gov/assets/research_reports/PRBDataOverviewReport2007-2011.pdf

Ravitch, D. (2013). *Reign of error: The hoax of the privatization movement and the danger to America's public schools*. New York, NY: Knopf.

Rice, J. M. (1913). *The scientific management in education*. New York, NY: Hines, Noble & Eldredge.

Rich, M. (2014, April 26). A Walmart fortune, spreading charter schools. *New York Times*, p. A1.

Schafft, K., Borlu, Y., & Glenna, L. (2013). The relationship between Marcellus Shale gas development in Pennsylvania and local perceptions of risk and opportunity. *Rural Sociology*, *78*(2), 143–166.

Scott, J. (1985). *Weapons of the weak: Everyday forms of peasant resistance*. New Haven, CT: Yale University Press.

Scott, J. (1998). *Seeing like a state: How certain schemes to improve the human condition have failed.* New Haven, CT: Yale University Press.

Scott, J. (2012). *Two cheers for anarchism: Six easy pieces on autonomy, dignity, and meaningful work and play*. Princeton, NJ: Princeton University Press.

Shannon, T. (2006). The economy of Appalachia. In G. T. Edwards, J. Asbury, & R. Cox (Eds.), *A handbook to Appalachia: An introduction to the region* (pp. 67–84). Knoxville, TN: University of Tennessee Press.

Shaw, T. C, DeYoung, A. J., & Rademacher, E. W. (2005). Educational attainment in Appalachia: Growing with the nation, but challenges remain. *Journal of Appalachian Studies, 10*(3), 307–329.

Solomon, S. (2010). *Water: The epic struggle for wealth, power, and civilization*. New York, NY: Harper Perennial.

Streifel, J., Foldesy, G., & Holman, D. (1991). The financial effects of consolidation. *Journal of Research in Rural Education*, *7*(2), 13–20.

Teets, S. (2006). Education in Appalachia. In G. Edwards, J. Asbury, & R. Cox (Eds.), *A handbook to Appalachia: An introduction to the region* (pp. 119–142). Knoxville: University of Tennessee Press.

U.S. Census Bureau. (1995, March 27). *West Virginia: Population of counties by decennial census: 1900–1990*. Retrieved from http://www.census.gov/population/www/censusdata/cencounts/files/wv190090.txt

U.S. Census Bureau. (1996). *Populations of states and counties of the United States: 1790 to 1990. Part III: Population of counties, earliest census to 1990*. Retrieved from http://www.census.gov/population/www/censusdata/pop1790-1990.html

U.S. Census Bureau. (2014). *State and county quickfacts: McDowell County, West Virginia.* Retrieved from http://quickfacts.census.gov/qfd/states/54/54047.html

Weber, E. (1976). *Peasants into Frenchmen: The modernization of rural France, 1870–1914*. Stanford, CA: Stanford University Press.

Weisman, A. (2013). *Countdown: Our last, best hope for a future on earth?* Boston, MA: Little, Brown.

West Virginia Department of Education (WVDE). (2005, November 14). *Governor announces national partnership to focus on 21st century skills for students* [Press release]. Retrieved from http://wvde.state.wv.us/news/1099/

Whisnant, D. (1980). *Modernizing the mountaineer*. Boone, NC: Appalachian Consortium Press.

Williams, R. (1973). *The country and the city*. London, UK: Verso.

Williams, W. A. (1969). *The roots of the modern American empire*. New York, NY: Vintage.

Woodrum, A. (2004, September 7). State-mandated testing and cultural resistance in Appalachian schools: Competing values and expectations. *Journal of Research in Rural Education, 19*(1). Retrieved from http://jrre.vmhost.psu.edu/wp-content/uploads/2014/02/19-1.pdf

Yahn, J. (2014). *The affectionate agrarian: An interview with James Scott* (Working Paper Series, The Center for Higher Education). Athens, OH: Ohio University Patton College of Education.

BIOGRAPHIES

ABOUT THE EDITORS

Sheneka M. Williams, EdD is an Associate Professor in the Program of Educational Administration and Policy at the University of Georgia. Her overarching research interest includes students' access to educational opportunity, and her specific research interest includes student assignment policies in urban and rural contexts, school governance, and school-community relations. Her research has been published in Teachers College Record, Urban Education, Education and Urban Society, and Peabody Journal of Education. She has also presented aspects of her research at the National Press Club in Washington, DC and on CNN. Dr. Williams is a graduate of Vanderbilt University's Peabody College of Education and Human Development.

Ain A. Grooms, PhD is a recent graduate of the Educational Administration and Policy program at the University of Georgia. Her research interests include racial/ethnic stratification, residential segregation, school choice, and equity and adequacy. Dr. Grooms also served as a founding administrator of a small, college preparatory charter high school in Boston. She received her M.Ed in Organizational Leadership from Vanderbilt University and her B.A. in Educational Studies from Emory University. Dr. Grooms works as a policy analyst with the Southern Regional Education Board.

Educational Opportunity in Rural Contexts: The Politics of Place, pages 155–157.

ABOUT THE CONTRIBUTORS

Daniel Boyd, PhD, has served as superintendent for Lowndes County Public Schools in Alabama since August 2006. As the chief executive officer of the school district, he manages a budget of 23 million dollars and supervises over 300 employees. From August 2007 through May 2015, Dr. Boyd served as the governor-appointed Chairperson of the Black Belt Education Commission. Dr. Boyd was also a finalist for the Alabama Superintendent of the Year Award in 2010 and in 2013.

Janeula M. Burt, PhD is assistant professor in the Department of Educational Leadership, in the College of Education at Bowie State University, where she teaches graduate courses, is a Co-PI on two research grants, is an evaluation researcher, and advises doctoral dissertations.

Karen Eppley, PhD is associate professor of education at Penn State University. Her research interest is at the intersection of literacy education and rural education. Her work explores ideas around contextually relevant teacher preparation, placed literacies, textual representations of rurality, and rural education as a matter of social justice.

Ain A. Grooms is a policy analyst with the Southern Regional Education Board. Her research interests are educational policy, access and opportunity, school choice, and racial and residential segregation. Dr. Grooms holds a PhD in educational administration and policy from the University of Georgia.

Annelise Hagedorn is obtaining her Master's degree in Rural Sociology at The Pennsylvania State University. Her research interests include issues of rural education, youth, and growing up in the rural context. Her current research focuses on participation in extracurricular activities among rural high school students in Pennsylvania.

Caitlin W. Howley, PhD, an educational sociologist, directs the Appalachia Regional Comprehensive Center and evaluates K–12 education and college access programs. Her research focuses on rural and Appalachian schooling, pathways to adulthood, and the dynamics of social stratification in rural places.

Craig B. Howley, EdD, has published widely on the relationship between culture, political economy, and rural schooling. Previously he directed the research initiative of an NSF-funded center, and--prior to IES's deformation of the ERIC system--an ERIC clearinghouse. Retired from Ohio University, he now conducts research and evaluation for WordFarmers Associates.

Jerry D. Johnson, EdD, is professor of educational leadership at the University of West Florida. His scholarship focuses on rural education, educational policy, school leadership, and educational equity. Johnson is a former high school teacher and principal, and served as a policy analyst for the Rural School and Community Trust.

Stephen Kotok is an assistant professor of Educational Leadership and Foundations at the University of Texas at El Paso. His research focuses on charter schools, school climate, and educational policy. Specifically, his research examines organizational features of schools and districts and how these institutions promote equity for minorities and low-income students.

Erica Lopatofsky Kryst is a doctoral candidate in the Department of Education Policy Studies at The Pennsylvania State University. Her research interests include issues of educational equity, rural youth out-migration, and the college access and academic achievement of students in rural areas.

Wesley A. Kuemmel is a photographer and a student in the graduate humanities program at Marshall University. His research focuses on Appalachian studies, labor history, and the influence of neoliberal policy on higher education.

Patrick Shannon teaches reading specialists and runs the Summer Reading Camp at Penn State University. His recent books include *Reading Wide Awake* (Teachers College, 2011), *Closer Readings of the Common Core* (Heinemann, 2013), and *Reading Poverty in America* (Routledge, 2014).

John W. Sipple, PhD, is associate professor in the Department of Development Sociology at Cornell University. He studies and teaches about the intersection of education policy and community development. He also directs the New York State Center for Rural Schools and the Community and Regional Development Institute (CaRDI), both at Cornell.

Yuan Yao is an undergraduate student in the School of Operations Research & Information Engineering at Cornell University. He conducts quantitative research on education and municipal policies at the Community and Regional Development Institute (CaRDI) at Cornell.

Brian P. Zoellner is assistant professor in the Foundations and Secondary Education Department at the University of North Florida. In this capacity he works in secondary science education and supervises student teachers. His research interests include STEM curriculum development and implementation, teacher theorizing and decision making, and educational policy.

Made in United States
North Haven, CT
03 May 2023